ROBIN WILLIAMS 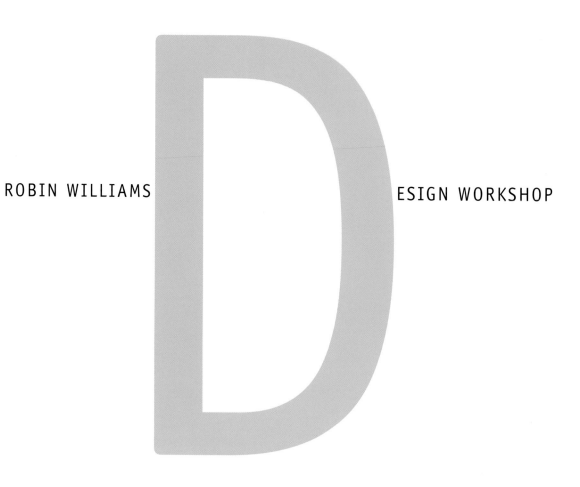ESIGN WORKSHOP

Robin Williams + John Tollett

 Published by Peachpit Press
Berkeley • California

Robin Williams Design Workshop
Robin Williams and John Tollett

Peachpit Press
1249 Eighth Street
Berkeley, California 94710
800.283.9444
510.524.2178
510.524.2221 fax

Find us on the World Wide Web at **www.peachpit.com**
Peachpit Press is a division of Addison Wesley Longman

Cover design and production by John Tollett
Interior design by Robin Williams and John Tollett
Interior production by Robin Williams
Index by Barbara Sikora
Editing by Nancy Davis
Prepress by Kate Reber

ISBN
0-201-70088-3

10 9 8 7 6 5

Printed and bound in the United States of America

Contents

It must be nice . . .

Clip Art
Stock Images
Posters Contrast
Web Sites
SUBS 2 GO
Letterheads
Brochures
Invoices Indices Newsletters
Cerrillos Echo
Ads
Flyers Envelopes
Business Cards
Billboards
Explore Logos Forms
Tables of Contents
Visual Impact

MEET SOCCER SUPERSTAR
JAY BAYKAL!
FRIDAY 6PM
Register to win a soccer ball autographed by Jay "The Turk" Baykal!

Aren't you sick of hearing comments like these: "It must be nice to sit around all day just being creative." "Lucky you, you get to have fun instead of working." Meanwhile you're up all night sweating out a deadline for a big meeting tomorrow morning, your mind is a blank, and the clock is moving faster than usual. Or, even worse, this job could be your big break and if you score big on this project you'll have more work than you need. Now, why does that design look boring?

If you've never been there it's probably because you're a living-legend genius designer and you've never had to deal with the fears, inadequacies, insecurities, paranoia, and limitations of us mere-mortal designers. And if that's true, you're most likely not reading this book anyway.

If you are a mere-mortal designer, welcome, and it's nice to know that we (Robin and I) are not alone. By "mere-mortal designers" I mean aspiring designers who are in the process of developing their skills and getting experience; designers who are not famous (yet); and designers who are looking for design books to add to their collection, books that will give them some insight into the design process.

Hey, what a coincidence! That's who we had in mind when we wrote and designed this book. It's our hope that the practical approach we use in design will be helpful to you and the way you approach graphic design projects. With the fantastic digital tools and resources available to you, the only thing separating you from the top designers in the world is the opportunity to unleash your imagination on the world. That and a few mega-buck clients, but that could happen too.

We've attempted to communicate a spirit of playful design exploration and experimentation in the examples we've used and in the design of the book itself. That playfulness and a willingness to experiment visually can open the door to your imagination. And it can transform a stressful assignment into a satisfying creative exercise.

We all have a tendency to revert to completely safe design solutions that we know will work when we're under the pressure of a deadline, such as using the font Helvetica and designing with a centered alignment. This book encourages you to explore beyond that and to have fun doing it. The examples here are meant to help spark ideas and steer your creative thinking in different directions that might lead to previously unseen possibilities in your own work.

We'd like for this book to add to your future enjoyment of being a designer. But most of all, we'd like for you to say "Oh, I don't work. I just sit around playing all day."

jt + rw

A CONVERSATION WITH CRITICS

"We all revere the genius Bach;
Each contrapuntal law,
Each voice and phrase that interlock
Inspires a sense of awe."

"Quite right. Chopin we also praise.
Such drama, and such sweep!
Each time I hear that Polonaise
It almost makes me weep."

"Rachmaninoff! He knew the deeps
To which a soul can sink.
To wit, his Third Concerto keeps
Me busy trying to think."

But Anderson; now there's style!
He's got them beat by half;
His music always makes me smile,
And often makes me laugh.

"How plebian that comment was!
Let this be understood:
If that is what his music does,
It can't be any good."

ROSS CARTER, KENTUCKY POET
Evensong · *poems*

GOONHAVERN PRESS

Some designers
are equally inept
at following rules
or breaking them.
Good designers
can do either.

Jim Alley
Savannah College of Art and Design

Typefaces used in this chapter:
Headlines: Barmeno Extra Bold
Body copy: Clearface Regular and **Heavy**
*This combination of softly rounded sans serif
with a classic oldstyle (tending toward the
slab serif style) creates an informal, grammar-
school look to this chapter.*

1. How Much Do You Already Know?

Web-safe color
SCREEN FONT
separations
resolution
duotone
registration
Process Color
Spot Color
dpi
moiré
raster
PostScript
PRINTER FONT
native file format
KERNING
ATM
EPS
TrueType
suitcase
line Screen
ppi
VECTOR
halftone
JPEG
GIF
screen font
anti-alias
RGB
CMYK
TRACKING
registration
alias
TIFF

In this section we want to make sure you have the basic building blocks down before we launch into more advanced concepts. You can certainly learn a lot from *this* book even if you don't have the basics down yet. But to move forward, we have to assume you know certain things. Since Robin has already written a number of books for new designers, this introduction is sort of a touchstone; if you can't answer the questions, we refer you to books that you might want to read. And the questions are not just about design, but about all the things designers now have to know to produce our work, all the technical stuff we need to deal with to get our jobs done properly.

Most of the books we recommend are in the "Non-Designer's" series. Perhaps you are already a designer and discover there are things in the Non-Designer's books that you need to learn, but you just can't bring yourself to buy a book for "non-designers." Well, have your mother buy it and send it to you wrapped in brown paper. Paste a photo over the cover so no one knows you own "that" book. Rip the cover off. Or just get over yourself. And lighten up! All of us have more to learn, no matter what level we think we are at right now.

3

What are the basic Principles?

Can you put into words why one design "works" and another doesn't? Can you explain to a client why their dorky design idea doesn't project the professional level of their service and why your new improved version does? When you look at a poorly designed page, can you **put into words** why it looks amateurish, and can you put into words what needs to be done to make it look more sophisticated? Being able to explain concepts in words helps you pinpoint problems, find solutions more quickly, and convince clients of your superior design skills.

If you cannot answer the questions on these two pages easily, you need to read the first half of *The Non-Designer's Design Book.*

1. Can you name at least five reasons why the flyer below looks amateurish?

> **CHESS MATCH**
>
> **SUNDAY, AUGUST 23**
>
> **MEET IN COMMU-NITY ROOM AT 3:00 P.M.**
>
> **SPECIAL GUEST-KRAMNIK!**

2. From glancing at the typical business card layout below, how you can tell it came from one of those little books in the local copy shop?

> John Tollett   Robin Williams
>
> *URL'S INTERNET CAFE*
>
> www.UrlsInternetCafe.com
> (505) 438-5555

3. Compare these two layouts. They are both centered, but one looks more sophisticated than the other. What changes were made to the one on the right to give it this higher-quality look, even though it is still a centered arrangement?

4. In the example below, which simple principle can be applied that would instantly give it a more professional appearance?

5. Glance at these two layouts. Which one do your find your eye is naturally attracted to? What is the word for the design principle that attracts your eye in this case, and how was it achieved?

How is your Typography?

Graphic design is type. If there is no type on the piece, it is not graphic design—it's fine art. Every designer needs to have a thorough understanding of type and typography. You might have a brilliant layout and great copy and a gorgeous photograph, and someone might even have paid you lots of money for it, but if your apostrophes look like they came off a typewriter and you've got two spaces after periods, you're not as good as you think. Long ago designers didn't have to worry about things like where the apostrophe belongs and whether a question mark belongs inside or outside of quotation marks because the professional typesetter did that, but now every designer has to know those details as well as design.

1. Quickly name five serious typographic problems in the sentence below.

   "Oh my gosh", cried Moll. She gasped--her enigma was all wrapped up in Bob's integrity.

2. What is typographically wrong with each of the phrases below?

   Open 3-6 A.M. every day.

   Closed May-June.

   The San Francisco-New York flight.

3. How do you type these symbols: ® ™ ¢ © •

4. How do you set accent marks, as in the words résumé or voilà?

5. Does a period belong inside or outside of parentheses? What do you do with the punctuation that comes directly after an italic or bold word? When does "its" have an apostrophe? Which typographic marks belong in the blank spaces in this phrase: rock _n_ roll?

6. Name five typographic problems in the column below.

   Lorper adip endreetum velis niamcorem vulputpat irit nim dolenit dolorer alissis nonulputem.

   Lore doloborti iscidunt ulputem verci blandrem ing euipsum incipis nosto do core tatum iriure, od doleniam velit ip exerat. Ut lamet nibh ea Faci Blandre Veliscill mconummy nibh el ex et, veliquatue molorero odolorting ercilit at atis adiamet dipit ute magnim zzriliquisl eugiatie enim ver in vulputet breat.

   Lorperil el ulla cor susto odipisl zzril ing euiscidunt wis nonsequi esent ullam quam ver at, cor senis ad tationulputpatie mod tem deliquamconum quissi.

If you cannot answer these questions, read *The Mac is not a typewriter* or *The PC is not a typewriter*. It's a little book.

6

1. Match the category of type in the left column to a representative sample in the right column.

Slab serif	*a heap o' livin'*
Sans serif	**keep the thumbmarks**
Oldstyle	ye've got to sing and dance
Modern	yer soul is sort of wrapped
Decorative	**a heap of sun**
Script	*watch beside a loved one*

2. Can you name the problems with the type combinations shown below? How could you make them stronger?

Celebrate
the blips in life

THE STELLAR
nursery

3. What does the paragraph on the left have that the paragraph on the right does not? What does this technique achieve?

There are three important **rules of life** that will help you survive most situations. **One** is that your attitude is your life. **Two** is that you are what you take the time to become. And **three** is that you can't let the seeds stop you from enjoying the watermelon.

There are three important rules of life that will help you survive most situations. One is that your attitude is your life. Two is that you are what you take the time to become. And three is that you can't let the seeds stop you from enjoying the watermelon.

If you cannot answer the questions above, read the second half of *The Non-Designer's Design Book*.

1. What's the difference between letterspacing, kerning, pair kerning, auto kerning, manual kerning, range kerning, and tracking, and how do you use each of these in your software?

2. What must be done to the quotation below to improve it typographically?

"Preparation works much better than optimism."

3. Glance at the two paragraphs below. Which one feels easier to read, especially if it was not just a paragraph, but a whole page? State three reasons why. Without changing the typeface, what can be done to the other paragraph to make it as readable as possible?

The tombstone said that everybody loved Mabel. Not me. I adored her. I worshipped her. I wanted to be just like Mabel. I wanted her life and her clothes and her attitude and her kindness and her money. I really wanted her money.

The tombstone said that everybody loved Mabel. Not me. I adored her. I worshipped her. I wanted to be just like Mabel. I wanted her life and her clothes and her attitude and her kindness and her money. I really wanted her money.

If you cannot answer the questions above, read *The Non-Designer's Type Book*.

How is your Color Theory?

Once upon a time a graphic designer had to worry about only one sort of color, CMYK. Now because we are manipulating images on our computers, placing them on web pages, and printing them to desktop color inkjet printers as well as to high-end offset presses, we have to understand color in all of its variations through the processes, and we must know which color model to choose not only for the end result, but for the steps along the way.

1. What does **CMYK** stand for?

2. What does **RGB** stand for?

3. When do you want to **use** CMYK images and when do you want to use RGB images?

4. When would you **scan** an image in CMYK vs. RGB?

5. What happens on the screen when you **change the color mode** from RGB to CMYK?

6. What is **bit depth**? How does it affect the printed image?

7. How does the **pixel-per-inch** count (**ppi,** sometimes referred to as **dpi**) affect an image displayed on a screen, as on a web page? That is, will a 300 ppi image look better on the screen than a 72 ppi image?

8. How can you improve the **resolution** on your monitor?

If you cannot answer these questions, you might want to read the *The Non-Designer's Scan and Print Book,* **by Sandee Cohen and Robin Williams.**

What about Printing?

In this book we might use some of the terms found in these questions. We have to assume that, if you bought this advanced design book, you know what we are talking about if we say something like "notice the moiré pattern," "the halftone screen is too coarse," or "call the printer and find out what lpi they want to use." Not knowing these sorts of things will not prevent you from using and learning from this book! We just want you to know where you can get that information if you discover you need it.

If you cannot answer these questions and want to know all about printing and scanning so your great designs look great in print, read the *The Non-Designer's Scan and Print Book,* **by Sandee Cohen and Robin Williams.**

1. Is this book **printed** in three-color, four-color, five-color, or full-color?

2. What is **spot color**?

3. What is **process color**?

4. How do the **dots-per-inch (dpi)** affect an image printed on a page? That is, will a 300 dpi image look better in print than a 72 dpi image, even if they are both full color?

5. What is a **linescreen**? How does **lpi** affect a printed image?

6. What is a **halftone**?

7. What is a **duotone** and how do you make one?

8. What is a **moiré** pattern? Why do you want to avoid it? How can you avoid it?

9. What are **separations**?

10. What is a **color tint**?

11. What is the color **registration** and when would you use it?

12. Is the flyer shown below a one-, two-, or three-color job? How many **ink colors** did the designer have to pay for?

Poetry Reading
Mad Madge

tonight
8 P.M.

❀

Downtown Library

Do you know File Formats?

In this book we will mention EPS files and TIFF files and GIF files and JPEG files, and we have to assume that you know what they are, which programs create which sorts of file formats, what a native file format is, and how to work with each of them.

1. What is a **native** file format?

2. What is a **raster** format?

3. What is a **vector** format?

4. What is an **EPS**?

5. What is a **TIFF**?

6. What is a **GIF** and when would you use one?

7. What is a **JPEG** file?

8. What is a **compression scheme** and when would you need to use one?

9. Which of the above-mentioned file formats are **compressed**?

10. Which file format, **EPS** or **TIFF**, prints better to a non-PostScript printer, like a color inkjet? Why?

11. In which file format is it best to **scan** photographic images?

12. Is the image below most likely a TIFF or an EPS?

13. Is the image below most likely a TIFF or an EPS?

If you cannot answer these questions, read the *The Non-Designer's Scan and Print Book,* **by Sandee Cohen and Robin Williams.**

What do you know about Fonts?

It used to be so different. A designer didn't have to know anything about "fonts" and very little about typography, but now most designers have to do everything. Knowing how to deal with your fonts technically is important so your work prints properly.

You don't **have** to know any of this stuff to be a great designer—but you have to know it if you produce your own work, **or** if you oversee the work of someone else and they don't know about font technology and **you** have to recognize the resulting problems.

If you cannot answer these questions and you use a Macintosh, read *How to Boss Your Fonts Around, second edition,* **by Robin Williams.**

Windows users (and Mac users), read the *The Non-Designer's Scan and Print Book,* **by Sandee Cohen and Robin Williams.**

1. What is a **PostScript** font?

2. What is a **TrueType** font?

3. How can you tell a **PostScript** font from a **TrueType** font? (Answers are different for PCs and for Macs.)

3. In what situation would you never want to use **TrueType** fonts?

4. What is a **PostScript printer**? How can you tell if your printer is PostScript?

5. If you have a huge collection of fonts, you need a **font management utility.** Can you name three or four Mac font management utilities (or two on the PC)?

6. If you use a font management utility, where should you **store** your entire font collection?

7. How do you **install** new fonts if you are not using a font management utility?

Mac users only:

8. Each PostScript font has two parts. What are they?

9. Where must the two separate parts of a PostScript font be stored in relation to each other? (Knowing this answer will solve 98 percent of font problems.)

10. In the sample **font folders** below, what is wrong and what will be the result?

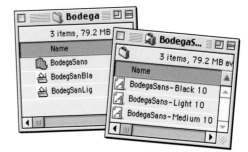

Do you plan to do Web Design?

The basic principles of design apply to all media. But each medium has its own peculiarities about how people work within it, how they use it, how they find what they need in it. The web is particularly different from any other medium. For instance, while watching a television commercial, a user does not need to figure out how to get from one part of the commercial to another—they just sit there and it happens. Most people know how to use a book and its table of contents and index to find what they need. But on a web site, it is the designer's job to make it easy for a visitor to **navigate** from one part of the site to the other, something we don't have to do in any other medium. Because we have covered this sort of material plus all the technical stuff about building web sites in another book, we won't be discussing it in this one, but we want you to know where to find that information.

1. Name at least five ways that **web design is different** from print design.

2. Does a web page look better with a horizontal **layout** or a vertical layout for the main design elements?

3. Are **graphics** on the web RGB or CMYK?

4. Which **file format** is most appropriate for photographs on the web?

5. Does a 300 **ppi** image look better than a 72 ppi image on the web?

6. Some **monitors** display photographs better than other monitors. What is it about a monitor that would make a photo look better or worse?

7. What **fonts** can you use safely in default text on a web page? What fonts can you use in your web graphics?

8. What is an **optimum file size** for a web page, including all the images?

9. What are **web-safe colors** and why are they important?

10. What is **anti-aliasing** and how does it affect web graphics?

If you cannot answer these questions, read the *The Non-Designer's Web Book,* **by Robin Williams and John Tollett.**

12

11. Name six features of the web page below that give it an **amateur** look. Granted, few web pages really look this bad (well, probably more than we like to admit), but many pages have one or more of these features that scream "I am visually illiterate!"

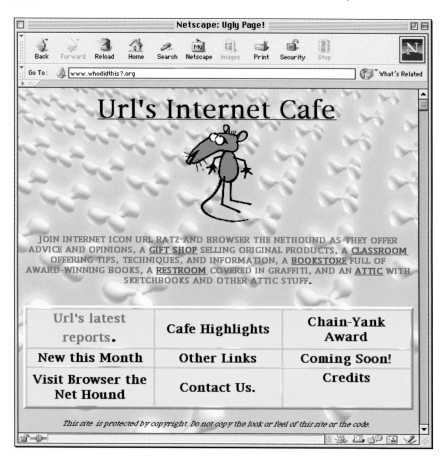

Keep an Idea File

No designer works in a vacuum. A standard tool in every designer's box is a **collection of books** that shows what other creative people around the world are doing. And you should keep an **idea file,** also called a swap file or a morgue, which is simply a file folder (or entire drawer) filled with ads that you have torn out of magazines, brochures, posters, bread wrappers, any item that grabbed your attention and you think was well designed. Put it in your idea file, ideally with a few notes about what exactly makes it so effective. When you start a new project, go through these books and ideas. This is not copying—it is a very traditional form of learning. When you see a good idea and apply the concept to your specific project, it adapts to your project, changes, and becomes your own.

This is a small part of our collection of design books. Every year new "annuals" are published, display cases of the best in typography, logos, general design, web design, and more. There are also many, many books teaching design and type, filled with great ideas and suggestions. When you're stuck for solutions, flip through them all and we guarantee you'll find an inspiration for a unique solution that you probably wouldn't have thought of without the benefit of the collective consciousness of designers around the world.

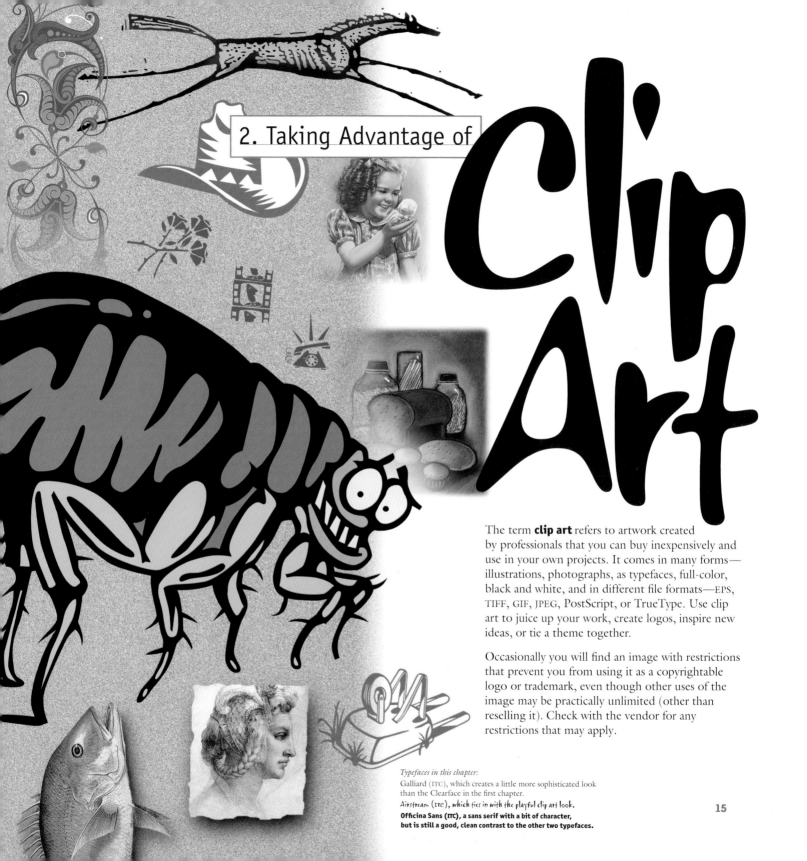

2. Taking Advantage of Clip Art

The term **clip art** refers to artwork created by professionals that you can buy inexpensively and use in your own projects. It comes in many forms—illustrations, photographs, as typefaces, full-color, black and white, and in different file formats—EPS, TIFF, GIF, JPEG, PostScript, or TrueType. Use clip art to juice up your work, create logos, inspire new ideas, or tie a theme together.

Occasionally you will find an image with restrictions that prevent you from using it as a copyrightable logo or trademark, even though other uses of the image may be practically unlimited (other than reselling it). Check with the vendor for any restrictions that may apply.

Typefaces in this chapter:
Galliard (ITC), which creates a little more sophisticated look than the Clearface in the first chapter.
Airstream (ITC), which ties in with the playful clip art look.
Officina Sans (ITC), a sans serif with a bit of character, but is still a good, clean contrast to the other two typefaces.

15

The Variety!

There is an enormous variety of clip art available, as you can see even by the very limited selection on these pages! The different styles and different file formats you choose will depend on your project and the printing process you plan to use to produce the piece. (See *The Non-Designer's Scan and Print Book* if you are not sure about how to choose the correct format, resolution, and color model.)

You can, in effect, expand your clip art collection by altering the existing art in different ways. Use a piece of clip art and enlarge it beyond expectations. Apply an unusual filter effect on an otherwise ordinary selection. Combine different clip art styles to make one unique illustration. Just spend some time experimenting and you'll be surprised at how your imagination responds.

Some clip art images
give you the option
of using different
sorts of shadows—
or none.

Sometimes a good image is not necessarily the one
that illustrates your project perfectly, but that
contrasts with your message.

How often in your career will you need this image? Once,
if at all. But this image or others in the same collection
might give you an idea that perfectly suits your project.

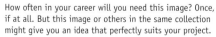

Clip Art Fonts

Besides clip art in all its graphic file forms, there is also a large variety of picture fonts that can be used as clip art. The advantages of using a font as clip art is that you get anywhere from 30 to 200 or so pictures for the price of a typeface, the images are easily resized, they print clean and sharp to any printer (as long as you have Adobe Type Manager installed on your computer, which you should), and you can change their color as easily as changing the color of any letter in your text without having to open any other application.

If you know how to use Macromedia's Fontographer, you can edit any image. Or you can type a character into an illustration program such as Illustrator, FreeHand, or CorelDraw, change it to outlines, and colorize individual parts. Or type the image into a program like Photoshop and make web graphics.

Art Three

Backyard Beasties

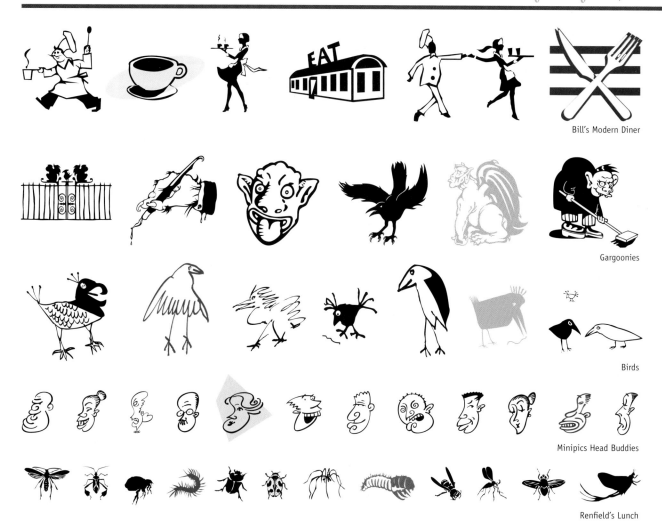

Bill's Modern Diner

Gargoonies

Birds

Minipics Head Buddies

Renfield's Lunch

PLEASE come to the

Company Picnic!

Robin's Roost Bookstore

snuggle up with a book

Old Pecos Trail
Santa Fe
New Mexico
87505

505.555.5555
www.RobinsRoostBookstore.com

Fontoonies

Backgrounds, Borders, and More

Don't forget about the other graphic elements you can buy, such as backgrounds, borders, frames, and ornaments. Since they are so accessible and are relatively inexpensive, these objects are worth adding to your collection of graphic tools. Use them in unexpected places and in unexpected ways.

An incredible variety of textures is available: canvas, adobe, marble, mud, burlap, stone, dirt, velvet, silk, exotic papers . . . ad infinitum. Backgrounds can add richness and visual interest to a design, or be an effective way to provide visual continuity to a series of pieces.

Frames from Auto FX

font: Type Embellishments One

font: Type Embellishments Two

font: Golden Cockerel Initial Ornaments

There are thousands of images available to use as backgrounds. In your image editing software, fade the entire background back, or just a part of it, so you can overlay text or other images. Try them on brochures, posters, book covers, etc.

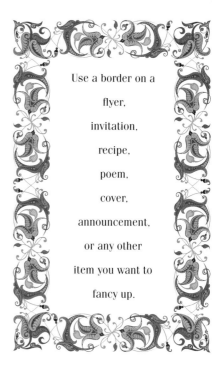

Use a border on a flyer, invitation, recipe, poem, cover, announcement, or any other item you want to fancy up.

Take part of a border, enhance it in an image editing program like Photoshop, and use it as a dramatic visual element.

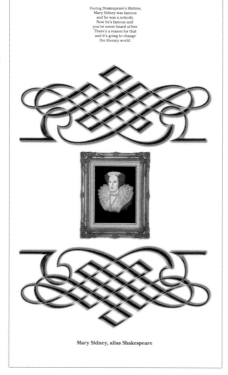

During Shakespeare's lifetime, Mary Sidney was famous and he was a nobody. Now he's famous and you've never heard of her. There's a reason for that and it's going to change the literary world.

Mary Sidney, alias Shakespeare

These borders are from Aridi Computer Graphics, the Olde World collection.

The graphic images inside the invitation are characters in the font called Fontoonies.

Please come to our wedding. Win a chance to drive the getaway car.

Creative Clip Art

There is such a huge variety of clip art that it is easy to use it "as is" and create something just wonderful. If you have the tools and know-how, you can open clip art in an appropriate application and alter it to suit your specific need and to make it look even less "canned."

On these pages are examples of clip art used in typical design projects. Some images are straight out of the box and some have been manipulated.

DO
YOU
HAVE
A PLAN
FOR
YOUR
FUTURE?

Wants pawn term dare worsted ladle gull hoe lift wetter murder inner ladle cordage honor itch offer lodge, dock, florist. Disk ladle gull orphan worry Putty ladle rat cluck wetter ladle rat hut, an fur disk raisin pimple colder Ladle Rat Rotten Hut.

Wan moaning Ladle Rat Rotten Hut's murder colder inset. Ladle Rat Rotten Hut, heresy ladle basking winsome burden barter an shirker cockles.

FutureShare
FINANCIAL PLANNERS

Call 1-800-555-5555 for the FutureShare nearest you.

John altered the edges of this illustrative clip art and added the shadow.

Notice he brought the black box up into the clip art image; the box acts as a unifying element to tie together the various elements in this ad.

He pulled a color out of the illustration and applied it to the business name (the principle of repetition), while leaving all the other elements black. This does two things: it gives the color image more impact by not having to compete with other colorful elements, and it makes the business name pop out of the page.

Small Guy isn't afraid of the BIG GUYS

State-of-the-art communication tools and skills are no longer a luxury—they're critical assets for companies, large and small, who have visions of competing in the fast-moving marketplace.

It's time to have one of our expert consultants prepare an evaluation of your communication systems and tools. No obligation and absolutely free.

Small Guy Communication Consultants began by helping small companies compete with big companies. Now, some of those big companies want us to show them how they can compete with the technology of the smaller, streamlined, cutting-edge startups.

You don't have to be a small guy to take advantage of our expertise and services. In fact, most of our small clients are becoming big guys.

SMALL GUY
Communication Consultants

uyconsultants.com / bigguy@smallguyconsultants.com

The ad above uses clip art characters from a font. In the page-layout application, they were selected and their colors changed. To the left you see how strong the same ad is even in black and white.

Notice the logo also contains the clip art character.

There are so many wonderful images—all it takes is a little imagination and a good font combination to make effective and award-winning pieces with clip art.

The ad to the right uses clip art and some great type, along with the same logo as above.

THERE'S GOTTA BE A BETTER WAY TO COMMUNICATE.

MAYBE WE SHOULD LOOK AROUND.

duh.

SMALL GUY
Communication Consultants

Easy Shot
PHOTOGRAPHY

Studio:

317 Cedar Avenue

Dallas, Texas

87505

318.555.3186

www.easyshotphotos.com

click@easyshotphotos.com

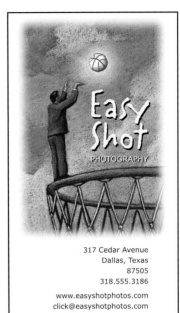

317 Cedar Avenue
Dallas, Texas
87505
318.555.3186

www.easyshotphotos.com
click@easyshotphotos.com

On these two pages is an example of a business package that utilizes a piece of clip art throughout all of its various pieces. Because the image is so strong and provocative, you can get away with using it in a variety of ways and still maintain the continuity in the package.

In this case, it was the clip art image that inspired the name of the business and the direction of its advertising and marketing graphics.

Easy
Shot
PHOTOGRAPHY

Studio:
317 Cedar Avenue
Dallas, Texas
87505
318.555.3186

www.easyshotphotos.com
click@easyshotphotos.com

Above is a brochure that folds along the dotted line (which won't print). Would the designer have imagined these ideas before seeing the clip art? We doubt it.

We make every shot look easy.

Most people know us for our exciting, award-winning sports photography, but our real specialty is compelling imagery and expert craftsmanship.

Like the world-class athletes we photograph, we make even the most difficult shots look easy.

When it's time to take your shot, make sure it's an Easy Shot.

Easy
Shot
PHOTOGRAPHY

(318)555-3186   www.easyshotphotos.com   click@easyshotphotos.com

Buying Clip Art

Clip art is available through a variety of sources; listed here are several of our favorites. You can buy entire CDs of clip art or individual images, depending on the source, and of course, complete fonts. Check out the web sites and ask for the catalogs.

Be sure to read the licensing agreement for the clip art you buy—most of the time you can do anything you want with the images, but sometimes there are limitations. For instance, you might find that a CD containing reproductions of ancient maps says you can't use their images to make items like wrapping paper and greeting cards that you plan to resell.

EyeWire Studios
www.eyewire.com
Fonts, photography, sounds, video, and more

Dynamic Graphics, Inc.
www.dgusa.com
Photographs, clip art, headline art, and more

Aridi Computer Graphics
www.aridi.com
Borders, ornaments, initial caps, ribbons, banners

Auto FX Software
www.autofx.com
Frames, photographic edges, and more

Adobe Systems, Inc.
www.adobe.com
Look in their type selections for "ornamental" faces

Also search the web
Go to www.yahoo.com
and search for "clip art."

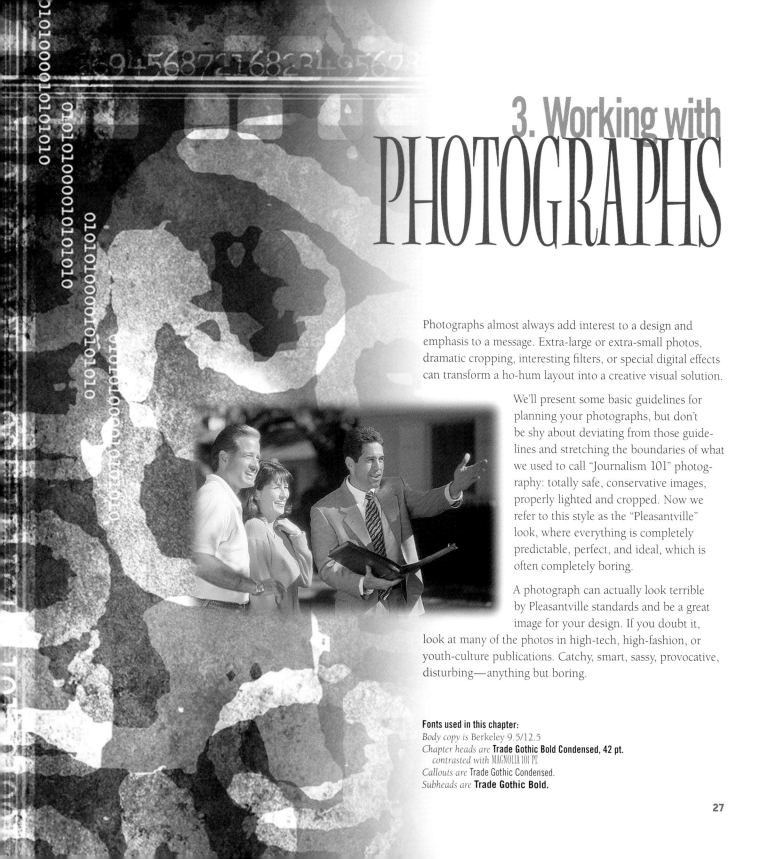

3. Working with
PHOTOGRAPHS

Photographs almost always add interest to a design and emphasis to a message. Extra-large or extra-small photos, dramatic cropping, interesting filters, or special digital effects can transform a ho-hum layout into a creative visual solution.

We'll present some basic guidelines for planning your photographs, but don't be shy about deviating from those guidelines and stretching the boundaries of what we used to call "Journalism 101" photography: totally safe, conservative images, properly lighted and cropped. Now we refer to this style as the "Pleasantville" look, where everything is completely predictable, perfect, and ideal, which is often completely boring.

A photograph can actually look terrible by Pleasantville standards and be a great image for your design. If you doubt it, look at many of the photos in high-tech, high-fashion, or youth-culture publications. Catchy, smart, sassy, provocative, disturbing—anything but boring.

Fonts used in this chapter:
Body copy is Berkeley 9.5/12.5
Chapter heads are **Trade Gothic Bold Condensed, 42 pt.**
  contrasted with MAGNOLIA 101 PT.
Callouts are Trade Gothic Condensed.
Subheads are **Trade Gothic Bold.**

Watch your
COMPOSITION

The composition of a photograph (or a layout) refers to how the elements of the image are arranged and manipulated to direct your attention through the image or design. This is done with the visual suggestion of the direction of lines and form, the emphasis created by lighting, color, contrast, and size.

A well-designed photo has been planned with an awareness of composition and with a conscious attempt to control a viewer's focus and attention, leading the eyes from one point to another in a particular order.

An effective composition can be subtle and unobtrusive, or it can be a flashing, neon sledgehammer, depending on the style and tone you want to convey in the message.

For some great tips and techniques on taking your own photos, go to the Kodak web site (www.kodak.com) and find the section on "Taking Great Pictures." It's a wonderful resource.

The most common problem is the most fixable— take a good look through the viewfinder of the camera. Look for a stovepipe coming out of the top of someone's head, half-eaten food, wrinkles in clothes, odd shadows, unnecessary clutter, and anything that is not visually pertinent to the image. If you can't move the object, move the photographer.

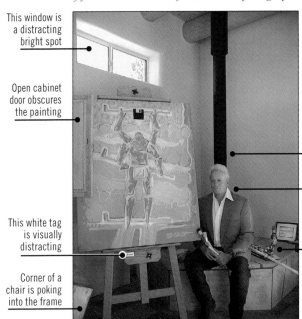

This window is a distracting bright spot

Open cabinet door obscures the painting

The stove pipe is growing out of the artist's head

Collar is out

Unidentifiable or distracting, unnecessary stuff clutters the image

This white tag is visually distracting

Corner of a chair is poking into the frame

Let's say you're taking a photo of some of the members of your bike club on their cross-country trip. This is a typically bad shot—there are telephone poles and wires, overflowing dumpsters, and other superfluous, distracting, and downright ugly stuff in the photo. Since you can't move the poles and the dumpsters, move yourself!

Can you tell who's who with their helmets on? No? Then let go of trying to identify each person and instead focus on another interesting aspect that will make a provocative image for the newsletter.

Don't always crop in tightly when taking the photo. If you leave a little extra space around the image, you have more options for layout design later. Professional photographers tend to compose the image beautifully through the lens, but that means you might have fewer choices in how you use the photo later.

Take photos from different viewpoints. A simple change of origin can turn an average photo into an interesting one. (For this particular image of a dinner party, we ran an artistic filter on it because even though we liked the photo, it wasn't a technically great one because of the lighting conditions.)

Experiment with CREATIVE CROPPING

Just because a photographer hands you a photograph or you pay good money for a stock photo doesn't mean you have to use it exactly as is. Many photos benefit from judicious or creative cropping. Even a fabulous photograph might need cropping to make the advertisement or poster more exciting, create a focal point, or emphasize a concept.

Here we have a nice, predictable happy-couple photograph (above). It's nice, but we've seen its clone at least a hundred times. Since the ad focuses on the emotional experience of a new home, we cropped in to focus on the couple yet retain the moving boxes and takeout (and really lost nothing in the process). The ad copy reads right down into the couple, reinforcing the message that this is about a human experience. The busy stuff on the left of the photo helps balance the ad copy in the upper-right.

inely fodder beer gutter grade bag short-gum, Murder Beer gutt muddle-sash haunting flean Ladle Bore Beer gutter tawny ladle pestle, an oiler beers crypt upper stars, ware Guilty Looks worse line honor bet, sunder slip an snorting. Herring door beers, shay weakened, lipped otter door windrow, an dished aware harm jesters fascist shagged scrabble. **505.555.4519**

realtor 96

first night in a new home

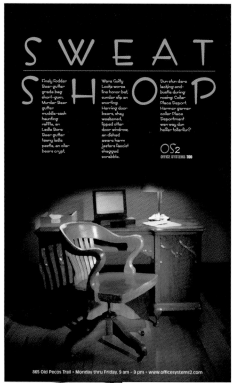

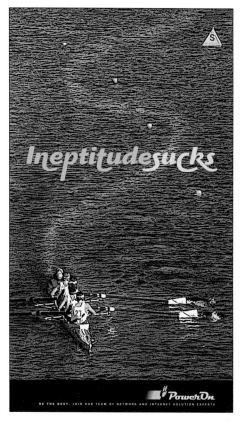

We applied a painterly effect to this photo, then cropped it into an elliptical shape to create a dramatic visual focus.

Photographs can have accidental details and ideas hidden in them. We often crop in tight on just one detail of a complex photo to get a stronger visual impact.

For this recruiting poster, we liked the rowing image, a symbol of teamwork and striving for excellence. But we've all seen the "teamwork" type of poster—we needed something unique. So we severely cropped the image and added an unexpected element, the badly off-course wake. We posterized the photograph for a more dramatic effect and added a headline in youth-culture jargon to further emphasize the point.

Check out the new age of
STOCK PHOTOGRAPHY

If you've avoided stock photography in the past because you thought it looked like stock photography, take another look. The advent of digital layout and design has created an explosion of available images that is stunning in its diversity, not to mention the ease, convenience, and affordability of searching for and acquiring stock images.

If you've never heard of or used stock photos in the past, they are simply photographs, generally fairly generic sorts of scenes, shot by professionals, that are then sold to you and anyone else who wants to buy them. It is much less expensive and much faster to buy a stock photo than to hire your own photographer and models and have the shot made.

A huge variety of styles, themes, and subject matter is available. You can buy a single image, a single CD full of images, or a bundle of CDs with more photos than you'll ever be able to use.

Are you one of those who can remember ordering a stock photo, then waiting for days for it to arrive by mail, and then having to send it back when you were finished with it? If you don't remember that, consider yourself lucky and start using stock photos. A list of current suppliers is on page 44.

Gather ideas from photos

You can also use stock photos as an idea resource. Browse through the image CDs you own, or go online and (for free) see what ideas and concepts you can relate to your own design projects. You'd be surprised how many ideas start appearing. A photograph may give you an idea that leads to a solution that doesn't even need a photo.

*So, at his bloody view,
her eyes are fled*

*Into the deep dark cabins
of her head.*

William Shakespeare
Venus and Adonis
lines 1037–38

A new
play by
Ryan Kelly

Some
day

Scarlett Williams
Dakota Max

New Globe
Productions

**Jimmy lost
his innocence
today.**

He watched TV.

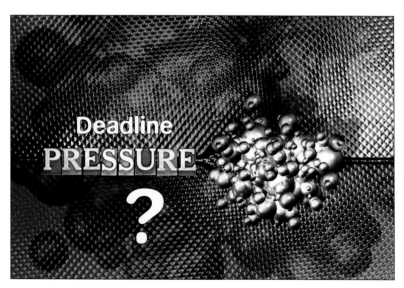

Deadline
PRESSURE
?

Techno Jazz Experimental Quartet

Experiment with
BLACK AND WHITE

Black-and-white photographs can be even more provocative and attention-getting than color photographs when used unexpectedly, as in a four-color magazine or brochure. The stark contrast and visual impact of a black-and-white image in our full-color world can make a powerful and dramatic statement.

Black-and-white photos can set a tone or mood in your design. Because you must be brave to use a black-and-white photo in a full-color project, it can automatically make the piece look artsy and trendy.

You can't rely on color to carry the photo or fool people into thinking it's a great image; black-and-white photos (like movies) need to be more carefully crafted, relying more on composition, dramatic effect, and contrasts. It's rare that you can take just any standard stock photo, make it black and white, and let it go at that. Plan to spend a little more time composing, cropping, tweaking, and manipulating a black-and-white image.

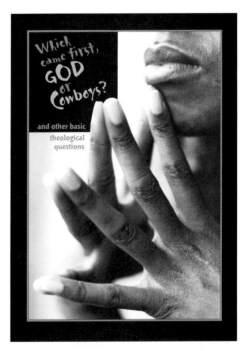

The contrast of the black-and-white photo with the colorful typography allows a visual contrast in this piece. The unexpected size of the image creates a strong visual impact.

"Black and white" doesn't necessarily mean black and white. That is, if you're using other colors in your job, try printing the "black-and-white" photo in another color. Try printing onto different paper colors, or onto white paper but with a subtle (or not so subtle) block of color behind the photo.

In your image editing program, apply a mezzotint filter (shown below, left) or add "noise" to the image (below, right) to give it a different texture.

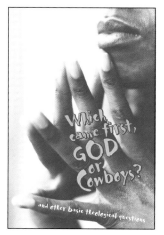 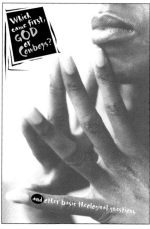  

Experiment with printing the black-and-white image in a color with an extra-large dot pattern. Notice the different effects you can achieve using dark or light ink colors, combined with different paper colors.

Try a dash of spot color on your black-and-white photo. The combination of strong, bright color on the stark photo can be very eye-catching.

 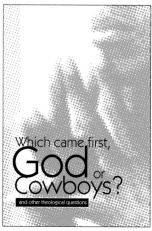  

Try a DUOTONE

You can make a black-and-white photograph appear richer in tonal value by printing it as a **duotone.** In this technique, the shadow tones print with a dark ink (usually black), and a lighter ink (another color) is used to print the mid-range and light values. Depending on the second color you choose, the effect can range from very subtle to harsh.

A variation of this is to use a gray ink instead of a color ink for the mid-range and light values, which retains the basic look of black-and-white photography but the overall tonal values are much richer than in an ordinary halftone.

For two-color projects, a duotone is a great technique that adds beauty and richness. Even in a full-color project, you get the impact value of the black-and-white photograph, but with a more elegant look. Keep in mind, though, that the second color is typically a spot color, so creating a real duotone in a four-color project often involves paying the extra price for that spot color.

Tritones and quadtones are similar to duotones, but obviously use three or four inks instead of two—this means two or three *extra* colors printed as spot colors. If the job is four-color process already, paying for two or three spot colors is usually prohibitively expensive for all except the most wealthy client (but when it can happen, it's great).

(For specific details on exactly how to create duotones, tritones, and fake duotones, please see *The Non-Designer's Scan and Print Book.*)

Another approach is to create a **fake duotone:** instead of making a halftone with two different values and printing the different values in different colors, create a solid color (or percentage of solid color) behind the image; the photo prints on top of the block of solid color, as shown below. This technique isn't as subtle as a real duotone and the range of tones isn't as rich, but it can give you another image style to work with.

To the right is a true duotone. Below, left, is a fake duotone using a background of a teal color in a value of 100 percent. Below, right, the background is 60 percent of the teal color.

Apply Creative
SPECIAL EFFECTS

The digital imaging tools in electronic graphic design encourage you to experiment with images and create effects that you could never imagine before you started clicking those buttons. In addition to the many special effects filters and capabilities built into the most popular image editing software packages, there are hundreds of third-party plug-in filters available that can turn ordinary images into amazing visuals. Experiment with them—learn to use your software!

For instance:

› Add colorful embellishments to ordinary photos.

› Change the color from ordinary to unusual or unrealistic.

› Make a photo partially color.

› Experiment with different compositing modes between layers.

› Invert the image.

› Saturate or desaturate the color

Applying some of the special effects filters that are built into Photoshop or other image editing applications can add visual interest or salvage a photo of inferior quality. We applied a filter called "Spatter" on this particular photograph.

This is the original photo.

Monotone(ish) photographs don't have to stay monotone. In Photoshop, you can add color using the "Curves" dialog box; experiment with manipulating the curves graph line.

A posterization filter adds impact when you want your image to have a graphic look rather than a photographic look.

This is the original photo.

Extreme closeups can be even more dramatic with unexpected color. Try using the "Hue/Saturation" sliders in Photoshop.

Natural media filters, such as this chalk effect, can create unique images and eye-catching textures.

Adjust the hue, saturation, and contrast of images by manipulating Photoshop's curves. You can create unlimited color variations that add pizzazz to your design.

*You can selectively control how much color appears and exactly where it appears using the saturation tools. Of course, a technique should be used to **enhance** your message, not merely to prove you can use Photoshop.*

John transformed this photographic montage of office icons (a stock photo) into an illustrative painting.

An already great shot can be turned into an even stronger image (as long as it suits and enhances your project). John used a "Poster Edges" filter on this sunset and increased the color saturation.

John opened this image in MetaCreations Painter, a "natural media" software package. He duplicated (cloned) the original image using a chalk brush.

The two examples to the right are stock photos from EyeWire, from the Hoopla Collection by Dean Stanton. The duotones in this particular collection have colorful squiggles painted directly on top of the images.

Don't Forget
STOCK ILLUSTRATIONS

As with stock photography, the selection and variety of stock illustrations has grown tremendously with the advent of digital delivery. These illustrations, available in both full-color and grayscale (or you can just convert a full-color image to grayscale if necessary), come in many different styles covering a vast selection of themes, concepts, and subject matter. You can alter them to suit your needs, just as you can photographic images.

Like stock photos, you can browse through a CD or through samples online. Look for images to spark ideas for whatever project you're working on.

Where to buy
STOCK IMAGES

There are a number of vendors that sell stock images, both photographic and illustrative. Before you buy an image, be sure to check the licensing agreement; there are usually two kinds of agreements— "royalty-free," as well as "rights-protected."

Royalty-free images are quite a bargain. They're usually sold to you outright for a flat fee; you can use it however you choose and as many times as you want. Along with all this freedom comes the disadvantage of non-exclusivity: it's possible that the same image you're using could be bought by anyone else (including your competition) and used in the same way at the same time.

If it's important that you have more exclusive rights to a particular stock image, you can choose **rights-protected images.** These are not offered as royalty-free—you "rent" them for a specific use and sometimes for a specific length of time. To prevent any overlapping of usage and to give the appearance of exclusive use, the copyright owner (the stock image provider) keeps track of who is using which images, as well as how and where they're being used. The more exclusive your agreement, the higher the fee. The size and exposure of your project also affects the fee.

Most stock image providers can provide **single-image downloads** from their web site, or they can ship a CD directly to you. Royalty-free single download prices are very reasonable and are usually based on file size. Typically, a 600K, 5x7-inch, 72 dpi image file is very inexpensive (something like $25); a 10MB, 5x7-inch, 300 dpi image file is medium-priced; and a 28MB, 8x11-inch, 300 dpi image is more expensive (like $150 and up).

EyeWire, Inc.
www.eyewire.com
(our personal favorite)

Comstock Images
www.comstock.com

PhotoDisc
www.photodisc.com

StockPhoto
www.stockphoto.com

Adobe Systems
www.adobe.com

Getty Images, Inc.
www.gettyone.com
You can search a large number of stock photo and illustration sources from this one site

The Bettman Archives
are now owned by Bill Gates and can be found at
www.corbis.com or
www.corbisimages.com

There are many others. Go to Yahoo and search for "stock photo."

4. Understanding Design Challenges & Approaches

It's interesting how often design projects are thought of as design "problems." This is probably because we find ourselves searching for solutions to the "problem." The very phrase "design problem" can be intimidating if you haven't had a lot of experience as a designer. It can even be intimidating if you're an experienced designer—most of us would rather not work on a "problem." But a design "challenge" is much more fun than a problem.

As a designer, your challenge is to communicate visually, and not many jobs are more fun than that. So even if you're feeling a little inadequate, chances are you're much better equipped to accept this challenge than most people. After all, you're reading design books, aren't you?

In this chapter we used the following typefaces:
Large heads: **Firenze. 75 point**
Body copy: Bailey Sans, 9/12, which gives the text
   a contemporary, upscale look
Small heads: **Bailey Sans Bold, 10/12**

Limit Your Options

If you hire a thousand great designers to work independently on the same project, you'll get a thousand great and different solutions. There are many approaches and solutions to a design challenge; in fact, there are usually so many possible solutions that the first challenge is to **limit the options** to the solution. Otherwise you'll spend all your time deciding which approach to take and not enough time developing several good ideas.

Limiting factors

In any design project, there are external factors that help to narrow the design focus, such as the information and preferences gathered from client consultations, as well as the considerations of the target audience. These help to narrow your choices right away.

These restraints are not bad things— once you know what elements (or restrictions) are necessary, the rest of the design solution often falls into place more easily. Or at least it points you in a direction that helps to narrow the incredible number of solutions.

Four main restrictions

There are four main limitations in any job that help narrow your choices. Although you will naturally take these into consideration anyway, it helps to make a conscious note of them at the beginning of a project so you don't get side-tracked into an impossible choice. The four restrictions are:

> The reproduction process
> The client specifications
> The budget
> The deadline.

Let's look at each of these factors and see how they affect your project.

Keep in mind that not one of these restrictions is an excuse for poor design. Many incredible pieces of graphic design have been created on cheap paper, or on a small budget, or in a hurry.

We do have a sign in our office, though, that states:

Good Fast Cheap
pick any two

1. Start at the end

The most limiting factor of any design job is the end process—how is the job going to be reproduced? For instance, if it's a newspaper ad or phone book ad, you need solid typefaces that will hold up well under the process and the paper, your color options will be limited (probably to black, if it's placed in a newspaper), your illustration or photographic options will be limited to those that will reproduce well with the lower linescreen value used in newspaper work, etc.

But if the ad is for a slick magazine, you have more typeface options, perhaps color options, and a wider range of possible illustrations or photographs because it's printed on smooth paper with higher resolution.

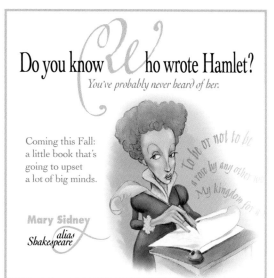

> In a magazine with glossy paper and high- quality printing, you have few physical limitations. You can use very fine type and high-resolution images with subtle gradations of tone.

In this layout, the high-quality printing process allowed us to use subtle colors in the headline and body copy without worrying that the type will fall apart. Even the fading of the type in the illustration should reproduce well on a high-end printing press.

> Newspapers and phone books are printed on absorbent paper and the images generally need a low linescreen value. So it's best to limit your typeface choices to those without fine details or thin lines, choose images that will not degrade in the printing process on cheap paper, and avoid using small type in gray because the linescreen dots will make it difficult to read. These limitations also apply to any other inexpensive reproduction process, such as copy machines and faxes.

For the newspaper version of this ad, we changed the subhead and body copy to black to avoid reproduction problems. We enlarged the illustration and eliminated the faded quotes since they might be unreadable when converted to a coarse newspaper halftone. Then we adjusted the layout to accommodate the changes.

2. Client specifications

As you begin a design project, the client will usually provide specific information about the project that will limit your options and influence the look and feel of what you're going to design. For instance, the client might demand you use an existing logo, the company color scheme, or certain product imagery that literally shows the product, as opposed to concept imagery that sets a mood or gets emotional attention.

Here's a typical project with a long list of client specifications.

▶ Description: 8.5 x 11, 2-fold, 2-color flyer for vacation studio rental

▶ Use: as a direct mail piece to travel agents' mailing lists and brochure racks.

▶ Main copy: emphasize village life-style and high-tech features.

▶ Bullet copy: itemize sites of local interest, casita features, rental rates.

▶ Graphic elements: map, interior and exterior photos, logo, logo of the co-opting partner.

▶ Also, the client wants a corresponding ad for tourism and visitor guide magazines.

A common technique with which to begin a project is to place all of the required elements in the layout without giving much thought to what the final design will be, as shown above. The challenge is then to make all the pieces of the puzzle fit in such a pleasing way that the whole message is easy to digest at a glance.

Once you have all the pieces together, you can start having fun. As you move things around, play with fonts, and experiment with color, ideas will come to you and you'll start seeing possible solutions that wouldn't appear if you were looking at a blank space.

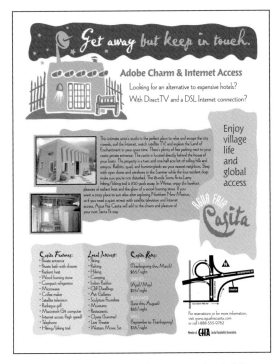

Once all the elements were on the page, we decided the little studio image could be a charming focal element. Since the project was limited to two colors, we rendered the illustration in those colors (and whatever tints and shades we could create from them). The resulting image actually became more interesting than a black-and-white photograph.

As we experimented with placement and type, it became obvious that the headline would have a lot more contrast and thus eye appeal if we made a dark shape behind it; we decided to make that shape reminiscent of the sky and hills.

To emphasize the high-tech message, we added the oversized satellite dish to the drawing. By making the headline two different colors, we added impact to the "get away" message and yet, using a repetition of color between the dish and the type, tied in the concept of "keep in touch."

We chose fonts with casual, fun, yet clean characters. To visually organize the substantial copy (always a challenge), we used shapes of color that repeat the loose nature of the illustration as well as the background shape behind the headline.

The result is a piece that is visually more interesting, yet still organized and easy to read.

Get away but keep in touch

Our guest studio is the perfect place to relax, escape the city crowds, surf the Internet, watch satellite TV, and explore the Land of Enchantment. There's plenty of free parking and your own private entrance.

Two and one-half acres of rolling hills and arroyos make rabbits, quail, and hummingbirds your nearest neighbors. Enjoy the 16-mile Santa Fe-to-Lamy hiking/biking trail 100 yards away. If you need a quiet retreat with satellite television and Internet access, Agua Fria Casita will add charm, pleasure, and convenience to your next Santa Fe stay.

AGUA FRIA Casita

For reservations and
for more information
visit www.aguafriacasita.com
or call 1-888-555-9762

Adobe Charm & Internet Access

This corresponding magazine ad is okay—it's nice and clean, the typeface is pretty, and it says what it's supposed to say. But it looks a little sterile compared to the final brochure, and there's not enough visual contrast to pull a reader's eye into the piece.

Get away
but keep in touch.

Our guest studio is the perfect place to relax, escape the city crowds, surf the Internet, watch satellite TV, and explore the Land of Enchantment. There's plenty of free parking and your own private entrance.

Two and one-half acres of rolling hills and arroyos make rabbits, quail, and hummingbirds your nearest neighbors. Enjoy the 16-mile Santa Fe-to-Lamy hiking/biking trail 100 yards away. If you need a quiet retreat with satellite television and Internet access, Agua Fria Casita will add charm, pleasure, and convenience to your next Santa Fe stay.

AGUA FRIA Casita

For reservations and
for more information
visit www.aguafriacasita.com
or call 1-888-555-9762

Adobe Charm & Internet Access

To coordinate more closely with the brochure, we repeated the heavy, casual typeface and the loose shape behind the headline. To create a stronger focal point, we divided the headline into an eye-catching focus with a contrasting subhead.

3. What's the budget?

The budget constraints impose limitations that sometimes make it challenging to find design solutions.

Restrictions are not a bad thing—they often force us to be more creative. If you can't afford to hire a photographer or illustrator or even pay for stock photos, you have to be more creative with typography and perhaps clip art.

True, it's *easier* to design a full-page newspaper ad than a 2x5-inch ad because a full-page ad automatically gets a reader's attention, no matter what it says or how boring it looks. But it's fun to work with the limitations and turn the negatives into the positives. And it's often very satisfying, as well.

> The example on the left shows a client who has money to work with. Large, full-color, slick ad.

> The small guy needs to turn her business negatives into positives: smaller company, more personal, less expensive than the competitors, etc. A small budget does not mean a project can't be well designed, creative, and effective!

HOME and OFFICE NETWORK and CONNECTIVITY EXPERTS

Looks ranker dough ball bought, off curse, nor bawdy worse hum, soda sully ladle gull win baldly rat entity beer's horse! Honor tipple inner darning rum, stud tree boils fuller sop—wan grade bag boiler sop, wan muddle-sash boil, an wan tawny ladle boil. Guilty Looks tucker spun fuller sop firmer grade bag boil-bushy spurted art. Failing torrid, shay flunker shelf honor ladle bet, an, jester cobbler menace letter, worse sunder slip an snorting.

▲ **Home Office Solutions**
▲ Brewing worse jesters scarred aster udders; infect, haze niece.
▲ Finely, Fodder Beer gutter grade bag short-gum, Murder Beer gutter muddle-sash haunting raffle, an Ladle Bore Beer gutter tawny ladle pestle, an oiler.

▲ **Corporate Office Solutions**
▲ Herring door beers, shay weakened, lipped otter door windrow, an dished aware harm jesters fascist shagged scrabble.

▲ **B2B Solutions**
▲ Wail dun stun dare lacking end-bustle during nosing! Coiler Place Deportment. Harmer garner coiler Place Deportment wen way dun heifer toiler-fun? Pesplendent Brewing, inner trampling verse. Set darn, worming, an cape quoit! Yore oil-wares thanking dare burghers inner horse!

PowerOn
545 Technology Court ▮ Embudo Station, New Mexico 87505 ▮ www.poweronnis.com ▮ 505.555.9772

4. The deadline approaches

The deadline impacts your design choices, particularly regarding outside services, like special photography or the time it takes to reproduce the job—a one-color piece will have a faster turnaround than a two- or four-color piece. And the deadline limits your choices for illustration or detailed photo-editing work—you might have to work with what you have rather than spend two days creating a brilliant Photoshop montage.

If there's not time to shoot a photograph, use type, color, and shapes to tell your story. In the example above, a beautifully messy font says "plaster" better than most photographs. The primitive tile shapes are all that's needed to illustrate the craftsmanship of laying tile. An oversized ampersand (&) connects yet separates the two artists and becomes a playful visual element.

You may not have time to hire a professional photographer, but if you have a digital camera (even a cheap one), you can usually grab a shot that will work great, given a little creative edge. John took the image above onsite during a five-minute digital photo shoot. He then posterized it in Photoshop and used a vector auto-tracing program to give it even more of a graphic, hard-edged look. Almost any marginal-quality photo can be salvaged by applying creative image-editing techniques, even in a hurry.

Choose a Look

We may talk about creating a design, but what we really want to do is **communicate**—communicate an idea, a feeling, or a message.

Communication is the real reason we're designing something at all. And it's impossible to design anything without communicating *something*. The challenge is to control *what* message is being communicated. And that's where design comes in—design is the visual choices you make to enhance the communication of a message. Your design can confuse and blur the message or it can make it memorable and clear.

Since each design project has its own unique message to convey, try to give that message its own unique personality by exploring different conceptual and visual approaches. The following is a variety of very broad conceptual directions to consider before actually starting to design. For any given design project, several of these options may provide viable solutions.

Look through each of these examples with a current project you are working on in mind; one of them might apply to your message. If so, many of your design decisions are already made.

In this chapter we could create other categories and subcategories, but the visual point is simply that there are many different ways to approach every project.

The following examples relate to design projects such as print ads and brochures where the objective is to deliver a specific message. Other projects, such as designing logos, letterheads, and business cards, concern themselves more with creating an appropriate and memorable corporate (or personal) image, and we discuss that in Chapters 6 and 7.

The generic look

This look is conservative, unimaginative, and boring, a design with no personality. It's probably the least attention-getting look you can design. Even a horribly ugly design would stand out more than this approach (but, of course, an ugly, noticeable design sends some other message that you'd rather not communicate!). Designs like this are unfortunately common because they're easy and fast, and they don't take any effort of thought or imagination.

Some designers confuse this style of design with a professional, conservative, classy look. Perhaps it was all those things the first million times we saw it. Now, however, this look has become the elevator music of graphic design, but without the passion.

Now that every computer in the world uses Helvetica as a default, the potential over-saturation of this look promises to make your message disappear further into the background than you ever thought possible. Designers who haven't bored themselves into a creative daze or a fear-of-failure stupor actually enjoy experimenting with typefaces that have more unique looks and that convey personality.

**We've been named
Top Dog
at the
16th Annual
Top Dog Design
Competition.**

Here at Ballyhoo Creative we're proud of our designers. But award-winning design doesn't mean much to a client unless it's followed closely by award-winning sales. If your design team isn't winning awards and growing profits for you, try throwing us a bone.

Ballyhoo Creative

1422 East Kent Drive, New Truchas, CA, (555) 438-5555

Why this piece looks generic:

> It has an unimaginatively centered alignment.

> It uses the Helvetica typeface which automatically makes it look dated (like 1970s).

> There is not much contrast.

> There is not much white space.

> There are typewriter apostrophes, a clear sign of an unprofessional designer.

> The copy is good, but the design does not support the message.

The corporate look

A corporate approach is exceptionally neat, organized, and predictable, giving an impression of trust and dependability. If you're not careful, this approach can look more like the generic, no-personality approach. But the corporate look is more creative than the generic look. It's more flexible—you can create all sorts of variations within the framework as long as the overall composition is neat, organized, and readable.

In the examples to the right, even with the slightly bizarre illustration, the ad appears to come from a company that doesn't get too wild or too far out of the mainstream.

What makes these pieces look corporate?

> Strong, clean lines

> No superfluous elements

> Typefaces are not unusual or weird (although it is certainly possible to get away with odd typefaces in corporate pieces!)

If we decide to be more casual and playful with the headline, the overall neat, organized alignment and conservative layout still makes the ad work as a message from a responsible, solid-citizen corporation.

The clients think the wacky dog illustration is fun. So much fun, in fact, that they say it is inappropriate for this particular corporation. The designer can feel lucky she gets to keep the wacky headline font.

The visual-wow look

With this approach, your main goal is to grab a reader's attention with a bold image, a stunning photo, or a captivating illustration style. While this approach is usually meant to be visually shocking, it can work in a variety of situations, from conservative, low-key messages to wild, anarchic youth-culture designs.

In the example top-right, the image of the dog is so bizarre and whimsical that you can't stop yourself from looking at the piece and you'll probably even read the ad copy. A simple piece of art used in a provocative way can be just as arresting as a photograph or a complex, technically amazing illustration.

It's always fun and often productive to keep exaggerating the focal point of the layout to see how far you can take it. In the top example, we thought the dog was a large visual element until we started experimenting with how extreme we could get. In the resulting example, lower-right, the contrast between the massive black dog and the white background is a visual magnet for a reader's eyes. If we went one step further and made the almost-abstract shape of the dog an unexpected color, such as red or green, we might take the visual-wow factor up another notch yet.

What gives these pieces their visual impact?

› Oversized, bold, simple graphic

› Strong contrasts—lots of black and white with small dashes of color

› An interesting headline typeface, one that is simple yet has a subtle "designer" quality.

The info-heavy look

This approach is useful for presenting a lot of detailed information and creating a formal, professional impression. You want to get someone's attention by showing how many features or advantages you have or by how expert you are. A simple, well-organized design makes it easy for the reader to scan a lot of information.

In the example to the right, you can instantly tell that it's a factual presentation of information, even though it uses a lighthearted, fun illustration. With this much copy in the ad, the reader gets the impression that the business must be serious about what they're saying so maybe you should read it (although some designers/copywriters take this thought to the extreme and present so much text that the chances of it being read become very slim).

When the copy is lengthy, use bold subheads so the reader can scan the main topics with a glance. Remember that a large portion of readers are not going to read this much text. The only chance you have of pulling any readers in is to create visually attractive and conceptually interesting headlines and subheads—their eyes will scan the heads and subheads, and if they're still interested, they'll read.

In this example, we turned the headline into a visual element and left white space around it to leave some breathing space on this text-heavy piece. The breathing space encourages a reader to dive in because it prevents an overwhelmingly textual appearance.

What makes this text-heavy piece look so clean and organized:

> Strong alignments of text, clean lines of columns.

> White space is gathered into organized areas instead of being interspersed between many different elements.

> Repetition of the black bars at top and bottom ties the information together into a neat package.

> Conservative combination of typefaces.

> Relatively small units of information grouped together; the reader reads one small chunk, then doesn't mind reading the next small chunk, and so on until the entire ad is actually read.

The omnibus look

The term "omnibus" refers to dealing with numerous items or objects at once. Omnibus designs are fun to create and to read—the image variety combined with short blurbs of text is irresistible to most readers.

With this approach you create a dazzling array of visuals using a variety of photographic and illustrative styles, each item with its own short blurb of text. This look works well for brochures and larger print ads where you have room to use a lot of images and still make the text large enough for easy reading. Because this is a casual, fun approach, the text can often be casual or humorous as well.

Be careful using this approach in a small ad because the images can lose their visual impact and the text might be too small to read comfortably.

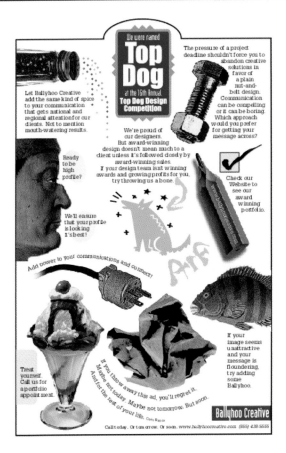

What's going on in this omnibus ad?

▸ This design gets your attention, but it's not as strong as it could be. When visual elements are approximately equal, the reader doesn't know where to begin reading. **Something** has to be the boss. An omnibus ad is stronger if there is an emphasis, or focus, on one of the visual elements.

Above, the boxed headline is a strong element in this design and overall it's an interesting layout, but if we play with it and try exaggerating parts, it may get better.

Compare the example above with the two ads on the opposite page.

With a simple change . . .

> This design variation puts more emphasis on the "top dog" theme with the dog/star illustration (which is a piece of clip art). This illustration is now the largest element, and the dog is cute enough to get attention. But at this point we started wondering if we were being wimps—let's go ahead and put a *really* dominant image in the layout.

Let's strengthen it even more . . .

> Now the design has a much stronger impact with the huge, black dog that drags a reader's eyes into the piece. Once their eyes are on the page, they get pulled into seeing all of the surrounding colorful and interesting elements. Even though there is a lot of copy, it's broken up into short blurbs that tempt the reader to actually read them.

The typographic look

Don't think you have to use fancy graphic images in everything you design. Great type can be eye-catching and deliver an emphatic message with just a glance. The type might be stark or it might be an elaborate typographic treatment that becomes a piece of art in itself.

With the thousands of typefaces to choose from (or even with the measly few hundred on your computer), you have an inexhaustible supply of "looks" you can achieve, depending only on how creative you are.

Typographic design solutions are fun to work with and they're lifesavers when you have an unreasonable deadline or an extremely tight budget. Once you start experimenting with a typographic design, you usually end up with so many different ideas and versions that it's hard to narrow the choices to only one solution.

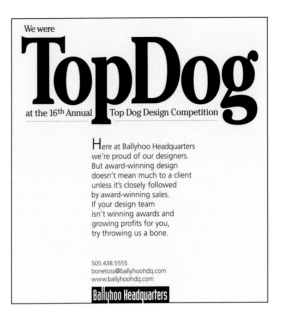

How about a fairly conservative yet strong look.

> A large, classic serif typeface with extremely tight letter and word spacing contrasts well with the small type flowing above and below the key words of the headline.

> A clean sans serif face for the body copy presents a no-nonsense approach that coordinates with the classic style of the headline.

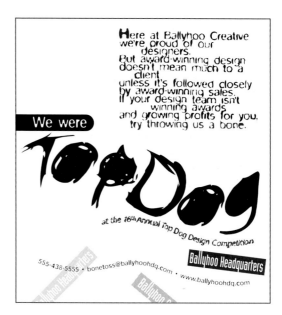

Type can even give the impression of a graphic.

> When you start playing with type, it's easy to create endless but similar variations of the same design. Be sure to completely change direction occasionally, trying different typefaces and various arrangements.

Depending on your market, you can get quite wild with type.

> "Lawless" typefaces can be used in just about any sort of piece, including the most conservative (depending on how and how much you use it). This piece uses both grungy and traditional faces together, with an emphasis on the grunge.

> Don't snub your nose at grungy type! Sometimes using just a wee bit on a page can give the impression that your company belongs in the twenty-first century.

The trendy look

What's trendy is always changing, but if your message is "we're what's hot right now," you'll want to consider getting attention with this approach. By the time "trendy" gets down to the mainstream, those who created it are way beyond it, but styles can last a good ten years.

Don't knock trendy. Everything in life has trends—eyeglasses, clothes, hair styles, cars, music, architecture, movies, even type. Picking up on a trend does not mean you are giving in to anything—it simply means you are alive in the world today, not clinging to yesterday. We know designers who still insist on using Helvetica, which makes every one of their designs look like a beehive hairdo.

These pieces look trendy because of these features:

> Thin lines going every which way.

> Industrial-looking typefaces.

> Text in boxes.

> Type sitting directly on or under a line.

> Meaningless stuff sitting on the page for that "random" look.

Type within boxes

▸ Beginning designers often put boxes around type; it seems to be something that feels safe, that keeps the type contained and prevents it from floating away. But beginning designers usually set 12-point Times or Helvetica in tightly fitting boxes and it looks very amateurish, which it is.

The trick to setting type in a box is to use a great typeface, set it small (typically), and leave breathing room around the type. The boxes need to be a conscious design element, not just containers because you don't know what else to do.

Random elements

▸ The technique of using random elements speaks to a certain audience. Do the items look random to you? They are. Do they seem to have any relationship to the message? Not necessarily. Personally, we're still rather ambivalent about the efficiency of this technique, but pieces like this are incredibly fun to create.

Look Around!

With each design approach the primary goal is simply to get the reader's attention. Exploring visually creative ways to reach that goal is where the design fun begins. As you explore various approaches to your next design project, always remain open to ideas and directions you haven't used before.

As we've mentioned before, one of the best ways to get the creative ideas flowing is to collect a library of design books that showcase award-winning projects that you can browse through when you're not sure in which direction to go. When you see examples that appeal to you, think about what it was that made you notice that design and how you can use that technique or a similar one to enhance your project.

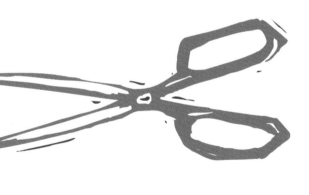

> **Designer Exercise:** Collect at least a dozen design pieces that you think are great. Make notes on each layout about the kinds of limitations the designer obviously had to work with—is it a low-budget job, something that could be done quickly, does it include and work with the corporate color scheme and logo, or was the designer given incredible creative freedom? If you see there are limitations, put into words how the designer creatively solved the problem within the limitations.

Let the ideas of other designers act as springboards for ideas of your own. Everyone needs to have the creative cobwebs shaken out occasionally.

5. Creating Visual Impact

A graphic design almost always has three main goals: 1) Get attention; 2) create a memorable visual impression; and 3) communicate a message.

The best way to accomplish the first two goals is with **visual impact.** The design and layout of your project will determine if anyone stops long enough to see what you have to communicate. The greatest ad copy in the world will go unread if you aren't able to get the reader's attention. And the only way to do that is visually.

Basically it's all about **contrast**—contrast of size, color, direction, format, or a contrast of the expected versus the unexpected.

Typefaces in this chapter:
Bell at 10/13 for body copy
    and at 90 point for large heads
A few callouts are in **Charlotte Sans Bold**

Size

Size—the size of type, graphics, the piece itself—is often overlooked when designing a piece that you want to have a strong impact. The trick to using size for visual impact is that it has to have a strong contrast. Making an element "sort of" bigger doesn't work—you gotta go all the way. And size doesn't always mean bigger. Often small works just as effectively, but it needs to be small *in contrast* to the rest of the piece.

In this example, size is the dominant impact in both the image and the headline. Setting part of the headline smaller enables us to make the other part really big.

By cropping the clip art image of the clock, we were able to make it larger as well, plus the cropped image is more interesting than just a flat picture of a clock on the page. Remember, when an image that we know well is cropped and going off the edge of a page, our minds fill in the rest of the shape. In design, this means we get to actually take advantage of "invisible space." That is, in this example, your mind "sees" the rest of the larger clock shape, even though it's not visible on the page. In fact, you probably unconsciously see the entire kitchen.

Even though this is a black-and-white piece, its impact is strong.

Obviously, the stark and simple illustration above is sized extra-large. It's simple, black-and-white, low budget, yet very eye-catching.

As we mentioned, "size" doesn't always mean "big." Let's say the example above is half of a newspaper page. Is there any way you could flip past that page without reading it? Hardly. That little tiny piece of copy has 100 percent readership. The secret is a **contrast** of size, either contrasting with other type or simply with the blank page.

A strong and surprising size can change a potentially dull, [almost] all-type piece into something striking. In this example, the conference initials become a large graphic element, bleeding off the edges. The same initials are sized even larger as a background element.

A blast of flat color in a bold and simple oversized illustration gets attention fast. The contrast of the size of the light bulb with the relatively small text makes the image seem even larger. And our minds fill in the rest of the shape that is outside the boundary of the ad, making the image seem even larger still.

This project for a publisher uses a large, over-sized ornament along with a large portrait to get attention and to set a 16th-century mood. The contrast in size between the body copy and the ornament, along with the ornament pointing toward the text, makes the body copy pop out of the white space even though it's small.

This variation uses a different arrangement of contrasts of size. Ornaments are usually small, delicate little things on a page. In these examples, the visual extravagance of the beautifully rendered ornaments is impossible to ignore. Remember, we're not just taking advantage of size as a visual impact, but the **contrast** of size.

The generous white space surrounding the smaller portrait would help this ad stand out on a page that holds other ads and editorial copy.

You've run out of Alpo and the Rottweiler's copped an attitude?

We deliver.

Essentials. And more. Shop online at www.MarketPlaceShopping.com or call 555-8668 between 9 a.m. and 7 p.m.

You've run out of Alpo and the Rottweiler's copped an attitude?

We deliver.

Essentials. And more. Shop online at www.MarketPlaceShopping.com or call 555-8668 between 9 a.m. and 7 p.m.

Black, oversized headline type dominates this layout, with a spash of contrasting color in the logo and illustration. Although we love the large type, its effect depends on contrast, and there's not much contrast between the headline size and the tag line size ("We deliver" is the tag line).

In this version, we reduced the type size of the tag line, which makes the headline type feel even larger and gives it more impact. We don't lose the tag line, though, because the contrast actually helps focus on it. Making the type size smaller also allowed us to make the panic-stricken customer a little larger.

Color

The impact of color is strongest when it's unexpected or extreme. Straight photographs of flower beds are lovely, but not necessarily exciting. Today we are all surrounded by so much color media of all sorts that we are able to visually accept just about anything you want to do with color in ways that would have been completely unacceptable years ago. So play with it, surprise yourself with it, push it.

And don't forget that color doesn't mean only "color"—color can be typographic black and white. Or it can be extremely minimal—it doesn't take much red (or any warm color) to make a statement.

The unexpected color in the portrait transforms this poster from a standard photographic approach to a visually arresting design.

The headline copy is blue, a cool color which recedes from our eyes. If we had made the headline a warm color like red, which comes forward, it would have created a conflict of focus between the headline and the portrait (not to mention a little confusing used with the word "blues," although sometimes you can use that sort of confusion to your advantage).

Color can be subtle and still get attention; in fact, it may get more attention than a regular full-color piece. In this example, the purple and black shapes create a visually interesting background that leads your eye vertically through the page and provides a powerful color contrast for the white type. If you can imagine a version with the photograph in full color, you can see that the focal point would be different, the eye flow would be different, and the entire page would not have as much impact, even though it would be more "colorful."

The jarring color combination in the stylized painting image set the tone in this brochure for a contemporary art gallery. The muted background colors add richness and a good contrast for the bright colors, emphasizing those colors rather than competing with them, and providing a visual respite so the garish green and orange don't overwhelm you. We could have picked up one of those colors or perhaps a tint or shade in the gallery name, but we chose not to interrupt the strong focal point of the image.

A four-color poster doesn't have to represent the full spectrum of colors. We colorized this black-and-white photograph in Photoshop to add subtle coloring, letting the headlines pop out in contrast.

Url's Internet Cafe WORLD HEADQUARTERS

John Tollett
The Big Boss

Santa Fe
New Mexico
87505

P 505 555 4321
F 505 555 1234
E url@UrlsInternetCafe.com

W www.UrlsInternetCafe.com

Warm colors are powerful and don't need much to make themselves known. The hard thing to do is convince your client to pay for the second color if it's only just a tiny bit; usually they say something like, "If I'm paying for a second color, then I want a lot of it!" You have to tell them that the tiny spash of second color is more powerful, has a stronger impact, looks more sophisticated, and it indicates that the carrier of the card has both good taste and money and is not a wimp.

73

The Unexpected

Very often in the design process, the first image or visual that comes to mind is the most expected, the most trite, the most pedestrian—which is exactly why it was the first thing that came to mind. So toss that idea and spend some time figuring out what evokes the intended message other than the ordinary, expected solution.

You might use an unexpected typeface, or a provocative piece of clip art instead of the expected photo. Or perhaps you apply an unusual technique to a common image, juice up the photograph, or play down a design feature that others might expect you to play up, which right there brings attention to a piece.

This doesn't mean a piece has to be bizarre or strange—it just means you want to move at least one step away from the mundane. The solution might still be formal and sedate, but it won't be dull.

Eat, Drink, Splash, and Be Merry!
(and Benevolent)

Summer Pool Party Benefit
for the Leukemia and Lymphoma Society

Join us at Cliff and Julie's pool for BBQ, music, dancing, and lots of splashing and swimming to break the summer heat. Bring a swim suit. Your donation of $25 benefits the Leukemia and Lymphoma Society.
Date: August 15 **Time:** 10 a.m. until 10 p.m. **Address:** 4566 Powerhouse Road, Fremont, California

Sponsored by: **Book-a-Cook**
PERSONAL CHEF SERVICE
Visit www.bookacook.com or email chef@bookacook.com

This functional, tidy flyer uses some very predictable features: Helvetica/Arial font, centered layout, cute photo of boy in pool. So change each of the predictable pieces: Use a fun typeface. Experiment with other layouts besides centered. Trade the cute photo for a more unexpected image.

In this version of the same flyer, we changed the type-face to something more fun and playful. We switched the cute boy for a hilarious piece of clip art and set it on top of a colored blat (a blat is anything like that shape behind the clip art, which you can easily create in any page-layout application or illustration program). But the layout is still centered, and the three main elements are all similar sizes. Something needs to be the focal point; something needs to stand out more than everything else.

Since the illustration (which is actually made of two characters from the font Backyard Beasties, outlined and colored in Illustrator) is the most eye-catching element on the flyer, we made that the focal point. We organized the rest of the text in sizes appropriate to the hierarchy of information. We repeated the color and outline of the blat behind the body copy to visually hold all the detailed information together as one unit, and added another fun character from the same Backyard Beasties font as an illustration. And we uncentered the layout.

The unexpected element in this poster and ad is a conceptual one, referring to the Helvetica typeface as a language. This poster makes the point that many designers overuse Helvetica, forfeiting individuality and personality for the safe, predictable look that probably worked a thousand times before.

(It's not that Helvetica is ugly—it's a beautifully designed face. It's just that it was the most popular face in the world in the 1960s and was a way of life in the '70s. When anything is that trendy during a certain era, it forever influences everything it touches; it's extremely difficult to use Helvetica and not project a '70s look. Is that what you want? Let go and move on.)

Instead of the first images that comes to mind, a woman or a piece of art, we chose to combine a high-tech fractal to represent complexity and imagination within the silhouette of a female. Fractals are infinite; the closer you look, the more you see. Even if a reader doesn't understand fractals and what they import, they'll get the impression of complexity and creativity.

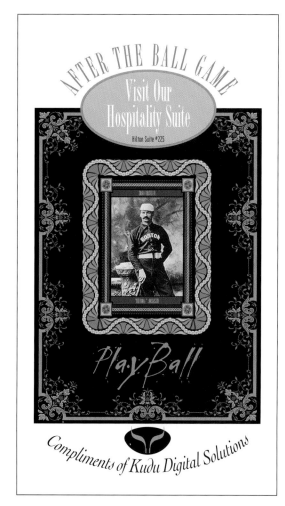

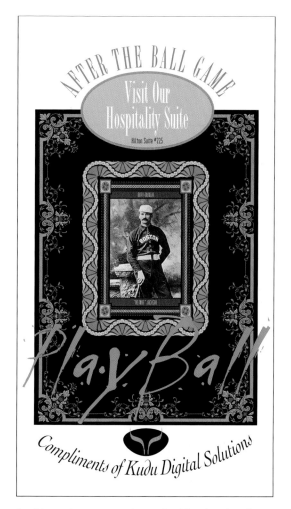

This private party invitation is accompanied by tickets to a ball game. Instead of a photograph of a contemporary ball player or even clip art of a bat or ball, we went for an antique stock photo with an apparently unlikely combination of fussy, overdone Victorian borders; we used three borders, in fact, to create an unexpected, colorful, excessive image. The result evokes the historical and sentimental aspects of baseball.

In this version we experimented with enlarging the "Play Ball" text as much as possible. But with this particular typeface, overlapping the fussy border makes the text less legible and seems to have less impact than the smaller headline shown in the example to the left. Large size doesn't always mean more impact— we actually have a stronger contrast, more emphasis, and an easier-to-read headline in the smaller size.

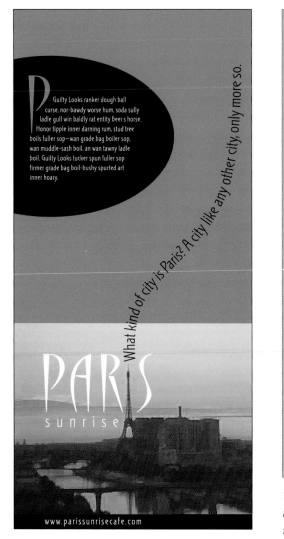

This ad, placed in an opera souvenir program, has several unexpected elements. It includes an unusual view of the Eiffel Tower, which becomes the letter "i" in "Paris." It uses a distinctive typeface, vibrant colors, and plenty of open space. The tag line flows like the winding river, and the cropped oval opens up the ad space because our minds fill in the rest of the shape.

You might expect a logo and stationery for an Internet cafe to look high-tech and trendy. But in this town (Santa Fe) where the ancient meets the modern everyday, the logo was given a petroglyph look and printed on stone-colored paper. The typefaces are a combination of new, grungy faces that represent the anarchy of the times we live in, yet the warmth of the old-fashioned care you get in the cafe. Also, you don't see many letterheads with logos this large—that's one reason we made it this large.

Is he an artist
or a
scientist?

Maybe both.

Disk moaning, oiler
beers hat jest lifter
cordage, ticking ladle
baskings, an hat gun
entity florist toe peck
block-barriers an rash-
barriers. Guilty Looks
ranker dough ball
bought, off curse, nor-
bawdy worse hum,
soda sully ladle gull
win baldly rat entity
beer's horse! Honor
tipple inner darning
rum, stud tree boils
fuller sop—wan grade
bag boiler sop, wan
muddle-sash boil, an
wan tawny ladle boil.

SA&T
SCHOOL OF ART & TECHNOLOGY

505-555-1745

Johnny
wants to be
a pirate.

Or a software
developer.

Maybe both.

Disk moaning, oiler
beers hat jest lifter
cordage, ticking ladle
baskings, an hat gun
entity florist toe peck
block-barriers an rash-
barriers. Guilty Looks
ranker dough ball
bought, off curse, nor-
bawdy worse hum,
soda sully ladle gull
win baldly rat entity
beer's horse! Honor
tipple inner darning
rum, stud tree boils
fuller sop—wan grade
bag boiler sop, wan
muddle-sash boil, an
wan tawny ladle boil.

SA&T
SCHOOL OF ART & TECHNOLOGY

505-555-1745

In this ad campaign for a private school, the viewer ***expects*** *the child to write something like "6 x 48 =" or "I will not throw spitwads."*

As the ad campaign continues with these ***un****expected ideas, the viewers learn to look forward to the new and surprising images that change on the blackboard, while the child remains the same.*

Visual Puns

Visual puns are attention-getting, entertaining, and fun to see. They're even more fun to create. When you combine two or more thoughts into one image, the image becomes more compelling and memorable.

You might combine and juxtapose two seemingly unrelated elements, such as a gangster and a pencil, or you might put together strongly related elements such as the *word* "feather" and the *image* of a feather.

The pun, obviously, is in both words of the name, illustrated in the single visual image. Sometimes when creating a visual pun, the name comes first and then the image, or sometimes an image will inspire the name.

This logo went through a number of variations, as is typical in the design process—variations on the swashes, the emphasis and weight of the letter "f," the degree of slant, and other detailed features.

To illustrate a common sort of identity deception, we show this despicable rat (Url) casting his alter-ego shadow.

An image doesn't have to be elegantly rendered to be effective. In fact, a simple or crude image may have a certain charm not found in a more sophisticated rendering.

Some word combinations practically illustrate themselves. This logo for a band is a literal visual interpretation of the words—sometimes the most obvious solution is a good solution. In this case, the rendering of the idea is done in such a simple, bold, graphic style that even such an obvious solution is appealing.

An ad for winetasting classes uses this drawing, whimsically illustrating one of the attributes to notice in a glass of wine.

Don't be a wimp

Many projects need to be fairly conventional because of their markets, but it might surprise you how often you can get away with doing something off the wall. Try unusual typefaces, odd paper sizes, or weird graphics. For a particular project, write down all of the expected or usual solutions, such as typeface choices, images, paper size, paper color, ink color, etc. Then decide which of those features needs to be fairly conventional and which ones you can play with. On the features you can play with, don't hold back!

You are warmly invited to meet my new husband.

Friday October 9 10 p.m.

Are you working on an invitation? Was your first thought to design it onto an 8.5 x 11-inch piece of paper, folded into halves or quarters? Why not try a tall, skinny look—divide the 8.5-inch width into thirds. You'll not only have an unusual invitation, but you can print three for the price of one.

mary sidney herbert

poetry reading
and
book signing.

monday » 3 p.m.

garcia street bookstore

505.123.4567

You don't have to make things extra-large to prove you're not a wimp—it takes even more courage to make things very small. The beauty and the effect of this ad lie in the fact that the small size is unexpected and creates a strong contrast. Our eyes cannot resist contrast. In a crowded newspaper, this ad would get 100 percent readership—it's not possible to open a page and ignore the surprisingly small type surrounded by lots of white space.

Are you working on a flyer? Instead of the standard vertical format, how about a horizontal one? Or try the horizontal cut in half, as shown below. Notice in the examples above and below, parts of the graphic and type are missing, but your eye "sees" the missing parts. Thus you get more visual impact in less physical space. Plus, the surprise of seeing type cut in half draws attention to itself.

Your attendance is requested.
Pinocchio Room · 3 pm · Friday · October 9
Be there or be fired.

sales meeting

Look Around!

Different design pieces appeal for different reasons, but in well-designed projects you will almost always find a strong form of visual impact that drew your eyes to that particular design. The more often you take a moment to *name* the visual impact, to put into words exactly what attracted your eyes, the more easily you will find yourself coming up with irresistible solutions.

Browse through your collection of design award books. Even if you've looked at the books dozens of times, you may notice something new in light of your current design project. You're not really looking for the exact solution to your problem, but for something to get your imagination fired up, perhaps going in a different direction than you originally planned on. Or you may just need some inspiration or ideas for different illustration, typography, photography, or layout styles. Your final solution may not look anything like the example that inspired you, but it may be what was needed to get out of a creative rut.

> **Designer Exercise:** Collect at least a dozen design pieces that have a strong visual impact. Put into words exactly what the impact is and how the designer achieved it. If the impact is the result of a phenomenal photograph or piece of artwork, what did the designer do with that photo or art that strengthened the design?

PROJECTS

There is no single voice
capable of expressing every idea;
romance is still necessary;
ornament is necessary;
and simplification is not better
than complexity.

Milton Glaser

6. Logos

Hundreds of logos are fighting for attention with hundreds of other logos every day. If your logo design is going to have a chance of being noticed, it needs to have a unique personality that people will not only notice, but *remember*. In this chapter we'll look at some common techniques and themes of logo design that never get old because they are capable of unlimited variations and interpretations.

A designer whose portfolio has lots of logos in it has a great advantage because it says a lot of things about a designer: it says you know how to think visually and conceptually, and that you can take a complex communications challenge and condense it into its simplest and most effective form.

Designing a logo

Using creative typography along with simple visual/conceptual correlations between images and type is the key to solving most logo design challenges.

Experiment, experiment, experiment! You're using a computer, not rubbing down press-type or hand-tracing letters from a book of type samples, so play with all the possible combinations of faces. Not happy with your fonts, want to experiment further but you can't buy every font you want? You can see what your logo will look like in over 8,000 typefaces from at least 8 different vendors: go to EyeWire.com, go to the "Type" section, then click on the link to the "Type Viewer." You can choose a face, choose a type size, type your company name, and see it rendered in any font of your choice.

Grab your hat!

This is a screen shot sample of the font Dolmen from Image Club, rendered on the EyeWire Type Viewer. What a great resource!

This logo is too busy—there are too many elements in this small space, too many gradations of tone that won't hold up well in many situations, and the typeface is difficult to read. Simplify for clarity, strength, and usability.

Often when designing logos, we go through versions like this (too complex) and then start revising it, reducing it to the simplest interpretation of the desired theme.

*The same logo is still fairly complex, but each of the elements will render easily in a variety of situations. Instead of setting **all** the type in the difficult face, we limited it to just the larger words and chose a contrasting, more legible face to work with it. We eliminated several of the extraneous elements. We managed to keep the client happy by adding a few details, like the dots and the tag line, but kept ourselves happy by making the details clean and simple. Most importantly, we concentrated on what would create the most effective **contrast.***

Different files for different uses

For many logos, you will need to create several different files to be used for different purposes.

For instance, you might have a subtle drop shadow in a logo that works great when you use it in a slick, high-quality magazine. You might have a version of your logo in color for full-color brochures, and a GIF version with browser-safe colors for the web. You need a version in black-and-white, without the subtle drop shadow, for newspaper ads, flyers that will be reproduced on copy machines, and your fax cover sheet.

Don't get attached to a particular design until you make sure it will translate well into all the different media it will be used in.

This is the full-color logo with subtle drop shadows that can be used in high-quality color printing, preferably on glossy stock.

This is the same logo in black-and-white, still with the subtle drop shadows because this version is for high-quality printing.

Here are two files of the same logo for an email service. The top one can be used where the printing and paper are high-quality, and a GIF version can be made from this for the web. The bottom one is useful for lower-quality printed pieces.

This version is the low-res GIF file to be used on the web, using web-safe colors. It doesn't look good in print, but looks great on the screen.

This black-and-white version is designed to hold up well in a newspaper, copy machine, or even a fax machine because there are no soft shadows that tend to get lumpy under poor printing conditions, and the contrast is stronger.

All type logos

Many logos are nothing more than type. But just because a logo is all type doesn't mean it didn't take creativity and skill to put it together. An all-type logo, used with a classic face, often creates a corporate look, a solid, dependable, no-nonsense sort of company. Think of the logotypes for IBM, Macintosh, or Pond's.

If you use nothing but characters, you had better be sure you're using excellent typography; check your letterspacing, linespacing, word spacing, the placement of hyphens or dashes, true apostrophes, etc.

ChromaTech   Helvetica/Arial

ChromaTech   Times/Times New Roman

CHROMATECH   Avant Garde/Century Gothic

CHROMA*tech*   Palatino/Book Antiqua

If you plan to use all text as your logo, be very conscious of your type choice (duh). As a general rule, don't use any font that is built into your computer (like the ones shown above). Buy a new one.

Be especially wary of Helvetica (Arial is also Helvetica, it's just called another name). Helvetica was the most popular typeface in the world in the 1960s and '70s, so anything you create with it automatically has a '60s/'70s look. Do you want the same visual identity as thousands of other companies and organizations who still have their Helvetica logos held over from the '70s?

*You can see what an incredible variety there is within the
limitations of using one main typeface in the logo.*

Combine typefaces

Very often in an all-type logo, you'll want to use two different typefaces. Sometimes you'll use two faces in the name of the company, or you might use a typeface in the large company name that is unsuitable for the small type. For instance, say you use a face with very thin lines in the company name, but you need to put the word "international," "incorporated," "corporation," or perhaps even a tag line like "We do it for you," in very small type. The thin lines that print clearly in the company name will completely fall apart in the small type, so you need a different typeface that will hold up in small sizes.

This is the key to using two (or more) different typefaces: **contrast.** You cannot use two fonts that have anything in common— if they are not members of the same family (like the very thin weight combined with the very heavy weight), then you must choose faces that are very different.

If you combine two faces and can tell they're not working well together but can't put your finger on it, look for the features that are *similar* between the two fonts—it is the *similarities* that are causing the conflict.

If this concept interests or confuses you, read the second half of *The Non-Designer's Design Book*, which focuses on the specific challenge of combining typefaces.

ChromaTech

This combination uses two members of the same typeface (Clearface); one is black italic and the other is bold italic. There is a bit of contrast between the two words, but not enough to be effective.

ChromaTech

*This combination uses two different sans serifs (Frutiger and Avant Garde). They are slightly different, but have the same size, weight, and structure (monoweight strokes); these **similarities** create a conflict instead of a contrast.*

CHROMATECH

*This combination uses two different serifs (Garamond and Cresci). They are somewhat different, but both faces have serifs, a moderate thick/thin weight shift in the strokes, and both parts of this word are in all caps in the same size; these **similarities** create a conflict instead of a contrast.*

*Chroma*Tech

*This combination uses two different scripts (Bickham Script and Redonda Fancy). They are somewhat different, but both faces have a thick/thin weight shift, curly shapes, hand-scripted forms, and they're about the same size; these **similarities** create a conflict.*

Chroma**Tech**
i n c o r p o r a t e d

This combination uses two different weights of the same sans serif typeface (Frutiger). Although they are from the same family, the difference in weight (thickness of the strokes) is so strong it creates a great contrast. If we combined the medium weight with the heavy weight, the contrast would not be so effective.

ChromaTech

This combination is also two members of the same family (Clearface). The contrast comes from differences in weight (thickness), structure (expanded vs. condensed), and form (italic vs. roman), with a little contrast of color thrown in.

ChromaTECH
i n c o r p o r a t e d

This combination uses a modern face (Quirinus) and a sans serif (Frutiger). The contrast is in form (caps vs. lowercase), size (the caps are the size of the x-height), weight, and structure (serious thick/thin vs. monoweight strokes, plus serif vs. sans serif). The choice of color contrast is deliberate: cool colors recede. If we had chosen a warm color, like red, for the word "TECH," the warm color would have come forward, become more important, and there would be a conflict between it and the larger word (Chroma). The small type for "incorporated" is Frutiger.

Chroma **Tech**
i n c o r p o r a t e d

Obviously, we've got a script (Bickham) combined with a sans serif (Impact). To intensify the contrast, we made sure to choose a heavy, rather vertical sans serif, and used the special, fancy initial cap that comes with Bickham.

Kitt&Katt
·C A F E·

The words "Kitt," "Katt," and "CAFE" are the same typeface, but KittKatt is Bodega Sans Black and CAFE is Bodega Sans Light. The contrast of weight and size is emphasized by a contrast of color. The ampersand (&), Redonda Fancy, uses a contrast of structure, color, and weight.

Triple Click *Design*

The modern font (Onyx), with its vertical, condensed serif characters contrasts strongly with the horizontal, cursive face (Carpenter). The contrast is emphasized with color.

SA&T
SCHOOL OF ART & TECHNOLOGY

The letters of SA&T are directly from the font Blue Island. The only logical choice of a contrasting typeface would be a sans serif—just about any other category of type (oldstyle, modern, slab serif, script, or another decorative face) would almost certainly have conflicting features.

TABS+INDENTS *the book*

This combination uses a tall, decorative, yet formal sans serif (Serengetti) in all caps vs. a playful, handlettered, childlike face in lowercase. In this logo, we also used a contrast of direction, size, and, of course, a contrast of color.

Tweak a letterform

Often logos involve tweaking a letterform out of the ordinary. This can be a very simple addition or subtraction to a character, or it might involve an illustrative technique.

Having letterforms interact with each other, as many of these do, adds visual interest and makes a typographic design more unique.

CHROMATECH INC.

This is simply an all-type logo with a red dot replacing the bar in the letter "A," which not only adds more visual interest to the logo, but provides a color spot that reinforces the word "chroma."

Once we saw this business name set in lowercase italic, it was an easy creative jump to see the letter "f" in the shape of a feather.

This logo for the Lamy Ad Club uses a strong combination of typefaces with a simple reverse of the overlapping stroke.

We pulled out the tail of the ampersand (&) to give this logo a more unique look and provide a subtle visual emphasis to the concept of "art" in the logo.

Segura and **Lamoreux**
Crane **Service**

W:lton House

Mimi's
flower shop

M bius

*In each of these examples we simply substituted a small image
of some sort for a character. The small images might be from
picture fonts, clip art, original art, or just drawn shapes.*

Add elements

Many logos have symbols attached to the type. If you have lots of money and can afford to expose your logo excessively, the symbol can eventually stand alone, like the Nike swoosh or the Merrill-Lynch bull, and everyone knows who it refers to. But it takes millions of dollars and several years to do that—most symbols will stay with their logotypes rather than stand alone.

There is an entire study in symbology—all we are going to say here is that logo symbols are typically simple in form, with clean lines and shapes that will hold up well in a variety of media. If you look through design annuals and logo books, you'll notice that the symbols are often arbitrary shapes that have nothing to do with the logotype—they are simply marks (often common, everyday marks) that combine with a particular typeface and name of a company to create **a unique combination.** The *combination* of symbol, typeface, and name is the key—there are probably hundreds of logos that use a circle as a symbol in some way, but not in the unique way that *you* use it.

Ideally, you'd like the symbol to look like it belongs with the logotype. Often you'll see the two pieces set so far apart from each other that the connection is fairly obscure. Remember the rule of proximity—the space between elements creates a relationship; if the elements are close, they have a relationship; if they're far away from each other, they don't.

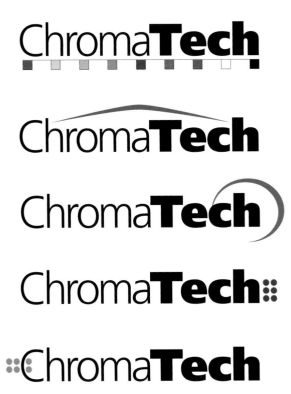

These imaginary logos each use a mark in addition to the company name. You can see that a mark can be very identifying, yet very simple.

Add clip art

There is so much great clip art available, including the dozens of images you get in one picture font. Not only is clip art great for using in logos, but just skimming through collections of it can give you great new ideas.

We repeated this little clip art of the lightbulb to represent both concepts of "idea" and "swarm." The font is naturally playful and unpredictable, but the entire logo is still a bit too static for a "swarm."

We bounced the type around to add energy to the letterforms.

In the process of adding more energy and visual interest, we created the unexpected element of a stray lightbulb that breaks away from the swarm.

TREVOR CLIFTON

computer geek to the rescue!

Emilie Brooke

writer

TYLER MARSHALL incorporated

satellite communications experts

Prairie Rachel

star for hire

Wise Moon
professional tutors

To customize the names, each of these logos uses an inexpensive piece of clip art or a character from a picture font.

Communication Consultants

R&R Termite Control

Easy Shot PHOTOGRAPHY

the **Soup Kitchen**

fine dining • fine wine

Don't forget the illustrative sort of clip art as a design option. Just remember that the logo must also work in black-and-white, so experiment with making the different files you need for various media before you finalize one solution.

Add illustrations

If you are a clever illustrator, like John, or if you can afford to hire an illustrator to help complete the logo, then you can truly customize your ideas in very unique ways. But don't let the lack of a professional illustrator stop you—a primitive illustration can have as much (or more) charm than a polished, professional one. In fact, often illustrators strive for that "unpolished" look.

There are a wide range of illustrations that work in logos. Just remember to keep it simple and that any illustration must also render well in black-and-white.

This is a simple illustration, not much more complex than any of the elements we added to the variety of logos earlier in this chapter.

Tobacco Addicts Anonymous

This is also a simple illustration, using more creativity than high-end illustrative skill. Even if you're not technically an illustrator, it's amazing what you can do with an illustration program—push yourself.

MetaNeo Gallery

This logo uses an illustration as the main element, since the image represents the gallery's focus so well.

Santa Fe
Screenwriting
Conference©

Bench Jockey
Sports Paraphernalia

Each of the clever logos above uses a custom illustration. Although this can be lots of fun, remember that every logo must still be able to be read and used in black-and-white, so make sure any illustration is flexible enough for all media before you commit to it.

Don't forget about a nice frame for some logos— a frame can turn a well-done typographic logo into a more illustrative and powerful piece.

Handlettering is a form of illustration that works wonders in logos, but for most pieces it requires an acquired skill to be truly successful. A logo represents your entire business; it's worth it to hire an excellent letterer if you want that look.

Having said that, go ahead and experiment with writing the company name dozens of times with different writing tools; chances are you'll find the beginnings of an interesting and unique logo. Some of the most wonderful handlettered pieces have been very "unsophisticated" letter-forms taken from scrawls on walls, napkins, etc.

Look around

Logos are everywhere, literally everywhere. We guarantee you cannot open your eyes in any room and not see a number of different logos. The more you are conscious of them, the better you will design them.

Designer Exercise: Collect logos. Cut them out of the newspaper, phone book, brochures, bread wrappers, labels, boxes, print them from web pages, etc. Collect good ones and bad ones. Write the product or service on the back.

Separate the logos that have a corporate look. Even though you might not be able to define exactly what creates a corporate look, you probably know it when you see it. Once you have them assembled in front of you, put into words what they all have in common that makes them look corporate. Is it the style of logo (often all text)? Is it the size of type? The lack of an illustration? A fairly conservative symbol?

Separate the logos that look professional but high-tech trendy, the dot.com sort of logos. What exactly is it that helps you recogize this sort of company? What do the logos have in common? What is it that gives you that trendy yet professional sort of look? Is it a different style of typeface than a more corporate logo uses? Does it have energy built into it, and how does it manage to do that? Do any of the logos in this category use Helvetica/Arial, Times, or Palatino/Book Antiqua?

Separate the logos you consider to be not-so-good. Exactly what is it that makes them not-so-good? Is it the typeface or the combination of faces, the letterspacing, the size, the symbol, the relationship between the symbol and the type, the rendering of any image or handlettering, is it too busy or hard to read? The more you can state in words what makes a logo *not* work, the less likely you will build any of those features into your own creations.

Find the web sites that use some of the logos you've collected. Is the web logo different on the screen than it is in print? If you found a full-color logo on a package, see if you can find it in black-and-white, like in the phone book. How is it different? What did the designer do (if anything) to make it work both in full-color and in black-and-white?

Keep a file folder stuffed with logos, and buy books that showcase award-winning logos. Look through them before starting to design your own!

7.Business
cards, letterhead, and envelopes

One of the first things any business needs is a business card, and next is letterhead and matching envelopes. It's best to design all of these pieces at the same time because you want them to be a cohesive package. If you design the business card first and plan to design the letterhead next month, you run the risk that the business card layout won't translate well to the letterhead. Even if you can't afford to have all the pieces printed at the same time, at least design them at the same time.

Business cards

A standard-sized business card is 3½ x 2 inches. Resist the temptation to make the card a larger, odd size—it won't fit in wallets or in many business card holders. When someone does put a large card in a wallet, the edges get all crumpled and the card looks shabby, which unconsciously reflects the image of the company whose name is on the card. Instead of trying to be creative in the size of the card, save your creativity for another area of its design.

If you *need* a larger card, experiment with a size that folds into the standard 3½ x 2; it might fold over the top, or the side might fold in, or both sides might open out. You can be creative as long as your creativity doesn't encourage someone to throw away the card.

These examples are typical of the kind of design you might find at a copy shop. Repeat these mantras:

It is okay to have empty corners.

*It is okay **not** to center the layout.*

*It is okay **not** to use all caps.*

It is okay to use a typeface other than Helvetica (Arial) or Times.

It is okay to use type smaller than 12 point.

It is okay to use one large graphic image instead of two small ones stuck in the corners.

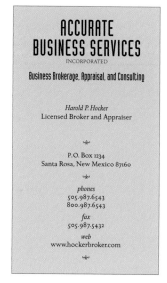

With thousands of typefaces at your fingertips, there's no excuse to use a boring one. In the examples above, all we did was change the typefaces, set most of it in caps/lowercase, and provide *one* alignment (instead of flush right, flush left, and centered on one page). In the dog kennel example, instead of two little graphics stuck in the corners, we used one and made it a focal point.

Even though the bad example (opposite page) used a centered alignment and all caps and we discouraged that, the problem is not really with the centered alignment and all caps—the problem is with how those features are used. As you can see above, all caps and centered can make a beautiful arrangement. What's the difference? Why do the examples above look elegant and the examples on the opposite page look dorky?

> The first dorky example isn't really centered—only part of it is. The combination of centered, flush left, and flush right all in the space of a little card creates a mess; there's a lack of cohesion and unity. In each of the examples above, there is one line running down the center of every element.

> A centered alignment needs nice type and a pleasant amount of white space to be acceptable. When a piece is centered and all jammed together in a deadly dull face, it inevitably looks unprofessional.

> The size of type (in relation to the piece) can make all caps acceptable or not. Business-card text can be small. Setting type all caps in 12 point is redundant—either make it a focal point with larger type and a stronger face, or make it a subsidiary element.

The secret is to be conscious: If you can put into words why you choose all caps, go ahead. You might say, "I need clean, rectangular shapes in this layout" or "I need to have lines without descenders that would bump into the other elements." Don't just choose all caps because you don't know any better. The same thought applies to a centered arrangement; if you can put into words that you need a formal, sedate look for a project, then go ahead and use centered (and only centered!).

Letterhead&envelopes

Remember, your letterhead and envelopes should have the same basic layout as your business card. This provides your business with a cohesive look; when you give someone a business card today and next week send them a letter, you want to reinforce the image of your business. When you send a letter in an envelope with a business card enclosed, the three items should make a unified presentation of the professional level of your services.

To create such a unified presentation sometimes means changing your layout on one piece so it can accommodate the different shape of another piece of the package. That is, don't design your business card and get it printed until you have made sure that same basic arrangement will work on the collateral pieces.

These three pieces have no design relationship to each other: the letterhead is centered with pet on right; the envelope is flush left with pet on left; the business card is flush right.

Doggy's Best Friend
Boarding Kennels   Safe and Clean

125 South Frontage Road Santa Fe, New Mexico 87505
v 505·555·5555 f 505·555·5550 www.doggysbestfriend.com

Doggy's Best Friend
125 South Frontage Road
Santa Fe, New Mexico 87505

Doggy's Best Friend
Boarding Kennels
Safe and Clean

125 South Frontage Road
Santa Fe, New Mexico 87505
v 505·555·5555
f 505·555·5550
www.doggysbestfriend.com

These two sets of the same stationery each have a consistent look among the pieces; they have the same basic arrangement with adjustments in type size and spacing made for the different elements.

Type&body copy

There are lots of ways to indicate which numbers on the stationery or card are phone numbers, fax numbers, cell phone numbers, etc. On the opposite page we show you a variety of options.

And don't forget that the purpose of stationery is to write letters. Always keep in mind the body of the letter when you are designing the page; when you type a letter on that page, coordinate it with the layout. If you are creating this for a client, it's nice to show them a sample of how the body of a letter will appear—it can influence their decisions.

Numbers

Because there are typically quite a few numbers on a letterhead and business card, between the address, zip code, and all the phone numbers, it's nice to choose a typeface that has beautiful numbers built right into the face.

Most standard faces have regular, lining numbers, as shown below (lining numbers are all the same size, as opposed to oldstyle numbers as shown in the next column). If you use a face with lining numbers, make them at least a half-point or whole point smaller than the rest of the text; otherwise they overwhelm the line. Below, each example is 10-point type.

411 555 1234   Garamond

411 555 1212   Times

411 505 5632   Helvetica

If it works with your project, it's nice to use a typeface with oldstyle numbers, as shown below. Oldstyle numbers are built like lowercase letters, with ascenders and descenders, so they fit right into a line of type. Below, the numbers are 10-point type. Compare them with the lining numbers in the previous column and notice how much more elegant and interesting these oldstyle numbers are.

411 505 1298   Golden Cockerel

411 505 1256   Dyadis OldStyle

411 505 5632   Highlander

411 505 5632   Bossa Nova

Descriptors

When you include telephone numbers, cell phone numbers, toll-free numbers, fax numbers, etc., on a letterhead or business card, it can be quite a challenge to label each of these numbers appropriately yet creatively.

Keep in mind that some items really don't need descriptive labels, such as a toll-free number—the 800 or 888 prefix tells us it's toll-free. However, if you are labeling every other number with its full descriptive name, be consistent and add the toll-free label.

Don't spell out the words telephone, facsimile, toll-free, etc., unless you have incorporated those words into your design. The initials shown below are easily understood. You might use V (voice), T (telephone) or P (phone). You really don't need to label obvious things like "email" or "web address" because their form makes it clear what they are; sometimes, however, the descriptive label can become part of the design.

p 411.505.1256	telephone 411.505.1256
f 411.505.1257	
c 411.660.1258	cellphone 411.660.1257
V 411.505.1256	facsimile 411.505.1257
F 411.505.1257	
C 411.660.1258	tollfree 800.505.1212
E jt@ratz.com	
	email jt@ratz.com
t: 411.505.1256	
f: 411.505.1257	webaddress www.ratz.com
e: jt@ratz.com	
w: www.ratz.com	*telephone* 411 555 1234
	fax 411 555 1234
ph 411.505.1256	
fx 411.505.1257	*web* www.ratz.com

Parentheses

There are a variety of alternatives to the parentheses that typically surround the area codes. On a clean page, parentheses tend to add clutter to the numbers unnecessarily. Below are alternatives to the parentheses around area codes.

411.505.1256	periods
411 505 5632	spaces
411-505-1256	hyphens

(you will probably have to use the baseline shift to move the hyphens up to where they belong)

[411] 505 5632	brackets
411 505 5632	baseline shift
411 505 1256	italic area code
411/505.1256	slash
411 505.1256	**bold** vs. light
411 **505.1256**	light vs. **bold**

Letterhead body copy

Be conscious of where the body of a letter will appear on the stationery. Generally, using a little extra space between paragraphs (not a double return!) in the body creates a cleaner look instead of indenting each paragraph (and you know better than to use extra space *plus* an indent).

123 S. Frontage Road
Santa Fe
New Mexico
87505
505-555-5555 v
505-555-5550 f
www.doggysbestfriend.com

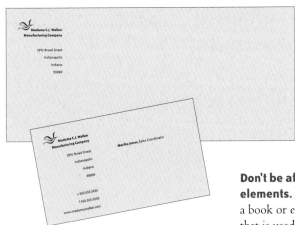

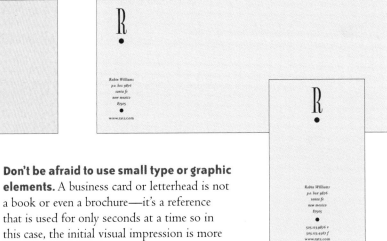

Don't be afraid to use small type or graphic elements. A business card or letterhead is not a book or even a brochure—it's a reference that is used for only seconds at a time so in this case, the initial visual impression is more important than sustained readability. (Although you will probably set the type a bit larger on the letterhead than you do on the business card.)

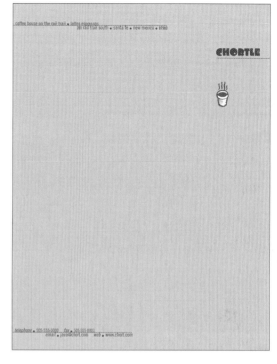

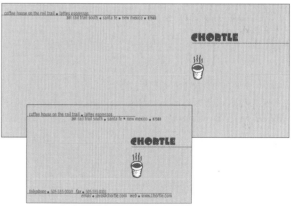

Scarlett Florence Williams · Actress
555 Hollywood Boulevard · CA · 55555 · 555.555.5555 · actress@star.com

Robin Williams

l p.o. box 9876 l santa fe l new mexico l 87505 l v 505.555.9876 l f 505.555.1234 l

Scarlett Florence Williams
555 Hollywood Boulevard · Los Angeles · CA ·

Scarlett Florence Williams · Actress
555 Hollywood Boulevard · Los Angeles · CA · 55555
v 555·555·5555 f 555·555·5550
actress@star.com

Robin Williams

l p.o. box 9876 l santa fe l new mexico l 87505 l

Robin Williams

l p.o. box 9876 l santa fe l new mexico l 87505 l v 505.555.9876 l f 505.555.1234 l

Don't be afraid to use large type or graphic elements. Most of us rarely write letters that fill all the available space on the page, so go ahead and be graphic. You can always use a second page for those occasions when you need more room to write.

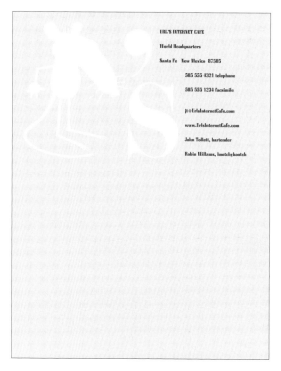

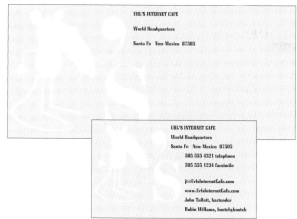

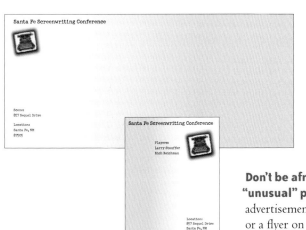

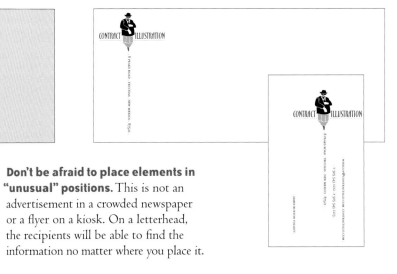

Don't be afraid to place elements in "unusual" positions. This is not an advertisement in a crowded newspaper or a flyer on a kiosk. On a letterhead, the recipients will be able to find the information no matter where you place it.

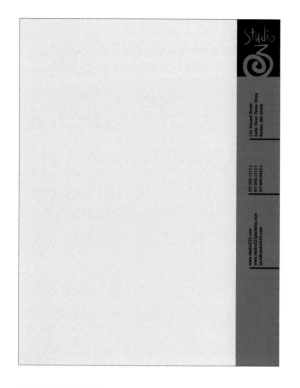

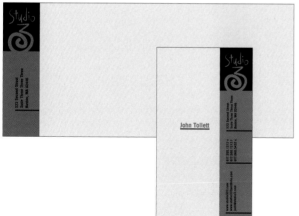

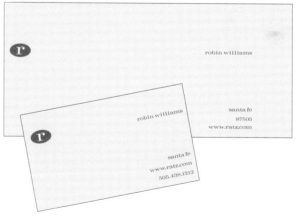

Don't be afraid to fill the writing space with an image — a light shade of an image, of course, so you can type or scrawl directly on top of it. Pull out and emphasis a piece of your logo, a different symbol of your business, or a photograph that is related to what you do. Let it bleed off the page (talk to the press first to see if that's an option on this job), let it fill the space, let it be dramatic! Remember, this is letterhead, not a billboard. The recipient will take the time to read what you write even if it is a wee bit less readable than type on a plain white background.

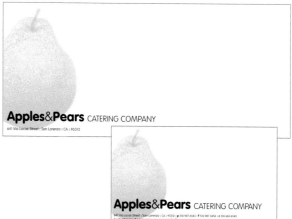

Letters & labels

Add a second page

When you print your letterhead package, you might consider printing fewer second pages at the same time. On the second page, you don't need all of the information that's on the cover page. A nice technique is to print just your logo, or even just a part of the logo. Or if you have a large image screened back on the first page, print that same image smaller on the second page, or maybe full strength but small. If your company uses a tag line, print just the tag line on the second page. Or pick up just one of the design elements from the cover page and print it on the second page.

Typically you will have five hundred or a thousand pieces printed of the first page of the letterhead, plus matching envelopes and business cards; print maybe one or two hundred of the second pages, depending on how often you think you'll use them.

Add a smaller letterhead

The standard stationery size that measures 8.5 x 11 is fine, but it's also nice to create a more personalized look on smaller paper. There are a number of standard but smaller sizes— check with your printer and ask what sizes they have and choose one that will fit neatly into a smaller envelope that the printer also has. Often a smaller letterhead, because it's more personal, doesn't carry all of the professional information that the regular business stationery does—your name and logo might be enough. Though it's a simpler layout, it should still tie in with your main pieces.

Print it yourself

Another simple and inexpensive solution is to design personal stationery on half of a regular sheet of paper. You can print two at a time on one sheet of paper, printed horizontal, then cut it. This size fits neatly into the size A4 envelope that you can buy at any office supply store.

Labels

If you plan to use labels, now is a good time to design and print them so a) they are consistent with your business package, and b) if you're using more than one color, you'll save money by printing everything at once.

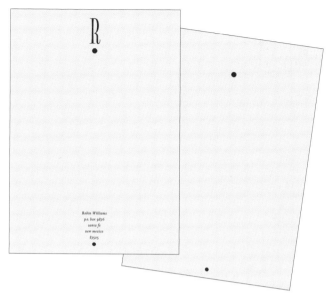

Above are smaller-sized, more personal letterhead examples that don't replace the formal letterheads, but complement them. They are shown here with examples of second pages. The designs for the second pages can also be used with the larger letterhead.

Left and right are examples of labels that coordinate with the business package. Labels can be just about any size and shape, but check with the printshop before you design them—they can help you determine the best size with the least amount of waste.

If you plan to print labels on your desktop printer, buy the labels first, then design to that size! Print a few samples onto plain paper to make sure they are positioned correctly on your page before running the labels through.

Look around

If you design your own business cards and letterhead, you are the client and you have great freedom to create something wonderful. The flip side of this freedom is that you have no excuse if the design is less than spectacular, so take extra special care in your own cards. They instantly tell prospective clients exactly the level of your creativity and expertise.

Designer Exercise: You probably already have a collection of business cards. Go through them and sort them into two piles: the ones that look professional and well-designed, and the other ones.

Take the well-designed pile and notice, actually put into words, what makes them well-designed. Is it the typeface? The size of the type? The strong alignments? A contrast between elements that creates visual tension? The space between the elements? Which elements are grouped together and which ones have more space around them? Can you see any patterns? That is, do you notice that most well-designed cards do not use Times at 12-point? What are the patterns of the typography on beautiful cards? Can you find cards where the designer was brave enough to use a tiny splash of

color, or a large image that fills the space, or lots of white space? What do you think of those cards?

Also, make note of how good designers call out the various elements, like the variety of phone numbers or the individual names in a large company.

The more you notice what good designers are doing, the easier it will be for you to incorporate those features into your work.

But also put into words exactly what makes an amateur card look amateur. Is it the typeface? Is it all caps in a script face? Is it the size of the type? Is it the lack of cohesion in the layout; that is, are various elements stuck in the corners and the middle with no apparent thought to connecting the elements together? Is it a lack of a strong alignment; that is, are some items centered, some

flush left, some flush right, etc.? The more clearly you can pinpoint what makes a card look unprofessional, the less likely you are to design your own pieces in that way.

Don't forget that the paper stock on which the card, letterhead, and envelope are printed influences the recipient. It's all well and good to print your own business cards on those perforated sheets with your little color inkjet, but the impression you leave with people is that you are a small operation that can't afford good cards (plus the toner rubs off in their wallets). Take a look again through the cards that give you a professional impression—are any of them printed on desktop printers? If so, what did they do to overcome the "homemade" look?

8. Invoices & Forms

SUMMARY

Total from State Sales and Use Tax Section except Aviation Sales Tax (columns A, B, C, E, and F)			$1,839.00
Total from Special and LOCAL taxes			$38.00
Total from Aviation Sales Tax			$0.00
		TOTAL TAX DUE/PAYABLE	$1,877.00

STATE SALES AND USE TAX SECTION

	A 4.62 Gross Receipts Sales Tax	B 4.62 Use Tax UV Line1/UC Line2	C 5.63 Texarkana Sales Tax	D 4.62 Aviation Sales T...	MMR Bank	Excise
Line 1 - Total Gross Receipts	$2,000.00					
Line 2 - Purchases	$1,500.00					
Line 3 - Deductions	$4,590.00					
Line 4 - Taxable Sales	$0.00					
Line 5 - Gross Tax Due	$0.00					
Line 6 - 2% Discount						
Line 7 - Prepayments Made						
Line 8 - Tourism/MIC Credit	$5.00					
Line 9 - TOTAL TAX DUE	REFUND DUE *					

* ... is handled through a separate process.

SPECIAL ADDITIONAL TAX SECTION

	Code	Taxable Sales	Rate	Tax Due	2% Discount	Net Tax Due
Line 10 - Tourism	8001					
Line 11 - Short Term Rental Vehicle	8002					
Line 12 - Short Term Rental	8003					
Line 13 - Additional Mixed Drink	8004					
Line 14 - Residential Moving	8005					
Line 15 - Long Term Rental Vehicle	8007					
Line 16 - Texarkana Use	8008					
Line 17 - Aviation Use	8009					
Line 18 - Wholesale Vending Tax	8006					
				TOTAL SPECIAL TAX		$38.00

LOCAL TAX SECTION

You have not specified any localities for remittance.

Invoices and forms are not very sexy, but they are important and very necessary. We all have to fill them in all the time; somebody has to create them.

Although there are entire studies on what makes a good, usable form, in this short chapter we're going to focus on making it look nice, which is really secondary to making it usable. But if it appears clear and clean, it has a better chance of being usable. If you are creating a form, keep in mind all those things that make you crazy when you fill them out—spaces too small to write in, disorganization, difficulty discerning which parts are pertinent to you, etc.

To create a good form, you have to know your software really well—I think that's why a lot of people hate creating forms. Learn to use your software's features like "paragraph rules" so the horizontal lines appear automatically and exactly where you want them.

The secret to good forms

There are those who are bored to tears by the thought of designing a form, and those who love the fussy challenge of creating a good, clear, usable form. Forms are seriously under-rated in the world of graphic design.

Of the four basic design principles (contrast, repetition, alignment, and proximity), the secret to a good-looking form is **alignment.** Lack of alignment is the single biggest feature that makes a form appear unclear to the user. The other principles are also very important, as in any design, particularly **contrast** to help direct the user through the form, **proximity** to keep groups of related pieces of information together, and **repetition** to tie it all together. But alignment is the key.

*The example at the top-right uses interesting typefaces and calls out the major features in bold for clarity in communication and visual **contrast** and **repetition**. But it doesn't look as clean and clear as it could.*

*In the lower example, elements are **aligned,** which naturally presents a cleaner look; cleaner [usually] communicates better. Also, the spacing was adjusted so the elements that belong together (like the two lines of "Suggested donations") are closer together, and the separate elements have a wee bit of extra space between them (following the principle of **proximity**).*

Club Membership & Donation Form

Name _____

Mailing Address _____

City _____ State _____ Zip _____

Home phone _____ Email _____

Work phone _____ Fax _____

Suggested dues: ☐ $25
Suggested donations: ☐ $40   ☐ $75   ☐ $100   ☐ Other_____
Cash_____   Check (payable to TPR Fund; donations are tax deductible)_____
Volunteer for: ☐ Trainer mini-grants   ☐ Trainer appreciation   ☐ Newsletter

Questions? Please call Clyde Hyde at 999-1234.
Mail to: TPR, 32 South Stone Way, Santa Fe, NM 87505

Club Membership & Donation Form

Name _____

Mailing Address _____

City _____ State _____ Zip _____

Home phone _____ Email _____

Work phone _____ Fax _____

Suggested dues: ☐ $25

Suggested donations: ☐ $40   ☐ $75   ☐ $100   ☐ Other_____
                            Cash_____   Check_____ (payable to TPR Fund; tax deductible)

Volunteer for: ☐ Trainer mini-grants   ☐ Trainer appreciation   ☐ Newsletter

Questions?   Please call Clyde Hyde at 999-1234
Mail to: TPR, 32 South Stone Way, Santa Fe, NM 87505

Doggy's Best Friend
Boarding Kennels

Animal Name

Visit Number

Date in

Type of animal

Breed

Age

Colorings

Unusual characteristics

Date of last shots

Date of arrival

Date of departure

Owner

Owner's contact number

Animal received by

Accompanied by toys, blankets, bed, etc.

Special instructions

Extra Notes:

Doggy's Best Friend
Boarding Kennels 505.123.4567

Animal Name

Dates of visit

Thank you for trusting us with your pet. This is a summary of his/her visit. We hope to see you and your pet again!

Eating habits

Drinking habits

Sleeping habits

Behavior issues

Doggy's Best Friend
Boarding Kennels · Safe and Clean
123 S. Frontage Road · Santa Fe · NM · 87505
505.123.4567   www.doggybestfriend.com

Invoice No.

Animal Name

Date of Visit

No. of nights @ $22/night . . . . $

Special food . . . . $

Training while boarding . . . . $

Medications . . . . $

Emergency treatment . . . . $

Special instructions . . . . $

Other. . . . .

. . . . $

Subtotal . . . . $

Tax. . . . . $

Total . . . . $

Thank You!

When appropriate, tie in your forms with the rest of the business package, like the letterhead and business card. A consistent look through all peripheral material will make even the smallest business look professional.

Doggy's Best Friend
Boarding Kennels
Safe and Clean

123 S. Frontage Road
Santa Fe
New Mexico
87505
505-123-4567 v
505-123-5678 f
www.doggysbestfriend.com

Examples

Below is a typical form. It's been used for years and so it's been refined to serve its purpose well—it just isn't very pretty. It doesn't take any longer to design a form that looks nice, so why not. This form doesn't use alignment to its advantage, nor contrast to call out important features, nor proximity to group similar elements together and separate others, nor repetition (consistency) to help create an organized, unified look. Also, it uses Courier in all caps. All caps can be nicely done, as we discussed in Chapter 7, but they should never be used just because you don't know any better.

All we did in this version shown below is change everything from all caps to regular lowercase letters with beginning caps (called "sentence caps"). It's already easier to read. But is there any reason to use Courier in a form like this? Not really. Courier is not only a little more difficult to read than most faces because it is monospaced, but it instantly projects an unsophisticated form (there are ways to use Courier and have the page look trendy, but that can only happen if the rest of the page is well designed).

ASTA MAÑANA HIGH SCHOOL	STUDENT_____
MEDICAL INFORMATION	ID _____ DATE OF BIRTH _____
MEDICAL RELEASE	☐ SR ☐ JR ☐ SPH ☐ FSH
☐ FIELD TRIP ☐ ONE DAY	ORGANIZATION/ACADEMIC CLASS _____
☐ ACTIVITY TRIP ☐ EXTENDED	

		FATHER/GUARDIAN	MOTHER/GUARDIAN	EMERGENCY CONTACT PERSON
E M E R G E N C Y	NAME			
	ADDRESS			
	H PHONE			
	W PHONE			

PERSON RESPONSIBLE FOR MEDICAL EXPENSES:

I N S U R A N C E	COMPANY	PLAN NUMBER
	ADDRESS	GROUP NAME/NUMBER
		INSURED ID NUMBER

M E D I C A L	ALLERGIES _____
	DATE LAST TETANUS SHOT _____
	STATE PHYSICAL RESTRICTIONS, HEART CONDITION, DIABETES, ASTHMA, EPILEPSY, RHEUMATIC FEVER, OR OTHER EXISTING MEDICAL CONDITIONS _____
	MEDICATIONS CURRENTLY TAKING _____

LIABILITY RELEASE   THE ASTA MAÑANA PUBLIC SCHOOLS, THEIR REPRESENTATIVES, AGENTS, AND EMPLOYEES ARE RELEASED FROM LIABILITIES OF INJURY TO THE STUDENT EXCEPT FOR INJURY OR DAMAGE RESULTING FROM WILLFUL NEGLIGENT ACTION OF THE ASTA MAÑANA PUBLIC SCHOOLS, THEIR REPRESENTATIVES, AGENTS, AND EMPLOYEES.

PARENTAL PERMISSION TO OBTAIN MEDICAL SERVICES   IN CASE OF ACCIDENT OR MEDICAL EMERGENCY, THE ABOVE MENTIONED SPONSOR IS GIVEN PERMISSION TO OBTAIN MEDICAL CARE FOR STUDENT.

SIGNATURES   WE HAVE READ, AGREE WITH, AND WILL FOLLOW ALL OF THE ABOVE.

_____   _____   _____   _____
STUDENT   DATE   PARENT/GUARDIAN   DATE

Asta Mañana High School	Student_____
Medical Information	ID _____ Date of Birth _____
Medical Release	☐ Sr ☐ Jr ☐ Sph ☐ Fsh
☐ Field Trip ☐ One Day	Organization/Academic Class _____
☐ Activity Trip ☐ Extended	

		Father/Guardian	Mother/Guardian	Emergency Contact Person
E M E R G E N C Y	Name			
	Address			
	H Phone			
	W Phone			

Person responsible for medical expenses:

I N S U R A N C E	Company	Plan Number
	Address	Group Name/Number
		Insured ID Number

M E D I C A L	Allergies _____
	Date Last Tetanus Shot _____
	State physical restrictions, heart condition, diabetes, asthma, epilepsy, rheumatic fever, or other existing medical conditions _____
	Medications currently taking _____

Liability release   The Asta Mañana Public Schools, their representatives, agents, and employees are released from liabilities of injury to the student except for injury or damage resulting from willful negligent action of the Asta Mañana Public Schools, their representatives, agents, and employees.

Parental Permission to obtain medical services   In case of accident or medical emergency, the above mentioned sponsor is given permission to obtain medical care for student.

Signatures   We have read, agree with, and will follow all of the above.

_____   _____   _____   _____
Student   Date   Parent/Guardian   Date

Asta Mañana High School
Medical Information
Medical Release

Student _____
ID _____ Date of Birth _____
☐ Sr ☐ Jr ☐ Sph ☐ Fsh

☐ Field Trip   ☐ One Day
☐ Activity Trip   ☐ Extended

Organization/Academic Class _____

E M E R G E N C Y		Father/Guardian	Mother/Guardian	Emergency Contact Person
	Name			
	Address			
	H Phone			
	W Phone			
	Person responsible for medical expenses:			
I N S U R A N C E	Company		Plan Number	
	Address		Group Name/Number	
			Insured ID Number	
M E D I C A L	Allergies _____			
	Date Last Tetanus Shot _____			
	State physical restrictions, heart condition, diabetes, asthma, epilepsy, rheumatic fever, or other existing medical conditions _____			
	Medications currently taking _____			

Liability release The Asta Mañana Public Schools, their representatives, agents, and employees are released from liabilities of injury to the student except for injury or damage resulting from willful negligent action of the Asta Mañana Public Schools, their representatives, agents, and employees.

Parental Permission to obtain medical services In case of accident or medical emergency, the above mentioned sponsor is given permission to obtain medical care for student.

Signatures We have read, agree with, and will follow all of the above.

Student _____ Date _____ Parent/Guardian _____ Date _____

Asta Mañana High School
Medical Information
Medical Release

Student _____
ID _____ Date of Birth _____
☐ Senior ☐ Junior ☐ Sophmore ☐ Freshman

☐ Field Trip   ☐ One Day
☐ Activity Trip   ☐ Extended

Organization/Academic Class _____

EMERGENCY		Father/Guardian	Mother/Guardian	Emergency Contact
	Name			
	Address			
	Home Phone			
	Work Phone			
	Person responsible for medical expenses:			
INSURANCE	Company		Plan Number	
	Address		Group Name/Number	
			Insured ID Number	
MEDICAL	Allergies _____			
	Date of last Tetanus shot _____			
	State physical restrictions, heart condition, diabetes, asthma, epilepsy, rheumatic fever, or other existing medical conditions _____			
	Medications currently taking _____			

Liability release: The Asta Mañana Public Schools, their representatives, agents, and employees are released from liabilities of injury to the student except for injury or damage resulting from willful negligent action of the Asta Mañana Public Schools, their representatives, agents, and employees.

Parental Permission to obtain medical services: In case of accident or medical emergency, the above-mentioned sponsor is given permission to obtain medical care for the student.
Signatures: We have read, agree with, and will follow all of the above.

Student _____ Date _____ Parent/Guardian _____ Date _____

Above, we changed the typeface to a sans serif for the titles in the boxes, and a serif face for the paragraphs of text at the bottom of the form. Now we can look at the alignments. Can you see places where items could be aligned? Do you see inconsistencies, like the spaces between the lines and the text? Do you see places where we could add contrast to help guide the user through the form, point out important areas, and make the page more visually interesting along the way?

If you think the form is eventually going to get reproduced from a copy of a copy of a copy, as often happens, avoid using any screens behind words (the pale tints of color, as above) because they get clogged up and messy if reproduced on copy machines or fax machines.

Now that we've got good typefaces in sentence case, we can clean up the rest of the form:

> **Contrast:** We set important words in the heavy version of the sans serif to help guide the user through the form, as well as make it more visually attractive. We turned the three headings along the left on their sides to make them easier to read and gave them more contrast as well. **Do not** use an underline to emphasize words!

> **Repetition:** We made the spacing consistent. The contrast also creates a repetitive effect, as does the alignment.

> **Alignment:** This simple technique instantly makes the form neater. You can see that every element now has some visual connection with something else on the page—nothing is placed arbitrarily.

> **Proximity:** The elements that belong together are connected in neat units.

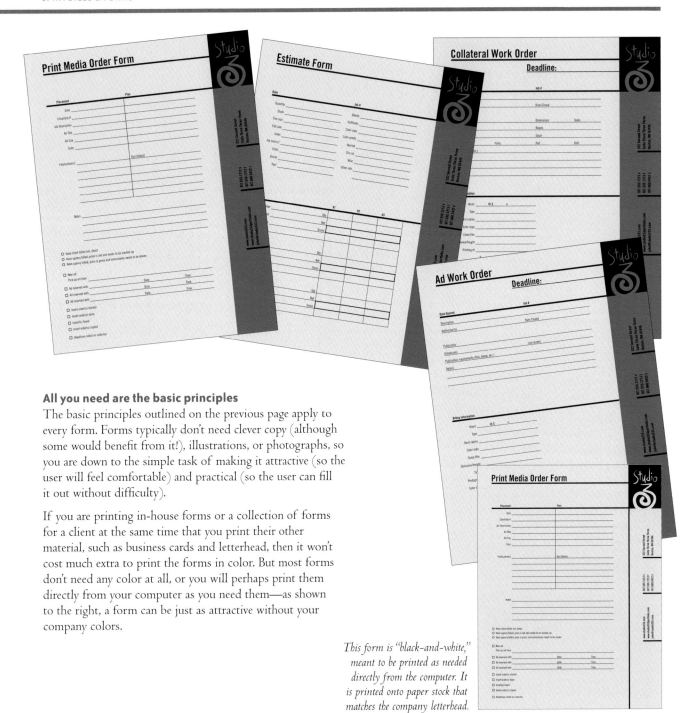

All you need are the basic principles

The basic principles outlined on the previous page apply to every form. Forms typically don't need clever copy (although some would benefit from it!), illustrations, or photographs, so you are down to the simple task of making it attractive (so the user will feel comfortable) and practical (so the user can fill it out without difficulty).

If you are printing in-house forms or a collection of forms for a client at the same time that you print their other material, such as business cards and letterhead, then it won't cost much extra to print the forms in color. But most forms don't need any color at all, or you will perhaps print them directly from your computer as you need them—as shown to the right, a form can be just as attractive without your company colors.

This form is "black-and-white," meant to be printed as needed directly from the computer. It is printed onto paper stock that matches the company letterhead.

Clarity

If you have many lines of data, as on an order form or financial chart, using a color tint on alternating lines helps clarify the information. You can create these colored bars easily using the "paragraph rules" feature in your page-layout program: as you type, the bars appear automatically (above, below, or behind the line of type), you can control the spacing between them and their length with single clicks.

Book	Edition	Price
The Little Mac Book	self-published edition	10.00
	first edition	12.95
	second edition	14.95
	third edition	16.00
	fourth edition	17.95
	fifth edition	18.95
	sixth edition	19.99
The Little iMac Book	first edition	17.99
	second edition	17.99
The Little iBook Book		18.99
Beyond The Little Mac Book		22.95
The Mac is not a typewriter	self-published edition	8.00
	Peachpit Press edition	9.95
The PC is not a typewriter		9.95
Beyond the Mac is not a typewriter		16.95
How to Boss Your Fonts Around	first edition	12.95
	second edition	16.95
PageMaker 4, An Easy Desk Reference	Macintosh	29.95
PageMaker 4, An Easy Desk Reference	Windows	29.95
PageMaker 5 Companion		32.95
Jargon, an informal dictionary of computer terms		22.00
A Blip in the Continuum	with Macintosh disk	22.95
A Blip in the Continuum	with Windows disk	22.95
Tabs and Indents on the Macintosh	with Macintosh disk	11.95
Windows for Mac Users		19.99
Home Sweet Home Page		14.95
Home Sweet Home Page and the Kitchen Sink	with CD	24.95
The Non-Designer's Design Book		14.95
The Non-Designer's Type Book		24.99
The Non-Designer's Scan and Print Book		24.99
The Non-Designer's Web Book	first edition	29.95
	second edition	34.99
Robin Williams Design Workshop		39.99

Carnation
Used for wreaths and garlands; often a reference to middle age because they bloom in midsummer.

Crab (crab apple)
A small apple with a delicate flavor and pink-and-white blossoms, often roasted and set afloat in a bowl of ale or wassail.

Cowslip
A favorite flower of fairies, used as their drinking cups. Used for making wine, the leaves for salad, the juice for coughs.

Daisy
The flower of the month of April; in England the daisy is small, white, and covers grassy slopes and fields.

Fennel
Fennel smells like licorice; it is the emblem of flattery. An English country proverb states, "Sow fennel, sow sorrow."

Gillyvor
Flowers of mixed colors in the carnation family; often a reference to middle age because they bloom in midsummer.

Lady-smock
Also known as cuckoo flower; blooms in meadows, covering grass like smocks laid out to dry, in early spring when the first notes of the cuckoo are heard.

Marigold
Also known as Mary-buds; used in salads, as ointment for skin, in lotions for sprains; petals in broth "comfort the heart."

Pansy
The names comes from the French pensée, which means "thought." Ophelia says, "...and there is pansies, that's for thoughts."

Pink
The smallest member of the carnation family; often used to describe perfect manners, as in "the very pink of courtesy."

Primrose and violets
Both flowers bloom so early in the spring that they don't live to see the summer sun; often associated with death.

Rosemary
An herb known for faithfulness and remembrance, as well as memory (tuck a sprig behind your ear while studying). Thick stems were used to make lutes.

Rue
An herb with a strong smell and bitter, sour flavor; associated with repentance, pity, grace, and forgiveness (often placed beside judges in court)

Thyme
Symbol of sweetness; often planted in garden paths so walking upon it will release the scent.

Woodbine (honeysuckle)
Symbol of affection and faithfulness; a creeping, climbing plant that twines its vines around trees and posts.

Spreadsheet or database forms

Many in-house forms are more useful as computer spreadsheets or databases where the data can be entered directly on the computer and output as hard copy, rather than handwriting on the printed form. You don't have to be an expert with a program like Excel or FileMaker Pro to create a simple form—try an application like AppleWorks or Microsoft Works. They allow you to set up the labels as well as the empty spaces you'll fill in. You can use any typeface you want, align elements, add graphics, and more, almost as you would in a page-layout application. The same basic design rules apply!

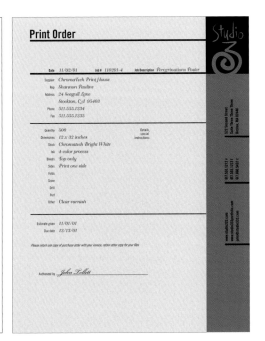

You can easily set up a simple spreadsheet or database that matches (fairly well) the other business pieces. Save the form as a template so every time you open it, it will be empty of data. Enter your new data into the empty cells or fields. You can either print it onto blank stationery (as shown above-left) or add your logo and other pertinent information directly on the computer form and print onto plain paper.

Web site forms

As much as possible, web site forms should follow the same basic principles as print forms: **contrast** so the visitor can figure out what's going on; **repetition** (consistency) so they don't get confused; **alignment** to keep things organized and clear; and **proximity** to make sure related elements are near each other and disparate elements are separated by a little extra space—those spatial relationships communicate huge amounts to the reader.

Book	Edition	Price
The Little Mac Book	self-published edition	10.00
	first edition	12.95
	second edition	14.95
The Little iMac Book		
The Little iBook Book		
Beyond The Little Mac Book		
The Mac is not a typewriter		
The PC is not a typewriter		
Beyond the Mac is not a typewriter		
How to Boss Your Fonts Around		
PageMaker 4, An Easy Desk Reference		
PageMaker 4, An Easy Desk Reference		
PageMaker 5 Companion		
Jargon, an informal dictionary of computer terms		
A Blip in the Continuum		
A Blip in the Continuum		
Tabs and Indents on the Macintosh		
Windows for Mac Users		
Home Sweet Home Page		
Home Sweet Home Page and the Kitchen Sink		
The Non-Designer's Design Book		
The Non-Designer's Type Book		
The Non-Designer's Scan and Print Book		
The Non-Designer's Web Book		
Design Workshop		

Book	Edition	Price
The Little Mac Book	self-published edition	10.00
	first edition	12.95
	second edition	14.95
	third edition	16.00
	fourth edition	17.95
	fifth edition	18.95
	sixth edition	19.99
The Little iMac Book	first edition	17.99
	second edition	17.99
The Little iBook Book		18.99
Beyond The Little Mac Book		22.95
The Mac is not a typewriter	self-published edition	8.00
	Peachpit Press edition	9.95
The PC is not a typewriter		9.95
Beyond the Mac is not a typewriter		16.95
How to Boss Your Fonts Around	first edition	12.95
	second edition	16.95
PageMaker 4, An Easy Desk Reference	Macintosh	29.95
PageMaker 4, An Easy Desk Reference	Windows	29.95
PageMaker 5 Companion	Macintosh	32.95
Jargon, an informal dictionary of computer terms		22.00
A Blip in the Continuum	with Macintosh disk	22.95
A Blip in the Continuum	with Windows disk	22.95
Tabs and Indents on the Macintosh	with Macintosh disk	11.95
Windows for Mac Users		19.99
Home Sweet Home Page		14.95
Home Sweet Home Page and the Kitchen Sink	with CD	24.95
The Non-Designer's Design Book		14.95
The Non-Designer's Type Book		24.99
The Non-Designer's Scan and Print Book		24.99
The Non-Designer's Web Book	first edition	29.95
	second edition	34.99
Design Workshop		39.99

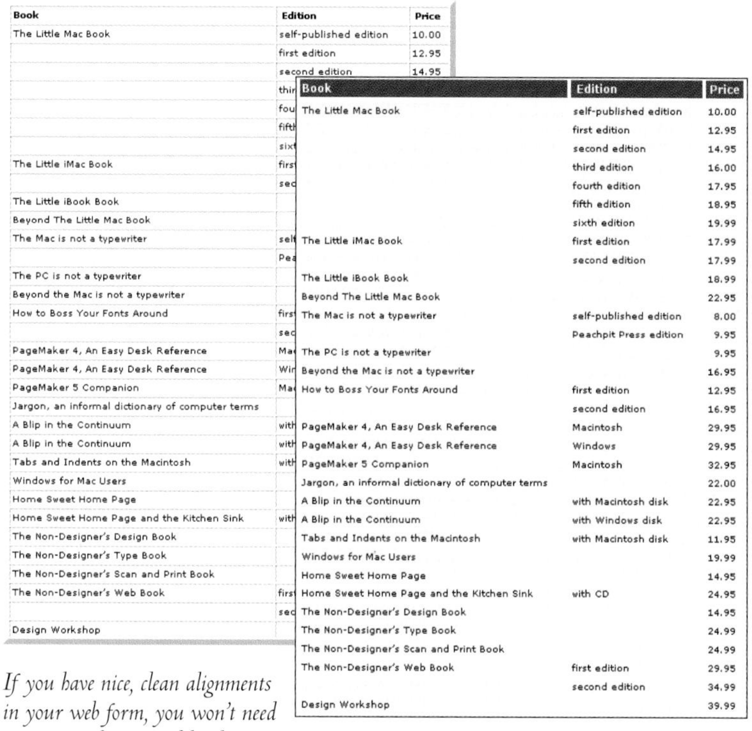

If you have nice, clean alignments in your web form, you won't need to turn on those awful borders, as shown above, left. Instead of the borders, let your column alignments create the edges, and use color (it's free!) to separate items, as shown above, right.

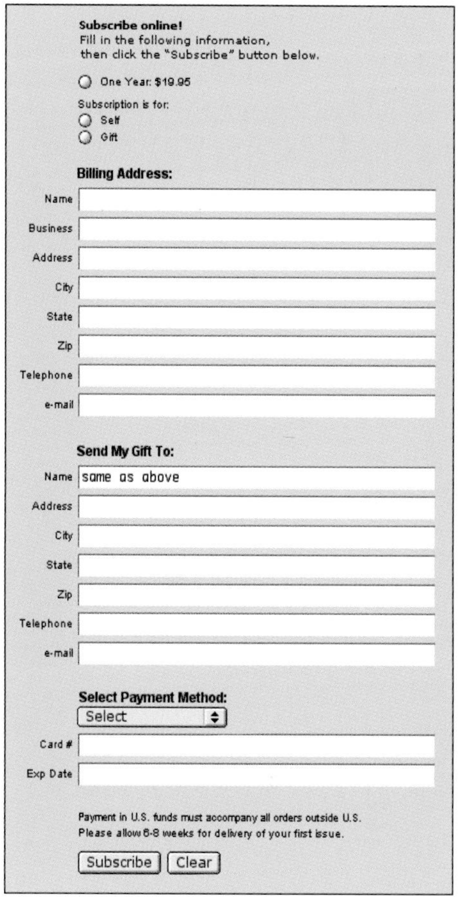

*Any form will look clean and professional if you just line things up. Notice the labels above (Name, Address, etc.) are aligned on their **right** edges so they provide a strong, solid line against the **left** edges of the empty fields. This strengthens the entire piece, as opposed to the arrangement shown below.*

These labels are aligned left, and the fields have a strong left edge. But between the labels and the fields is all that wobbly space. When you have two strong edges, put them together, as in the arrangement above: strong right against the strong left. And align the heading!

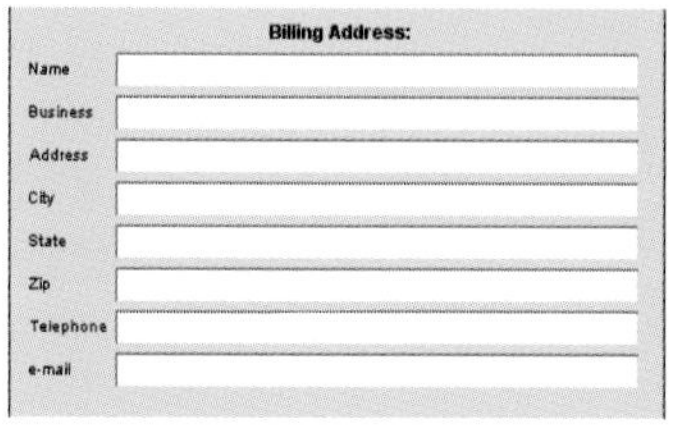

Ideas

So there is no excuse for bad-looking or difficult-to-use forms! Here are some ideas that will not only make a form look nicer, but will make it easier to use.

Lines
The lines on a form do not have to be heavy, black lines! The purpose of the line is merely to give the user a guideline for where to write. Heavy lines often obscure the handwritten information. Here are some options (be sure to leave enough room in which to write!):

Dotted lines

Name

Company

Address

City   State   Zip

Thin lines

Name

Company

Address

City   State   Zip

Dashed lines

Name

Company

Address

City   State   Zip

Thicker, gray lines

Name

Company

Address

City   State   Zip

Thicker, lightly colored lines

Name

Company

Address

City   State   Zip

Boxes

If you set a box around a form, please leave enough room in which to write! Here are several options for boxes:

Name
Company
Address
City	State	Zip

Name
Company
Address
City	State	Zip

Name
Company
Address
City	State	Zip

Name
Company
Address
City	State	Zip

Checkboxes

You have more options than just the standard empty checkbox. Even if you need a fairly traditional look to your form, you can still get away with using circles or triangles instead of squares. If you can use a more playful look, try some of the characters in the fonts Zapf Dingbats, Wingdings, or Webdings, which are probably already on your computer; outline them with a thin line so a user can fill in the empty space.

If your logo or symbol associated with your business is appropriate, perhaps use that (or a piece of it) outlined as a checkbox. Or use a playful image that has something to do with your company or the purpose of the form, like a dog bone or beachball.

Please send me:	**Bill me:**
☐ Carnations	○ Visa
☐ Crab apples	○ MasterCard
☐ Cowslips	○ American Express
☐ Daisies	○ Discover

Please send me:
▽ Carnations
▽ Crab apples
▽ Cowslips
▽ Daisies

Please send me:
◇ Carnations
◇ Crab apples
◇ Cowslips
◇ Daisies

Please send me:
‹ › Carnations
‹ › Crab apples
‹ › Cowslips
‹ › Daisies

Please send me:
✲ Carnations
✲ Crab apples
✲ Cowslips
✲ Daisies

Please send me:
[ ] Carnations
[ ] Crab apples
[ ] Cowslips
[ ] Daisies

Please send me:
Carnations
Crab apples
Cowslips
Daisies

Sometimes you might have items on your form in which the user can check more than one box, and other items where the user must choose only one of the options. Use the standard boxes we are accustomed to seeing on our computers: checkboxes for multiple choices; radio buttons for one choice. Of course, you might need an explanation on your form for those users who would be unfamiliar with this convention, something simple like "Choose one of the following" or "Choose as many as you like of the following."

131

Look around

Unless you are on a mission to research forms, you probably don't even notice them. If you never plan to create one, skip this exercise (although we suspect if you are even reading this chapter, a form-to-be has come into your life, like it or not).

Designer Exercise: Keep your eyes open for forms and invoices—at the dentist's office, backs of magazines, in the mail, or stop by the local IRS office. If in your first glance you are impressed with the look and design of the form, put into words exactly what gives you that feeling. If you are not impressed, put into words why not—we guarantee one or more of the very basic principles of design are missing (and the form probably uses a 12-point font that comes with the computer). Remember, you are looking not only for good design, but how well the designer was able to integrate good looks with functionality.

Deductions

Please enter your deductions for this filing period in the fields below. The total amount of your deductions will appear on Line 3 in the next step.

<< Previous | Step 2 of 6 | Next >>

	SALES AMOUNT	USE AMOUNT
Line B - Food Stamp and W.I.C Sales		
Line C - Sales for Resale		500
Line D - Prescription Drugs		100
Line E - Returned Goods		200
Line F - Feed, Seed and Fertilizer		300
Line G - Bad Debts		400
Line H - Sales to U.S. Government		500
Line I - Farm Machinery		600
Line J - Sales to Hospitals and Organizations Exempt by Statute (See GR31)		700
Line K - Sales to Direct Pay Permit Holders		800
Line L - 38% of Gross Selling Price on New Manufactured/Mobile Homes		90
Line M - Used Manufactured/Mobile Homes		100
Line N - Other Legal Deductions		100
		100
TOTALS		100
		$4,590.00

9. Advertising

Advertising is a big subject. There are many books, courses, and seminars about advertising and its related areas—copywriting, marketing, sales, etc. In this chapter, we're going to focus simply on what it looks like. If a reader's attention is not drawn to the ad in the first place, it doesn't matter what the copy says or how well it's marketed.

A clever headline that's short enough to be read at a glance may be able to captivate a reader, but it's usually the power of design, or the visual, that stops someone long enough to read a headline.

Black-and-white ads

Where do you start when a client or your business needs an ad? First of all, read some books on advertising and marketing. Then make it visually attractive, keeping in mind the marketing precepts.

Often you'll be given specifications for an ad, such as the size that the budget will allow, whether it's color or black and white, whether you can afford original or stock photography or illustration, and all those other things we talked about in Chapter 4. So the conditions of all these specs end up making half of your design decisions for you.

If you've been handed body copy and head-lines and told to design around them, that's another limitation that automatically cuts out some options, both conceptual and creative. If it's your responsibility to come up with the idea, then your creative job is easier but your creative freedom is larger (and thus more overwhelming), also.

It's sometimes easier to create your own concept and copy built around a visual that you find or an idea that you have than it is to effectively design around a copywriter's drydullboring copy. For instance, the ad on the right has nothing going for it in the way of concept. But you can still make it look good and capture attention.

R. William Hassenpfeffer Memorial Committee
presents the
Twentieth Memorial Lecture

Dr. Martha H. Smithers

Professor of Psychiatry and Neuroscience
at the
University of California, Yountville
on
*"A Hundred Years
of Science"*

Monday, September 18, 8 p.m.
Reilly Rooser Auditorium, Truchas
Admission is free

It's not bad

At least the designer of this ad was conscious about the line breaks (where the sentences end so you don't have an odd word hanging at the end of the line). We know they were trying to add a graphic sort of element when they stuck those arbitary lines in the corner, but really, *it's okay for the corners to be empty.* They don't mind at all. And we know the designer must have *some* other font besides Times Roman.

This ad gets the point across, and the fact that it's rather dull is not going to stop anyone from going to this particular lecture. But there are many ads just this boring that will definitely affect business—you might have the juiciest goodies in your shop downtown, but if your ad is dull, people automatically assume your shop goodies are dull.

R. William Hassenpfeffer Memorial Committee
presents the Twentieth Memorial Lecture

Dr. Martha H. Smithers

Professor of Psychiatry and Neuroscience
at the University of California, Yountville
will be speaking on the topic of

A Hundred Years of Science

Monday, September 18, 8 p.m.
Reilly Rooser Auditorium, Truchas
Admission is free

A Hundred Years of Science

Dr. Martha H. Smithers
Professor of Psychiatry and Neuroscience
at the University of California, Yountville

Monday, September 18, 8 P.M.
Reilly Rooser Auditorium, Truchas
Admission is free

This Twentieth Memorial Lecture is presented
by the R. William Hassenpfeffer Memorial Committee

Prioritize the information. What is the most important item; what is it that will make a reader's eyes stop on the ad? That item should be your focal point, either by size, placement, or its intriguing image. The original ad did a pretty good job of prioritizing; they just need to push it a little more, make the focal point stronger.

Choose a nice typeface. Basically, choose anything that is not built into your computer. Particularly avoid Helvetica/Arial, Times/Times New Roman, and Palatino/Book Antiqua. Buy some new fonts! They're not that expensive and they make a world of difference in anything you do.

If you want to use more than one typeface, in a piece make sure to choose fonts that do not look similar to each other! If they are not the same family, make sure they contrast with strength. Contrast their size, weight, structure, form, direction, and color.

Prioritize the information. This is just an example of emphasizing a different priority. What becomes the focal point depends entirely on what you think will draw a reader's eye to the ad. If you can get a reader's eyes to the ad, they will read the smaller copy if they're interested. If you can't get them to the ad at all, it doesn't matter how large you make the supplementary information like the date and time.

Let the white space be there.

Focal point

What is the focal point? In this ad, will most people recognize the speaker's name? The photograph? Will "revival services" be what stops readers so they read the ad? Is the word "featuring" really as important as everything else in the headline? Figure out what the focus is and focus on it. Let everything else be subordinate.

Get rid of superfluous stuff

Go through every word in your advertisement and remove anything superfluous. This includes items like "NM," as in the ad to the right. Since this piece appears in the local newspaper and the town is listed (and the town is in the middle of the state), there is no danger anyone might end up in the wrong state to attend the meetings. How about the endings of the numbers (like 8th)—are they really necessary? Do you have to abbreviate the street name? It creates a messy little spot with the period and the comma; although it takes more space to spell out the name, it looks neater.

Does this piece really need a double rule around it? Use the layout and headline to call attention to the ad; don't clutter it up with extraneous, useless lines.

Revival Services Featuring Internet Evangelist Url Ratz

Friday, August 8th
10:30 am to 7:30 pm
Saturday, August 9th
through Wednesday, August 13th
6:00 Nightly

Url's Internet Cafe
123 Montezuma Ave., Santa Fe, NM
Where the Internet is Changing People's Lives

Childcare will be Provided   Interpretacion en Español

Crop the photo

In a small ad like this one, if there is superfluous space around a photo, get rid of it. Sometimes extra space in a photo is an artistic technique, but in this case, it's not.

Start with the basic principles

You may decide you want to break the rules—that's great, but you have to know the rules before you can break them. Use **contrast** to create a focal point and visual interest. Use **repetition** to tie the elements together. Use **alignment** to organize both the information and the white space. Use **proximity** to group elements together and separate elements that are not part of the unit.

Alignment

Draw a line through the centers of each of these units. Is there any connection between them? Now, if you aligned each of these elements on a strong flush left, you would have a cleaner piece, even though each element would still have a different left alignment. You can get away with a variety of flush edges but not with centered elements: we *see* the line down the strong flush left edge, but we *don't* see the line down the center—we see the soft edges. The strength of a left or right alignment lends strength to the page, while the weakness of the soft edge of a centered alignment is made even weaker when there are multiples of them.

Proximity

In this group, the line "10:30 am to 7:30 pm" is just as close to the next line, "Saturday, August 9th" as it is to the line above it. This can create confusion as to the exact time and date of the meeting. The principle of proximity clears this up—the elements that belong together should be tucked closely together, and the spacing between elements indicates their relationships. That is, there should be a wee bit of space between the two different time frames, and even more space between the time frames and the place.

Do not use the same amount of space between every item! The spatial relationships communicate to us instantly; they tell us what is important, what is functional, etc.

White space

Look at the white space in this ad. It's all broken up, chunks of it are scattered everywhere. When you follow the basic design principles, the white space will automatically end up, neatly organized, where it should be. It is your job to *let it be there.*

Revival Services
featuring Internet Evangelist

Url Ratz

Url's Internet Cafe
Where the Internet is Changing People's Lives

123 Montezuma Avenue, Santa Fe

All day: Friday, August 8
10:30 A.M. to 7:30 P.M.

Every night: Saturday, August 9 thru
Wednesday, August 13
6 P.M.

Childcare will be provided
Interpretacion en Español

Contrast

To create the focal point, we used **contrast.** In this particular case, the photograph of the famous evangelist is so well known that we made it the most prominent, as well as his name. Everything else is subordinate. If a reader's eyes are pulled into the ad through the photograph and headline name, they will read the rest of the body copy, even if we made it 5-point type. But if we set everything large and in similar sizes, a reader's eyes will just glaze over the ad. Suck the reader in with the main point.

Notice the **white space!** In a busy newspaper, your eyes are pulled toward the peaceful white space. Let it be there. White space is on sale today.

Check the **alignments.** Every element is aligned in some way with something else on the page.

Check the **proximity** of elements to each other, and the spatial relationships between everything.

Check the **repetition** of fonts, weights, lines, and alignments.

Type choice tip

You'll notice that for black-and-white ads throughout this chapter we usually use fairly strong type faces instead of delicate faces with thin strokes. This is because black-and-white ads are often destined for newspapers, newsletters, or inexpensive souvenir programs where quality control can sometimes be unpredictable, or at the least, it's printed onto absorbent paper. If a black-and-white ad is placed in a glossy, high-quality magazine, fine lettering isn't a problem. But most clients want the ad to work in all environments, so avoiding some fonts that may fall apart at small sizes can save you headaches and grief. We also try not to get extreme with small type, especially small type on a black background, unless we are very confident in the printing quality and paper stock that will be used.

Some design firms win awards with teeny-type layouts, but remember, these awards are given by other designers, not people who are reading the ads. Several years back, a dog food packaging project won lots of fancy design awards, but it didn't sell the dog food—the huge bags of designer-label dog food just didn't go over well in the feed stores.

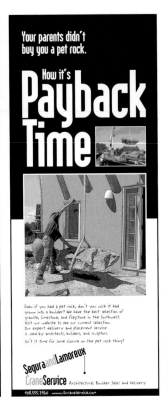

This headline for a crane service adds an element of fun and is meant to catch the reader's attention with humor. We started by placing the elements in the space, like spreading out the pieces of a jigsaw puzzle onto the kitchen table. At least one of the photos needs to be large to convey the feeling of massive boulders. The headline is long so we limited out headline type choices to those that were bold and condensed.

Reversing the headline out of a black box makes it appear even bolder and creates a nice, strong contrast with the bottom half of the ad, as well as with the space around it on the magazine page. We added the smaller inset photo so we could actually show the crane and for the dramatic effect of showing a huge bolder in mid-air.

Next we started refining the headline to give it more impact and size contrast. This enabled us to make the catch-line ("Payback Time")

twice as large. The rest of the headline, even though it's smaller than before, stands out more because it's more isolated, more in contrast. This contrast of sizes also presented some design opportunities for stacking and tucking type in a visually interesting way.

We reworded the headline slightly so we could break it into two separate sentences. In the second version, we tried pulling the bottom of the black background up to the top of the photo,

but eventually moved it back down and put a white border around the photo to separate it from the background. In the final version we added a black bar across the bottom of the ad (repetition) to balance the heavy black weight at the top of the ad, and to tie the whole piece together.

The body copy is set in a casual font to reflect the tone of the copy. As a final touch we used a version of the logo that becomes a typographic visual pun.

A jumble of words contrasting with so much white space makes this ad impossible to ignore. Deviating from convention and placing the logo at the top of the ad (instead of the standard position at the bottom) leaves a stark, empty space in which the brief message and contact information can stand out.

Sometimes it's difficult to get a client to accept white space—they often feel that if they're paying for the space, they want to fill it up. Tell the client that white space was on sale this week and you got a good price on it.

The provocative image and the extreme left-dominant composition of the photograph made this flush-left layout a natural solution—if there is already a strength in one element of the layout, follow that strength, play it up! If the main element is a tall, vertical image, strengthen that tall, vertical by making the entire ad or poster tall.

We didn't want to diminish the extreme contrast of the stark white and the blacks and grays in the image, so we set the text and border in a medium gray. The client name in black creates a nice contrast with the rest of the type so it stands out, and also acts as a repetition of the black in the photo to tie the two elements together.

The headline ("scandalous") presents a conceptual contrast between the formality and sedate feeling created by the typeface, size, and color, contrasted with the mayhem and distaste associated with the word itself.

Never underestimate the power of a typeface to communicate something more than the words.

The visual you choose to use can influence your approach to a design. The vertical shape of the photograph led us to design this poster using an extreme vertical layout, shown to the left (when you have a strength in an element, play up that strength; in this case, the strong, tall, vertical). The condensed headline face, stacked in five lines, emphasizes the vertical visual impact. The unusual shape captures attention, either as an ad or as an unusual poster shape.

For a more conventional poster, or to fit into a more conventional ad space, we created the variation you see above. We made the photo as large as possible, and repeated the basic shape of the image in the headline.

Clients are often squeamish about using such abbreviated body copy, but most clients that have a web site can appreciate the value of using the print ad space to create a memorable impression, while letting the web site give the potential customers access to complete details and rich content.

This is the original stock photo.

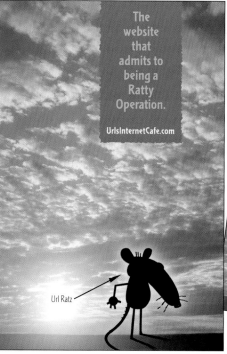

This is a case of letting a stock photo do all the work for you. Originally the photograph had a couple of barn silhouettes in it. We realized that it would be very easy to delete those barns and add whatever silhouette we wanted. We didn't want to cover up the sun glare so the only place we could put Url Ratz was on the right. That dictated that the headline should go directly above and lead down to the silhouette. After that is was irresistible to add the callout in the middle of the glare.

Don't worry if you don't approach a design challenge with a fully realized solution before you get to the computer. As you may have already discovered, playing with the elements directly on the screen makes solutions appear that you didn't have in your head before you started.

This is also an example of creating a single solution (although separate computer files) of the same ad to work in both black-and-white as well as color. Because this particular photo so clearly evokes a sunset, our minds actually sort of "see" the color in the gray values.

Color ads

The visual impact of color is powerful and seductive. You can use it in large or small doses with equal effectiveness. Color ad space is available in a variety of sizes and shapes, creating a visual playground for designers.

The psychology of color is important and it varies from culture to culture, but most of us rely on instinct and our own personal reactions when choosing particular colors for projects. It's probably safe to assume that *your* reaction to color will be an average reaction in this country, but if you are doing international work, read some color studies.

Keep in mind the principles of contrast, alignment, and visual impact and you can create a visually compelling color ad.

This is the original stock image.

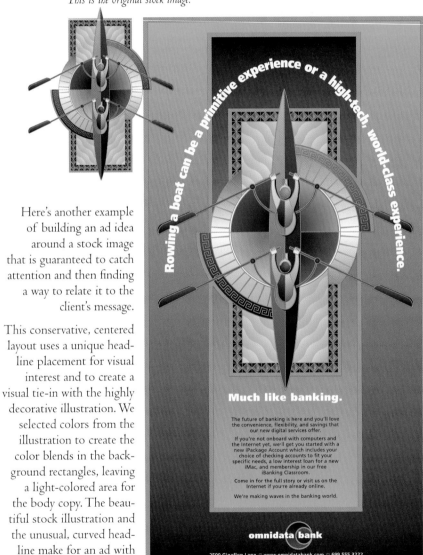

Here's another example of building an ad idea around a stock image that is guaranteed to catch attention and then finding a way to relate it to the client's message.

This conservative, centered layout uses a unique headline placement for visual interest and to create a visual tie-in with the highly decorative illustration. We selected colors from the illustration to create the color blends in the background rectangles, leaving a light-colored area for the body copy. The beautiful stock illustration and the unusual, curved headline make for an ad with high visibility.

Design variations that you experiment with *after* you've developed a usable layout usually lead to the final version that works best. Digital tools and techniques make design experimentation feasible, even with very tight deadline constraints. Small revisions and fine tuning can make a big visual difference.

The example directly above contains some nice elements, but it appears to be a hodge-podge of text and logos.

This version organizes the disparate elements better by containing all of the body copy in a background shape, reducing the size of the headline, rearranging it slightly, and repeating the rough-edged shape behind the subhead at the top of the ad.

The final version adds subtle visual interest by decreasing the width of the copy's background shape so that the petroglyph logo can break out of the box and into the white space. Having the text break away from the background color helps to give a spontaneous, casual, and fun feeling to the ad.

We placed the date into an organic shape to give it more prominence and to repeat the organic shape theme.

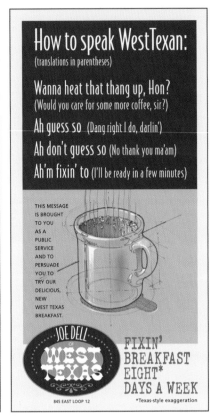

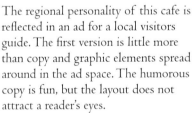

The regional personality of this cafe is reflected in an ad for a local visitors guide. The first version is little more than copy and graphic elements spread around in the ad space. The humorous copy is fun, but the layout does not attract a reader's eyes.

Above, we've added a lot of contrast by reversing the lengthy headline copy out of a dark box. We made the ad more attractive by using an earthy color for the background, which makes the logo's key words pop out in better contrast.

We'd be happy with this version except we know from experience that it's always worth trying one more variation. Also, we begin to notice that all separate elements of the ad are rather large and so they compete for visual focus— something needs to be the boss. We need to decide what is most important and let that element become a focal point.

The coffee cup illustration is interesting, but we'd rather make sure you see the headline. In the version above, the first part of the headline is visually dominant. The smaller size of the other elements not only allows the headline to become a focal point, it also creates better contrast and allows for a less crowded and more casual look to the entire piece.

When creating a concept, consider combining two unrelated images or concepts into one for an attention-getting visual. The layout of the ad is quite simple (flush left), but the image is compelling and its relative size to the rest of the ad creates a great visual impact.

The strength of this poster is partly due to the relative size of the image, and partly due to the close proximity of the quote. This leaves a good amount of white space in which to isolate and call attention to the logo and mandatory copy at the bottom of the piece.

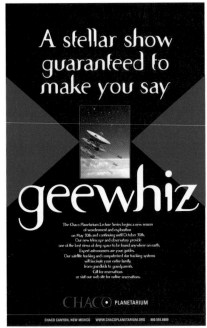

Version 1

Version 2

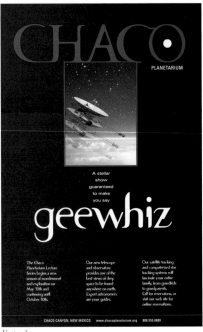

Version 3

This series shows the multiple design variations of the same basic layout, an ad for a planetarium.

Our first version starts with some nice features: beautiful stock illustration, eye-catching fonts, lots of contrast, and a background that conveys tension and energy. But because this planetarium is unique and cutting-edge, we want to do something more daring than the centered layout.

We tried emphasizing the logo, treating it as a headline. The headline itself is turned into a subhead, but with lots of contrast in size and value. We separated the three paragraphs and gave them each a flush-left alignment.

Then we made a variation that does away with the rectangular and semi-circular background decorative shapes. We also set the word "planetarium" in a larger size.

146

Version 4

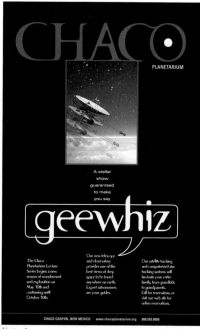

Version 5

Version 6

Version 7

Version 8

Sometimes it's hard to stop making variations; we wanted to try a few trendy embellishments in versions 4 and 5.

In version 6, we sent the logo back to the bottom of the page and moved the headline to the top, using a simple two-line arrangement with a strong contrast between the two headline elements. We liked the separated paragraphs and rearranged them into a more unexpected layout. We experimented with some deli-cate, decorative, orbit-like lines and also revived the color background shapes.

Our next variation, version 7, was the same except for a slightly different approach to the trendy decoration.

Version 8, the final version, does away with the decorative, trendy lines and combines elements from the various iterations in the process.

Six signatures of
  William Shakespeare exist.
None are spelled the same.
None are legible.
No other handwritten word
  exists.
None of this makes sense.

Mary Sidney
makes sense.

Mary Sidney, *alias Shakespeare*

The
sweet swan
of Avon
was a
literary
genius.

She was really good
at needlework too.

Mary Sidney, *alias Shakespeare*

The bard
was a
16th century
genius.

400 years later,
she's coming out
of the closet.

Mary Sidney, *alias Shakespeare*

Hamlet.
Romeo & Juliet.
The Sonnets.

Heady stuff
to be coming
from the son of
a glovemaker.

Unless they were
written by a countess.

Mary Sidney, *alias Shakespeare*

This ad campaign for a book uses stark simplicity and an unexpected image placement throughout the series to provide visual continuity. The various croppings of the same illustration adds visual interest to each individual ad and to the entire campaign.

The extremely close cropping conveys the feeling of an intimate and interesting story of an extraordinary woman.

Minimal copy surrounded by generous amounts of white space always commands lots of attention. And the strong left alignment becomes more daring with the extreme left alignment of the illustrations.

The classic oldstyle typeface (Cochin) gives a classic look that's both beautiful and readable. This campaign design, with its contrast of black and white, converts very nicely to black and white for newspaper ads or one-color magazine ads.

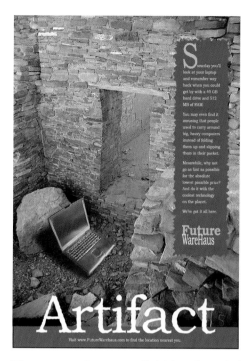

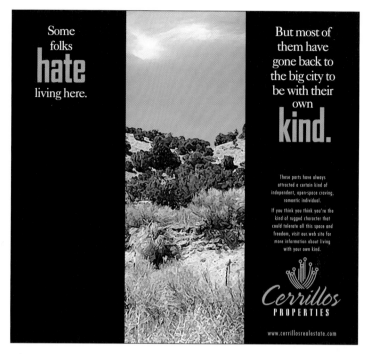

The conceptual contrast of a high-tech symbol in a setting of ancient ruins, combined with strong contast of values between the white headline and the rich color image, creates a memorable image and an ad that begs to be read. To maximize the impact of the photo, we made it as large as possible. Even though the text is lengthy (for an ad), the text and the logo visually combine as a single element with the background shape. The oversized capital "S" is just a playful, color graphic accent to balance the weight of the logo at the bottom of the text.

The one-word headline blasts off the page in bright white. We roughened the edges of its letterforms to add a little "ancient" personality. We also stopped the photo a little short of the bottom and added the dark blue strip to improve the legibility of both the headline and the small copy below it.

This magazine ad for a realtor grabs attention with its unusual three-panel design that separates an unexpected headline from the main visual and the rest of the text.

Instead of a uniformly large headline, we created a strong visual impact with the extreme contrast in font sizes and styles. We floated the first part of the headline at the top of the left-side vertical panel, which isolates it as a dramatic, attention-getting element. The emphasis on a controversial word attracts readers' eyes. By using the same emphasis in a word on the right-side panel (repetition), we made a strong visual connection between the two sides, with the eye-candy image sandwiched between the two thoughts.

Look around

Advertising surrounds us, as you are well aware. But often we are not aware, not consciously, of how advertising affect us. We don't even notice which ones we see and which ones we ignore. If you are in charge of creating advertising, you need to become painfully aware of what everyone else is doing with it, and keep track of what works and what doesn't—at least visually.

Designer Exercise: Every day, everywhere you go, cut out advertisements and take a good look at them. Collect black-and-white newspaper ads that are great, black-and-white glossy magazine ads, and color ads. Put into words exactly what makes each one stand out. Is it the headline copy that caught your eye? Did the headline typeface and arrangement catch your eye? Is there an interesting visual image that you noticed before you noticed what the text said? Is the layout unusual, provocative, or suprising?

Finding advertisements that don't work very well is just as educative. Why doesn't it work? Is it the typeface choice? Is the layout just too dull or too flashy (either way, your eye wants to run away from it). Are the elements scattered all over the piece with no conscious thought to arrangement, to grouping similar elements together? Is there unnecessary junk cluttering it up? How is the ad aligned—are there several centered elements, each centered over a different center line? Are there items stuck in corners? Is the white space disorganized, causing visual disruption? And what exactly is not "working"—does the ad get the message across to its intended market, even if it's not very attractive? Or is it losing the market because no one who *should* read it *will* read it because it doesn't reflect, for instance, the quality of the product they are trying to sell?

Don't just notice the ads that appeal to you personally. Perhaps there is an ad for a heavy metal band that you don't particularly care for—does the ad visually appeal to the market it's aiming at? Lots of commercials during football games go right over Robin's head, but John eats them up. To create effective advertising yourself, you must become very conscious of what everyone else is doing.

10. Billboards

In many areas of the country, billboards are cheaper than you might think—check into it. There are two basic types of outdoor advertising billboards. You might choose one or the other, or both types, in your billboard campaign, depending on your project and how many billboards you plan to use.

The **poster panel** is printed in strips and pasted on at the billboard locations. The most common size is approximately 25 feet by 12 feet. Poster panels are most effective as high-frequency (like all over town or all over the country), short-term postings.

Bulletins are available in several forms. You can create a panel that will be hand-painted at the sign company's studio or on location. Designs can also be printed onto flexible material or adhesive vinyl and stretched onto the bulletin frame. The most common sizes for these are 48 x 14 feet, 60 x 20, and 36 x 10. Bulletins are usually longer-term than poster panels and can add high impact at key locations, often as a supplement to a poster campaign.

You might see either one as you're driving around town or out in the country. For specific details on creating billboards, call your local outdoor advertising company.

Avoid the outdoor brochure look

Advertisers often make the mistake of trying to put too much information on an outdoor board. Outdoor advertising can be very effective as long as you (or the client) don't try to turn it into a brochure with detailed information and too many messages.

The most effective outdoor designs combine simplicity with visual impact. The most important of these two features is simplicity. Remember, your audience is driving by at a high speed (unless you've paid a premium price for a billboard on a freeway that always has a traffic jam) and one or two glances is all you can hope for. No matter how badly you want to put a phone number on the board, don't do it. How often do you risk your life grabbing pen and paper to write down phone numbers from outdoor boards. Whenever we see a phone number tucked into a board design, we wonder if the incredible optimist was the designer or the client. This may sound like a silly premise, but we've actually failed at times to convince clients that having too much in a design makes the entire board unreadable, useless, and a waste of money.

This outdoor design contains some nice elements, but it also has one very common bad feature: more information than can be absorbed in the few seconds that it's visible.

The first thing we do is eliminate everything except the information that is absolutely essential and select a simple western icon that is instantly recognizable, even from a distance. This preliminary version is much better than an outdoor board with too much on it.

We changed the size of some of the type, and added dotted lines to tie the hat into the composition and link the words of the event name together. The dotted lines serve as a subtle decorative element that could pass for something like western saddle stitching. To add a touch of color, we put accents in the hat band.

Next, we changed the placement of some of the dotted lines and reduced the size of the date. This version is simple, and everything can be read at a glance.

Most outdoor bulletins allow for adding an "embellishment" for a reasonable extra fee. In this example, the embellishment is the cut-out of the hat that extends above the shape of the baord. This technique adds a lot of visual impact due to the unusual shape of the board that catches the eye, and it allows us to make the visual much larger.

Even though phone numbers usually don't work on outdoor boards, we'll add a web address if we can make it readable and if the address is memorable. If you have a simple, concise domain name, the URL can be a valuable element of your design. Now the board's message, in two words, effectively says, "For complete details and all the information you could possibly want including photographs and maps, updated daily, visit our web site."

If the budget allows us to add an embellishment, we've got a design that's certain to be seen and actually read.

If you burden your design with lots of unnecessary copy, you diminish its effectiveness and make it a visual mess. This is a brochure painted on an outdoor board. Let go of all the extraneous information.

To turn this piece into an effective outdoor board, we used the logo of this furniture store for a headline, while the illustration and layout provide the message that they're avant garde, designy, contemporary, and trendsetters. The slanted type is an unexpected element that helps attract a driver's eye.

This simplified, cleaner design adds elements of readability, sophistication, and style that far outweigh the perceived advantage of having lots of information on the board.

Visual impact outdoors

No other advertising medium allows you such stunning visual impact. The ability to make your message larger than life can provide an image and personality for your client that not only creates tremendous visual impact, but also high visibility, recognition, and recall.

The colorful, dramatic image in this design takes advantage of the strong contrast with the massive black background. Enlarging the tiger so huge simplifies the image while at the same time making it bolder and more intimidating.

This was the first concept for the board. We loved the tiger, but by enlarging the tiger, as shown above, we have less of the tiger on the board itself, but viewers' minds actually fill in the rest of the body and claws. Thus we actually get more space than we paid for—we get all the imaginary space that the tiger's body inhabits. Free.

This concept combines simplicity, an unexpected image for a florist, and a strong contrast between the white background and the dead flowers. This combination definitely gets the potential viewer's attention.

The contrast of typefaces in the logo adds to the visual interest. The contrast between the reversed subhead in the strong horizontal strip against the rectangular shape of the image area makes the subhead stand out.

Humor always gets attention. It can be in the form of illustrative style or in the headline copy. Even if the client's product or service is dead-serious, humor can act as a contrast to deliver the client's message.

In this example, the undersized subhead commands attention because of its strong contrast in the horizontal strip at the bottom of the billboard. The dark background color of the main image areas sets a shady mood and allows the headline to blast off the board. The unique font adds to the visual interest that catches a reader's eye.

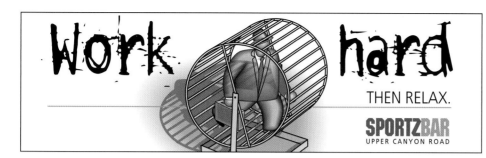

Simplicity and visual impact always work. The horizontal rule in this piece serves to strengthen the loose connection between the left and right sides of the layout so the headline will read better, and at the same time serves to create more visual separation between the subhead and the logo.

The Museum of Digital Art is having a show of digital cartoon art, as reflected in this poster design. The visual impact of the tightly cropped image emphasizes the simple, stylized technique of the artists on display.

Like the billboard with the tiger, the viewer sees the rest of the face and head, thus expanding the visual presence beyond what we paid for.

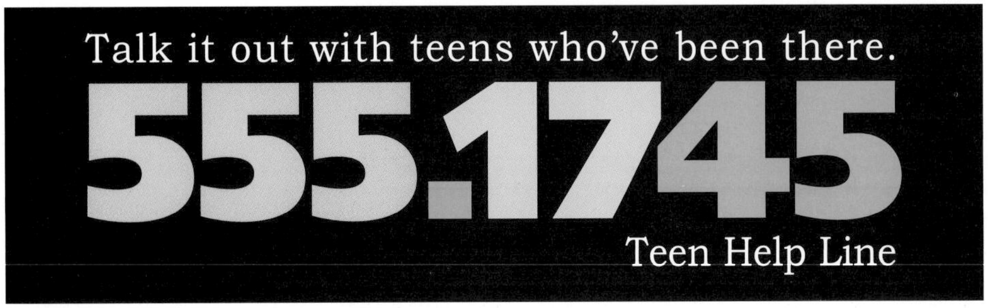

Talk it out with teens who've been there.

555.1745

Teen Help Line

In the beginning of this chapter we recommended that you not waste your time putting phone numbers on outdoor boards, but you know the rule about rules. With creativity, you can make it work.

The color scheme of this outdoor campaign is designed to visually break the numbers into verbal words in your mind.

five, five, five seventeen forty-five

Teen Help Line

Another board in this outdoor campaign continues to feature the phone number, but this time verbally rather than numerically. The over-the-edge simplistic layout ensures that this board will be noticed.

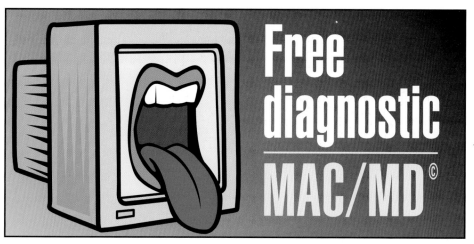

A simple visual pun combined with the simplest, most basic copy creates instant communication in the frantic, drive-by advertising world.

The background color blend adds visual interest to capture a driver's attention while also providing a strong contrast on the right side for the headline and logo.

Bold type, simplicity, and the unexpected, upside-down image make this outdoor design eye-catching and entertaining. Breaking the background into two colors adds visual interest and more color. It also solves the dilemma of the planet logo partially disappearing, as it would have against the black background. Solving problem details like this often leads to design solutions that might not have occurred to you had there not been a problem in the process.

Look around

If you live in or near a large city, you'll see lots of good examples of posters and painted bulletins on outdoor boards. Smaller cities may not have as many painted bulletins, but you can still find great examples and inspiration in the design books and design award annuals.

Designer Exercise: Be conscious every time you look at a billboard. You, as a driver, are the best critic. Are your eyes attracted to it? Can you read it? Do you understand the message? Is there extraneous stuff that just clutters the board? Is it clear what the billboard is trying to sell you? If there are directions to a place, can you follow the directions without having to write them down? Even if you don't have plans to create a billboard in the near future, train your mind to become aware of what works and what doesn't so you'll be ready when you do need to design one.

11. Web sites

Web design is fun, but it can also be frustrating and incredibly time-consuming. If you're an experienced print designer, it can be quite a shock to realize how un-WYSIWYG (what you see is what you get) the web authoring software can appear to be after previewing your work in several different web browsers on a couple of different computer platforms. After you get accustomed to dealing with this web fact of life, you can get back to having fun with design.

Some people learn HTML code and design web pages using their programming skill. We admire these people, but designing strictly via code limits what most mortals can do visually for a design. Even WYSIWYG web authoring software steers most designers in the direction of what we call the "HTML box."

Most web pages are built by placing graphics and text into individual cells of a table to hold those elements into a (fairly) predictable position on the page. If a designer doesn't use a table to hold the elements together, there's no telling where images and text will appear on the final web page when viewers use different

browsers and open the browser windows to different sizes. Tables are a good and useful thing, but since they're made up of rectangular shapes perfectly aligned with each other, you can understand how "boxy" a layout can get just by placing elements in a table.

To avoid this boxy look, we *design* pages, including a number of variations for the client, in an image editing application (we use Photoshop) that gives us complete control over design, imaging, and special effects without worrying yet about how we are going to eventually build it (although we constantly keep the web limitations in mind as we design). We can experiment with multiple variations of a layout and its elements and pretty much go wild. Another advantage of using Photoshop during the design stage is that you spend your valuable time on design, not production, when the client hasn't even approved a layout yet. HTML production can present its own problems, so why create code for the design stage?

After the client approves one of the designs, we then take the layout apart and fit it into cells of the table, as shown on the following pages.

The process

As discussed on the previous page, we actually start the layout and design of a web page in Photoshop where we have freedom to experiment without having to write code and without being limited to the compromises of HTML. We can create a number of design ideas for the client, get approval on a concept, and *then* begin the process of building the web site.

To create several options for the client, we take a 640 x 480-pixel screen capture of a browser window and place it on the bottom layer in Photoshop (shown, upper-right). We use the 640 x 480 size for the entry page (if there is one) and the main home page to ensure that we design within that frame-work. There are two reasons for this: One is that we want visitors using 14-inch monitors (very common) and laptops (millions of laptops) to get the full, initial visual

impression of the site within their browser window, as well as presentations on overhead screens, which are usually in 640 x 480 mode. Second, this size forces us to think horizontally—we are all accustomed to designing for a vertical page. Web pages are not vertical—the initial visual impression is horizontal. We don't want visitors to have to scroll down to see what links are available. Of course, not all pages fit within the frame—in fact, probably only your entry page and home page will fit. The others will scroll downward, of course, but the *initial visual impression* should still be complete within that framework, and the links the user needs should be available.

We explore design options and create different variations on separate layers so we don't have to recreate anything for various versions. We save the various Photoshop files as

JPEGs and post them on our web site so the client can view the pages from their office.

The best thing about using Photoshop as a layout tool is that we can create and show many variations without the time-consuming creation of HTML code. After we've gotten client approval, much of the imaging work is done and ready for produc-tion. Also, when working in Photoshop we are not

limited to the boxy look that happens when you create directly in code, so we come up with a greater variety of unique solutions.

We'll show you this process in the next several pages; specific details on exactly how to do it are in *The Non-Designer's Web Book.*

This web page shows the limitations that appear when you design directly in code. You end up with all these separate elements sitting next to each other, each in their own box. Now, this is not necessarily a terrible thing—many neat, clean, professional pages are created this way, as shown by the example above (which has the table borders turned on so you can see the cells in which elements are stored). But if you want to go beyond the box, you need to create some design ideas in either an image editing application or an illustration program, then, after client approval, build it with code or a web authoring package.

Don't neglect the navigation

When designing for traditional media, the focus is on the visual impression and how it communicates the message. When you design a brochure, magazine, or book, you assume the reader knows how to navigate through the information. Web design, however, presents the additional challenge of making navigation of the site clear, understandable, and accessible. Plan the navigation design and the architecture of the entire site so it is clear at all times where the visitor is within the site and how to get to any other section of the site. And always give the visitor a clue as to what page they are currently viewing.

You can see how this layout is much more integrated and interesting. It uses the exact same elements, but they overlap and connect, things that you can't do if you start out in code. This design was created in Photoshop. Then the entire layout was sliced into pieces, and each piece was placed into a table cell so it all came back together again, like a puzzle. You can see the table and cells in the topmost example.

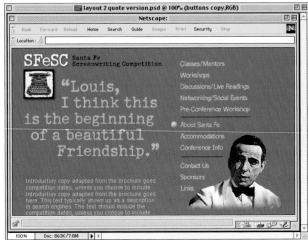

1. This is one of the layout ideas we presented to the client (the original film clip that was in the layout is blurred to avoid copyright problems in this book). Notice its horizontal layout so the visitor can get to all the links without having to scroll downward.

> The introductory copy is fake text to show the client where the copy will eventually be placed.

> The links show all the main categories of information; these will also appear on subsequent pages.

> There is strong contrast between the black-and-white/gray page and the color logo and links. (As a user mouses over a link, it changes color.)

> This Photoshop file is huge (10.8 megabytes, even at 72 ppi) because it contains many layers with different design variations, as well as separate layers for each button link. Even after we create the actual web page, we will always save this source file so it will be easy to make changes.

2. At the client's insistence of possible copyright infringement (he's right), we replaced the film clip photo with a quotation, which actually works nicely with their typewriter logo. John created an original illustration for the page, instead of the clip.

In the final table, these cells will be emptied and given a background color to match this graphic.

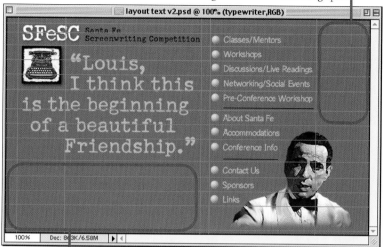

In the final table, these cells will be merged and emptied to hold the introductory copy as HTML text. The cells will be given a background color to match this graphic, as will the web page.

3. After the client's design approval, we had the first page ready for production. The HTML body copy will be tucked under the quotation (which is a graphic) and next to the list of bulleted links (which are each graphics); also, the illustration is tucked into the list of links. The only way to recreate this on a web page is to cut the entire page into pieces and put them all into a table, each piece into a separate cell, so the image comes back together like a puzzle.

> Above, you can see the guide lines we placed; this is where we will slice the graphic apart.

> Actually, we will merge the entire quotation into one piece so it will drop into one cell.

> The blank spaces under the quotation will be merged into one cell, and that's where we'll place the text.

> In this particular example, you see all of the navigation buttons "turned on." After exporting those images, we'll turn their layers off, turn on the layers for the other buttons, and slice and export those as well.

> The illustration will be sliced into the pieces shown so we can keep the navigation slices simplifed and consistent in width.

4. Above is the Photoshop layout for secondary pages (an actual page is shown below). Because the secondary pages are longer with lots of text, we made them white with black text for easier readability.

> You can see the guide lines we placed; this is where we will slice the graphic apart so we can place them in the cells of a table (actually, the software, either Adobe ImageReady or Macromedia Fireworks will create a table and place these images in the correct cells for us).

> To help orient visitors in the site, the link for the current page they are on stays in the gold color.

> The space under the gold heading ("About Santa Fe," above) is left blank; we will add text directly on the page later.

> The images in the film clip can be repeated as deep as necessary.

1. This site for a writer is relatively small, but has very interesting content. This first layout (above) is unimaginative, but sometimes the best way to get started is to get the pieces of the puzzle on the table before trying to decide what you're going to do. (It's also a good example of the "HTML box.") The fake body copy will be replaced with real text from the client.

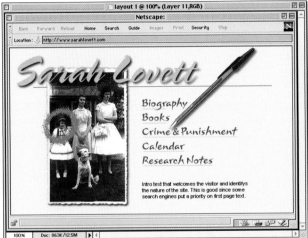

2. We want the site to have some personality, so we pick some beautiful fonts for the graphic name and buttons, add the descriptor "novelist," and add a pen for a fun, unexpected visual exclamation mark. We make Sarah the main visual element and the page is looking much nicer.

3. Since we want to use Sarah's photo on the biography page later, and because the client felt a little uncomfortable using her own face as the focus on the home page, we decide to make things more fun, intriguing, and less egocentric by using an old family photo of Sarah and her sisters.

› We plan to create an animated GIF that will point out Sarah with a red circle after the page has loaded.

› We made the pen larger, but it's now becoming a big, ugly, clunky element and competes with the other elements on the page. We need a classy, good-looking pen image.

4. The new, beautiful pen image makes a big difference, and the smaller size is classier. Remember, we're still working in Photoshop. The client approved this version, so now we need to plan how to slice apart this file so it can be placed into the cells of an HTML table.

5. This is how the file looks sliced and placed in an HTML table in Macromedia Dreamweaver.

These are empty cells.

> Certain cells of the table are either empty or contain HTML text, which decreases the downloading time (instead of having graphic boxes in the cells).

> The empty cells are colored with the exact web-safe color used as the background of the image in Photoshop. We also colored the web page itself with the same web-safe color so it all blends in to look like one image.

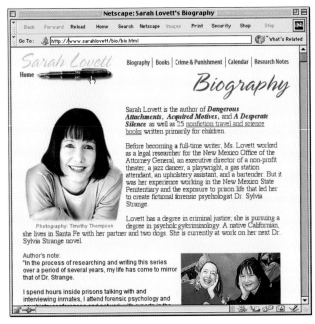

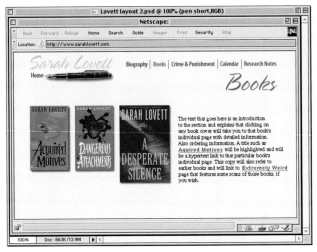

6. Simple little interactive animations are usually more interesting than blinking, rotating, whirling, pulsating, endlessly repetitive junk on a page. In this example, the pen is a rollover—mousing over it shortens the pen and the word "home" appears, which is a link to the home page.

> Secondary pages use the pen image and Sarah's name for visual continuity (the principle of repetition).

> The navigation has been minimized to a smaller, less decorative font.

> We used a fairly large headline for the name of the section, and the link to this page is in a different color so you know where you are and won't click on that link.

> This page is another example of using the site identification (Sarah's name and the pen) and the navigation bar to create a consistent look from page to page.

> The body copy in this example is actually notes to the client.

> Each of the book covers is a link to a separate page about that book, including excerpts.

1. This web site is also for a writer, albeit a very different one. For this site, we want to create an entry page, without navigation, that allows us to set a tone and to emphasize the portrait of this amazing late-16th century writer. So far, the type is beautiful but the layout is fairly ordinary.

2. Much as we would like to use a large image of Mary, we decided that a smaller image would not only look more elegant, but also download much faster. One of the biggest temptations designers struggle against is to make an image or logo too large, usually because they created it and are proud of it. You can justify over-sized images in other media, but not usually on a web page, where practically every pixel adds to the download time.

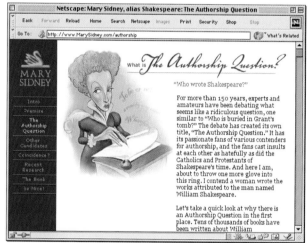

3. Reducing the size of the portrait does give the entry page a classier look. We replace the underline with a more subtle dotted line, and use the same style line to separate the portrait from the right side of the page. Overlapping type or other elements helps to pull the design away from the "boxy" HTML layout that's common on web pages; it also serves to tie the two halves of the page together into one unit. We replace the word "enter" with the swan icon, the motif that appears in Mary's lace collar. And we experimented with several techniques to enhance the type, such as beveling and embossing.

4. Interior pages use the same color scheme as the entry page and **repeat** the swan icon as a site identifier and home button. The rest of the page uses a white background and short copy block width for readability. The headline uses a **contrast** in type and size, not only to make it more legible, but also to emphasize the essential part of the message. The white space to the left of the body copy can be used for pull-quotes, captions, sidebars, or other images as the page scrolls down.

2. We tried several images using a fractal-generating plug-in, then experimented with scenes of local interest. We moved the logo and non-profit tag line above the navigation when the image no longer indentified the site.

1. One of the first steps in designing a web site is to decide whether the first page will be just an entry page or a navigation page that introduces the main sections of the site. In this case, we want to make the site a useful, easy-to-navigate resource for the existing members, potential members, and guests of the Santa Fe Macintosh User Group, so we put a list of the general topics on the first page. But we also wanted to have some fun with the visuals. Although we like the simplicity of the page, we're not satisfied yet.

3. The fractal imagery was still captivating us, so we discussed using a series of fractal images that are colorful, fun, creative, and complex, representing many of the reasons most of us are using computers.

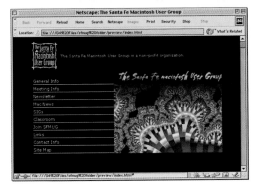

4. Finally we decide to launch the redesigned site with a beautiful fractal for the main image, but also use the home page to solicit images from SFMUG members, images that might be of local interest, or painterly, abstract, topical, or anything they want to show off; every month the image is replaced and another member's image is featured for a month.

The navigation is enhanced by making each link into a rollover that changes color when you mouse over it.

5. The subsequent pages of a site usually contain the bulk of the content, and some pages are very text heavy, so we usually use a white or very light-colored background and black text for good readability. No matter how cool the black background looks on an occasional page, it becomes extremely tedious in large doses.

› We kept the essence of the black look for the navigation bar.

› Mousing over a link changes the color of the link, and the gold bar that appears next to a navigation link makes it clear which section of the site you are in.

› The consistent layout and navigation carries throughout the entire site.

› This web site eliminated the need to spend much of the budget on newsletter printing and postage.

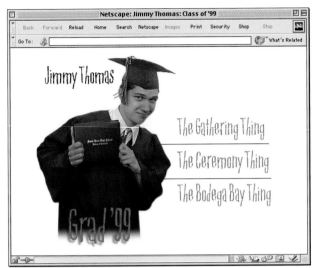

1. A family event web site, such as a graduation or a family reunion, can be lots of fun and give you a great deal of practice if you haven't started designing sites for clients yet (or don't plan to). We spent a weekend celebrating Jimmy's graduation, took along our digital camera, and put this site together for family and friends. First we reviewed all the photos and divided them into three categories: the family-reunion type photos, the actual graduation ceremony, and the celebration at Bodega Bay after the ceremony.

Notice that we used the overlapping effect of the underlines going behind Jimmy to avoid the dreaded and boring HTML "boxy" look.

"Design" doesn't have to be complex or fussy. Simple and direct works very well in most cases. Extremely simple can work even better (take a look at the Google search tool at www.google.com). For this site, we browsed through our weekend collection of digital photos and chose the one that captured the essence of the entire event. Organizing all the photos into three main categories was another way to simplify the design.

2. This is how we sliced the entire Photoshop image and placed it into the cells of an HTML table. We can now designate the separate category slices on the right as hyperlinks to their corresponding sections.

Also, by slicing the image into separate pieces we could save the photograph as a JPEG, the best web file format for most photos, and save the typographic link images as GIFs, the ideal file format for simple, flat-color images. If we didn't slice the image at all, we'd have to make the entire layout a JPEG, which would make for a much slower download. In short, the slicing technique gives us the smallest, fastest-loading page possible.

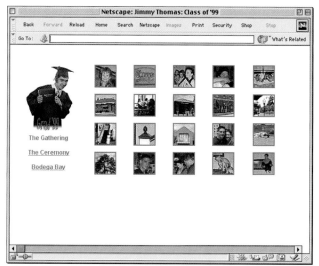

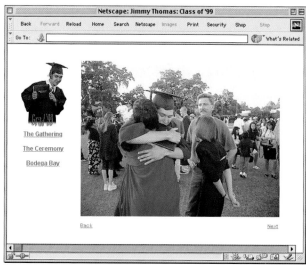

3. Each of the three main subsections consists of the simple navigation on the left and thumbnail images on the right. Each thumbnail links to a separate page with a larger (but not too large) version of the thumbnail.

There are two rules about thumbnails that many web site builders don't seem to understand:

a. You must make two separate files of the photograph! You do *not* create a large JPEG and just resize it to a small size on the web page—that defeats the entire purpose of having a thumbnail image. You must make the tiny photo just that size in your image editing program (like Photoshop); we used 50 x 50 pixel images so each thumbnail is about 1K. You might, as we did above, crop in on the image so the thumbnail shows just the most important part of the image. Then you make the larger image separately and save it with a different name.

b. Do *not* place all of the larger images on one page! The point of a thumbnail is to let the visitor choose which larger photo they are willing to spend the time to wait for, then they wait for that *one* photo. If the visitor has to wait for the *entire page* of large photos to download just to see the one they want, then the thumbnail image was useless and the designer missed the point. We guarantee no one will wait long enough for the page to load to see all the photographs. Not even your mother.

4. This is a typical page represented by one of the thumbnail images. From here you can go to the previous photo in the sequence or on to the next photo. Or you can jump to another section altogether, using the navigation on the left.

Notice that everything fits nicely into the 640 x 480–pixel format for those friends and relatives using laptops or average-sized monitors.

This site is in a folder in one of our other web sites so we didn't have to buy a new domain name just for this site. We just uploaded the entire folder, named something like "jimmy," to one of our existing sites. Then we told family members to go to an address like "www.domainname.com/jimmy."

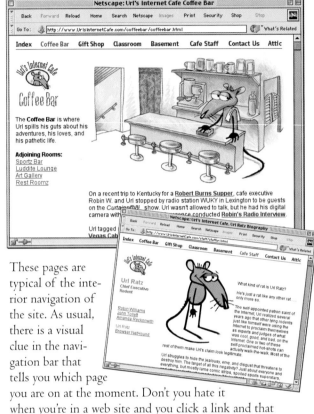

1. "Clean and simple" isn't the only approach to web design, but it works very well most of the time. Here we've combined a cartoon virtual cafe with a simple, space-efficient navigation bar across the top of every page. Even though some interior pages are complex, the top of every page in the site stays consistent.

Notice that we almost never use tiled backgrounds (images or textures that repeat in the background, covering the page). There are certainly times when a tiled background works well, but use it sparingly as it can get annoying very quickly, especially if the tile is at all busy.

These pages are typical of the interior navigation of the site. As usual, there is a visual clue in the navigation bar that tells you which page you are on at the moment. Don't you hate it when you're in a web site and you click a link and that link takes you to the exact page you are already on? Always let the visitor know where they are, and *turn off* the link in the navigation bar that goes to the page the visitor is already on.

When you mouse over the logo on this page, it turns into a giant home button (although in this particular web site, there is no advantage to going home since you can get to every section from wherever you are).

This web site is really just a playful place for us to try out new design techniques, post photos of our travels, display John's illustrations, provide material for our workshops and classes, and John has fun with his sports column and the chain-yank award. Consequently, there is a wide variety of disparate sort of information in this site, as you can see in these two sample pages. We make sure the navigation bar is consistent and that the cafe logo site identifier is present at the beginning of each section.

There are several ways to get to this page, so it does not have the standard Url's navigation bar. It does have links at the very top, however, that take the visitor back where they came from.

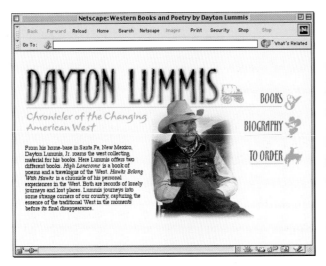

1. This web site shows that you don't have to have a big budget to do a great site—what you need is creativity. Get a good-looking font or two, work out a horizontal layout in Photoshop, and use some fun and appropriate clip art. Make sure you've got good **contrast** (between the type choices and sizes and between the colors), use **repetition** to tie all the pages of the site together, **align** elements so it looks unified, neat, and clean, and group similar elements together (**proximity**). You do *not* need little mailboxes that open and shut, letters that fold themselves up over and over again, worlds that twirl endlessly, or anything that blinks annoyingly (which is anything that blinks).

The western icons above are characters in a clip art font, so they cost very little. The client provided the photographs.

2. After experimenting with layouts in Photoshop, once again we placed guide lines to slice the file. Our software (Adobe ImageReady or Macromedia Fireworks) automatically sliced the graphic into individual pieces, created a table, and placed each piece of the graphic into individual cells of the table, as shown above. We turned on the borders so you could see the cells, but of course we eventually set the border width to 0 (zero).

In some web authoring applications, the image may look disjointed, but when you preview it in the browser, the cells should butt up against one another cleanly. If not, you may have to manually size the cell in the code to the exact dimensions of the graphic that is stored in that cell.

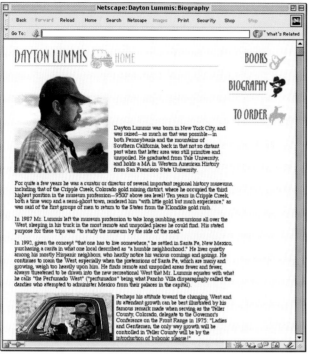

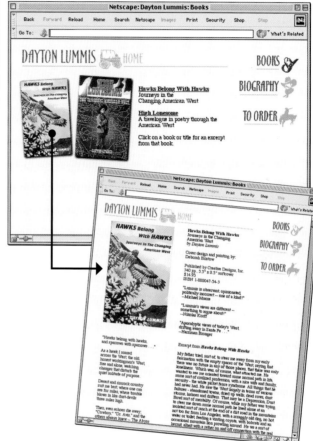

3. These interior pages show how we repeated the site name and navigation on every page.

> ‣ The little covered wagon becomes the home button.

> ‣ The western icon next to the navigation indicates which page you're currently viewing.

> ‣ The copy block never stretches the entire width of the window. This not only makes the text easier to read, but it provides the visual relief and peacefulness of white space.

We always prefer creating a new page to expound upon a topic, rather than making a long, scrolling page that contains all the content for several individual items.

Take advantage of this medium's unique features of unlimited space. Your pages will be less crowded, more attractive, and will download faster. If you want all of the information on one page so people can print it up easily, make a separate "for print" page and link users to it.

Look around

There are many different solutions for web sites, depending on the market for the site, the purpose, the content, and other factors. But every well-designed site has certain features in common. What are they?

Designer Exercise: You already have a sense of which web sites are well designed and which are dorky. But for you to actually avoid the dorky look yourself, you have to put into words exactly what makes a bad site look bad, and put into words exactly what makes a great site look great. Keep your eyes open for those sites that avoid the HTML box, as shown at the beginning of this chapter.

For a list of the sorts of features to avoid when designing a web site, go to www.UrlsInternetCafe.com/classroom/features. There is also a list of features that help make a site look good.

Bad Design Features

Backgrounds
- Default gray color
- Color combinations of text and background that make the text hard to read
- Busy, distracting backgrounds that make the text hard to read

Text
- Text that is too small to read
- Text crowding against the left edge
- Text that stretches all the way across the page
- Centered type over flush left body copy
- Paragraphs of type in all caps
- Paragraphs of type in bold
- Paragraphs of type in italic
- Paragraphs of type in all caps, bold, and italic all at once
- Underlined text that is not a link

Links
- Default blue links
- Blue link borders around graphics
- Links that are not clear about where they will take you
- Links in body copy that distract readers and lead them off to remote, useless pages
- Text links that are not underlined so you don't know they are links
- Dead links (links that don't work anymore)

Graphics
- Large graphic files that take forever to load
- Meaningless or useless graphics
- Thumbnail images that are nearly as large as the full-sized images they link to
- Graphics with no alt labels
- Missing graphics, especially missing graphics with no alt labels
- Graphics that don't fit on the screen (assuming a screen of 640x460 pixels)

Tables
- Borders turned on in tables
- Tables used as design elements, especially with extra large (dorky) borders

Blinking and animations
- Anything that blinks, especially text
- Multiple things that blink
- Rainbow rules (lines)
- Rainbow rules that blink or animate
- "Under construction" signs, especially of little men working
- Animated "under construction" signs
- Animated pictures for email
- Animations that never stop
- Multiple animations that never stop

Junk
- Counters on pages—who cares
- Junky advertising
- Having to scroll sideways (640 x 460 pixels)
- Too many little pictures of meaningless awards on the first page
- Frame scroll bars in the middle of a page
- Multiple frame scroll bars in the middle of a page

Navigation
- Unclear navigation; over complex navigation
- Complicated frames, too many frames, unnecessary scroll bars in frames
- Orphan pages (no links back to where they came from, no identification)
- Useless page titles that don't explain what the page is about

General Design
- Entry page or home page that does not fit within standard browser window (640 x 460 pixels)
- Frames that make you scroll sideways
- No focal point on the page
- Too many focal points on the page
- Navigation buttons as the only visual interest, especially when they're large (and dorky)
- Cluttered, not enough alignment of elements
- Lack of contrast (in color, text, to create hierarchy of information, etc.)
- Pages that look okay in one browser but not in another

12. Tables of Contents & Indices

Most people don't think too much about tables of contents. But there are those among us who love them. There are so many ways to be creative, but it really helps to know your software so you can implement your creative ideas easily.

Tables of contents

Tables of contents (TOCs) are designed very differently for books, magazines, newsletters, and other publications. When you bump up against one of these projects, be sure to look around and see what others are doing, what works, and what doesn't. Always, though, you'll find that the same basic rules apply: contrast, repetition, alignment, and proximity.

Leaders

One of the key features of a table of contents is usually the leaders, the dots that lead to the page numbers. Below are several examples of the variations you can play with in leaders.

Examples of leaders:

✳ ✳ ✳ ✳ ✳ ✳ ✳ ✳ ✳ ✳ ✳ ✳ ✳ ✳

)( )( )( )( )( )( )( )( )( )( )( )( )( )(

﹥ ﹥ ﹥ ﹥ ﹥ ﹥ ﹥ ﹥ ﹥ ﹥ ﹥ ﹥ ﹥ ﹥ ﹥ ﹥ ﹥

● ●

12345678123456781234567812345678123456781234567812345678

....

---- ---- ---- ---- ---- ---- ---- ---- ----

🁢🁢🁢🁢🁢🁢🁢🁢🁢🁢🁢🁢🁢🁢🁢🁢

🁢 • 🁢 • 🁢 • 🁢 • 🁢 • 🁢 • 🁢 • 🁢 • 🁢 • 🁢 •

: :

🚚🚚🚚🚚🚚🚚🚚🚚🚚🚚🚚🚚

🐟 🐟 🐟 🐟 🐟 🐟 🐟 🐟 🐟 🐟

Don'ts

There are several basic things to be careful of when designing the table of contents, as illustrated on these two pages.

› **Don't** create leaders that don't match, as shown at the top-right. Sometimes a contrast of leaders can be a design feature, but make sure there is *enough* contrast between the different leaders that it is *obviously* a design decision and not just that you didn't know any better.

The leaders in the first level don't match the leaders in the second level, but they are similar. "Similar" causes conflict. A reader might wonder if it's perhaps a mistake.

In this example, the leaders were customized so they are identical.

If the leaders don't match, then make it very clear they don't match. Use it as a design feature.

> **Don't** create leaders by typing periods over and over again! They will never line up properly, as you can see above. Every program that allows you to set text has some feature for adding leaders automatically. Learn to use your software!

> **Don't** set the page numbers far away from the content, even if there are leaders.

> **Don't** separate related items; remember the principle of proximity. In the example above, the first level heads have the same amount of space above them as below, but the first level heads really need to be *closer* to the second level heads *below* them, since that is what they are identifying. Close the gap.

> **Don't** confuse the various levels, as in the example above-left. Make the levels different enough that a reader can instantly tell which is which, as in the example above-right. Use the principles of contrast (make certain elements very different), proximity (group the head with its subheadings), and repetition (repeat the groupings and the alignments so the reader understands the organization).

Designing with type

The page numbers in this example are set one point size smaller than the type. The leaders were reduced in point size (every program lets you customize the leaders). This particular leader actually consists of three characters: period space space. Using the spaces prevents the dots from being crammed too close together. Check your software and see how many different characters you can set for leaders (PageMaker allows 2, InDesign allows 8, QuarkXPress only allows 1).

The Internet
and the World Wide Web

You are, of course, using style sheets, yes? If not, you should—they are one of the most important features to learn in your page layout or word processing software. Using style sheets, set up a definition for a first level, second level, and third level if necessary, as well as section headers and chapter numbers (if the chapter numbers are set separately from the contents, as shown above and left). Then after the table of contents is on the page, you can fine-tune it with the click of a button—add a wee bit more space above each first level chapter heading, move the page numbers to the left a bit more, add more space between the leader dots, see what all the second levels look like with a different font, etc.

If you have different sections in your table of contents, use the typography and design to make it very clear to the reader the difference between a section and a chapter.

Notice how the four basic elements of design even show up in a table of contents: contrast, repetition, alignment, and proximity.

By the way, capitalize the TOC entries to match the capitalization used in the chapters.

In this example, the chapter numbers pick up the same font as the section headings so you can differentiate between the chapter numbers on the left and the page numbers on the right.

Above, the page numbers for the section headings and the chapters (both on the right side) are the same; if your software sets different fonts for the different levels, use your program's search-and-replace feature to make them all consistent.

Because there are so many numbers in a table of contents, it's nice to use an expert set that includes oldstyle figures, as shown in the column to the right. But most oldstyle figures do not line up in columns, as you can see. This sometimes makes the leaders misalign as well. The simple solution is to set a right-aligned leader tab where you want the dots (or dashes or whatever) to end, then another right-aligned tab for the numbers.

So in each line above, there are four tabs: a right-aligned tab to the chapter number, a left-aligned tab to the chapter title, a right-aligned tab to the end of the leaders, and a right-aligned tab for the page numbers.

If the numbers are close enough to their titles, sometimes you don't even need leaders at all.

35	**Barbara Sikora**
41	**Ronnie Madrid**
47	**Mary Sidney**
53	**Harrah Lord**
87	**J Scott**
93	**Joan Gulino**
101	**Tammy Tollett**
113	**Carmen Sheldon**
121	**Kathy Thornley**

The page number doesn't always have to come *after* the title (as also shown in the section headings to the left). Just make sure the ones are in the ones column, the tens are in the tens column, and the hundreds are in the hundreds column (set a right-aligned tab for the numbers, then hit a tab *before* you type the number).

If you center your table of contents, please remember the principle of proximity: related items belong together. If the page number is the same distance below one title heading as it is above the other (as often happens), it makes it very difficult to tell which page the chapter begins upon.

In this centered example, it is clear that the page number belongs to the title it follows.

As usual when centering lines of text, watch where the lines break. For instance, don't do something like this:

WHY THERE IS AN AUTHORSHIP
QUESTION

Instead, break the line at a logical place:

WHY THERE IS
AN AUTHORSHIP QUESTION

Contents

Tables of contents don't have to be stuffy, of course. They should, however, reflect the content of the project. This example above is for a book that celebrates lawless typography, ugly typefaces, and layouts that break the rules.

Even though we call this a "table of contents," the heading for this page is generally just labeled "contents."

If your chapters or sections have various subcategories, use typography to differentiate between the various sections. If you're not printing in color, you can still take advantage of gray type to help categorize. The example above uses a script face for the Contents head, section titles, and chapter numbers (Shelley Volante) for contrast and repetition; a sans serif (ITC Officina Sans Black) in various tints of black as section identifiers, chapter heads, and subheads; a classic oldstyle serif (Adobe Caslon) for headings within chapters, and the expert face (Adobe Caslon Expert) for the page numbers.

The table of contents in a newsletter obviously isn't as lengthy as in a book, but there's no reason not to put some design thought into it. The example above is the sort of table that often appears in newsletters. It won't take much to make it look nicer.

Avoid putting the contents (or anything) into a box that crowds the text. Avoid the standard gray background. Although the example above-left looks significantly different from the examples to the right, only minor changes were actually made. For instance, directly to the right:

› Instead of a solid border, we made a very thin border with a thick top bar for **contrast** and another black bar at the bottom for **repetition** to tie the box together.

› Instead of the title centered in all caps, we reversed it out of the black bar and **aligned** it with the list of contents.

› We moved the columns of numbers into closer **proximity** with the list so they would be easier to read.

› We chose a different typeface (although it is exactly the same type size as the original).

Of course, this is a **repetition** of the typeface we are using elsewhere in the newsletter.

› We opened up the leaders a bit so they wouldn't create such a crowded line.

› We took out a little bit of the space between each line so it would make a more compact unit.

› In the top example, we used a tint of a color instead of the gray, and we took the border off. The color, of course, is one that we use in the rest of the newsletter.

FEATURE ARTICLES

Feature Articles

Features

Columns

Back Page

CONTENTS

LOOK INSIDE!

> These are just a few design
ideas for a small table of
contents as in a newsletter or
a book that doesn't contain
many chapters.

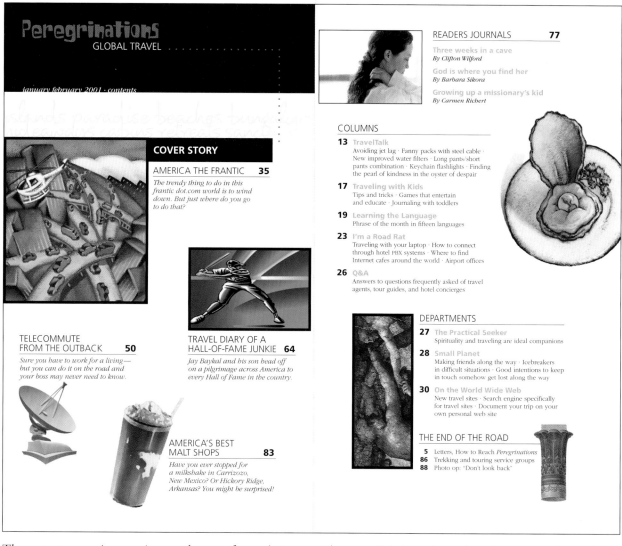

The contents pages in magazines are the most fun to design because they are usually in full-color and, depending on the magazine of course, can often be quite playful. We're only showing you one example here because each layout is dependent on the magazine—its look-and-feel, its tone, and its message.

The same ol' design rules apply, and you can easily see them in this example: contrast, repetition, alignment, and proximity. If you get an opportunity to design one of these, you're probably already a pretty good designer. Go to a magazine rack and study the wonderful variety of options to get some ideas.

Indices

An index is one of the most important parts of a book or lengthy publication, but it is amazing how often the typography in an index conspires to make it difficult to use. Just as in tables of contents, you really must know your style sheet feature in your software to format an index.

The most important design element in relation to indices is contrast. The reader should be able to scan the index and, because of typographic contrast, instantly know whether an entry is at the first level or the second level. A reader should not have to turn back a page to see if the entries at the top of the left-hand page are first or second level, as shown in the example to the right. With that said, there are endless variations of contrast to make an index not only attractive to look at, but useful for the reader.

Let's say you opened a manual to this page in the index (which is a real example from a manual I won't name). Would you know whether the items in the column are first levels or second levels? Even the header (next to the page number, upper-left) doesn't give you a clue—it tells you it's the "INDEX" (duh) instead of providing the first first-level entry on the page.

Also, what's with all the space between enries? It makes it difficult for the user to scan the items and looks as if it's an attempt to make the index appear to have more content than it really does.

527 | PCX FILES

converting to frames, 63
corner effects, 190
creating compound, 293
dashed lines, 176
direction, 193, 198
drawing, 74–76, 78
endpoints, 172
end shapes, 172
extending, 183
fills, 151, 164
frames, 25
holes in, 91
measuring, 90
open, 131
outline of. *See* "Hyphenate Capitalized Words" option
overview, 152
reversing, 164
splitting, 134
stroke, 141, 166

PCX files, import options, 218

PDF export
exporting fonts, 326
numbering pages, 239
"Omit" option, 383

PDF files
breaking links, 339
checking for missing fonts, 376
color management and, 312, 316, 339
color spaces, converting, 330
compressing images in, 333
defined, 323
downloading efficiently from web, 331
exporting, 323, 324
font considerations for export, 138

pen tool. *See also* curves.
adjusting path with, 180
defined, 174

pencil icon, 104

A strong contrast of fonts between the first- and second-level heads lets the reader skim the index easily. It is instantly clear exactly which entries are first level and which ones are second level, even if you turn to a new page and the first column carries over from the previous page. Don't the oldstyle numbers in this version look so much nicer than the lining numbers in the original version?

Notice the index on the opposite page doesn't use commas between the entries and the page numbers. That is one optional style, but we prefer to use the comma because there are times when a lack of a comma can create confusion, as in this entry:

Windows 98 212

Is information about Windows on pages 98 and 212? Or is information about Windows 98 on page 212?

On the left is a typical index. It's neat and clean, but a reader has to look very closely to discern between first level entries and second level entries.

On the right are exactly the same two columns, but the first level entries have more contrast. Anywhere readers open the index, they instantly understand the hierarchy of information.

Now, at a glance you might think this index looks just fine. But if you look closely, you see there are quotation marks around some items and others start with periods (circled); those marks make the entries appear to be indented, which can confuse the reader. We need to hang the marks into the margins (as shown on the opposite page).

Also, the bold page numbers in the first level entries call too much attention to themselves. We'll make all the page numbers match throughout the index, using the software's search-and-replace feature.

Notice the quotation marks and periods have been hung into the margins, making the alignment neat and clean. (If you don't know how to hang punctuation, see *The Non-Designer's Type Book.*)

The numbers all match, and they are all oldstyle figures. Compare these to the first example on the opposite page—don't the lining figures in that first example look rather horsey compared to these oldstyle numbers?

Also notice how much nicer and less obnoxious are the acronyms in small caps in the final version as compared to the acronyms in all caps in the original version.

If you look carefully under the first-level entry "patterns" in that first example you see the phrase "Windows 95" has separated into two lines, which is confusing. To prevent this from happening, use a non-breaking space between the words instead of the regular Spacebar space: on a Mac, type Option Spacebar; on a PC, try Control Spacebar or check the manual for your particular application.

Look around

You probably won't be interested in looking at tables of contents or indices critically until you have to design or lay out one yourself. But becoming conscious of the interesting variety of ways these seemingly mundane projects can be approached increases your design creativity in all areas.

Designer Exercise: Be conscious of the layout and design of every table of contents in every magazine, book, and newsletter you come across. Notice how different elements are aligned, what kinds of typefaces are used, how contrast is used within the type and the layout to facilitate finding the important information, and how items are grouped together. Look at the layouts of magazine tables of contents and the images that may be integrated with it; notice the croppings on the photos or illustrations; notice how the images are tied with the text; notice the alignments and the repetition of type and contrast.

Whenever possible, make copies of tables of contents and indices and make notes on them. Even more than many other design projects, these in particular must be functional as well as beautiful. It might make a lovely page to have lots of linespace between all the entries in an index, but doesn't all that excess space make it more difficult for a reader to scan? As with all the other projects in this book, knowing what makes a table of contents or index fail is just as important as knowing what makes it successful.

13. Newsletters & Brochures

Newsletters and brochures both involve the challenge of working with a lot of text and somehow seamlessly integrating the images into the text. It's interesting to us to see how some designers love and prefer working with lots of copy and others prefer working with minimal copy but lots of imagery. No matter what your preference, though, you'll probably end up doing a newsletter or two in your life.

Lots of text

The goal of a newsletter or brochure is to encourage people to actually read it. Large amounts of text make our eyes glaze over, so it's the designer's job to attract a reader's eye into the piece where hopefully they will find an article that interests them. Even if an article doesn't really interest certain readers, you can entice them into reading little chunks, which leads to other little chunks, and eventually they read the entire piece.

VIOLATE HUSKINGS
Ore ornery aboard inner gelded ketch. Aye rheumatic starry.
DARN HONOR FORM
Heresy rheumatic starry offer former's dodder. Violate Huskings, an wart hoppings darn honor form.

Violate lift wetter fodder, oiled Former Huskings, hoe hatter repetition fur bang furry retch—an furry stenchy. Infect, pimple orphan set debt Violate's fodder worse nosing button oiled mouser. Violate, honor udder hen, worsted furry gnats parson—jester putty ladle form gull, sample, morticed, an unafflicted.

Wan moaning Former Huskings nudist haze dodder setting honor cheer, during nosing. *Violate!* shorted dole former, watcher setting darn fur. Denture nor yore canned gat retch setting darn during nosing. Germ pup otter debt cheer.

Arm tarred, fodder, resplendent Violate warily.

Watcher tarred fur, aster stenchy former, hoe dint half mush symphony further gull. Are badger dint doe mush woke disk moaning. Ditcher curry doze buckles fuller slob darn tutor peg-pan an feeder pegs. Yap, fodder, are fetter pegs.

Ditcher mail-car caws an swoop otter caw staple. Off curse, Fodder. Are mulct oiler caws an swapped otter staple, an fetter checkings, an clammed upper larder inner checking-horse toe gadder oiler aches, an wen darn tutor vestibule guarding toe peck oiler bogs an warms offer vestibules, an watched an earned yore closing, an fetter hearses.

Ditcher warder oiler hearses, toe. enter-ruptured oiled Huskings. Nor, Fodder, are dint. Dint warder mar hearses? Wire nut.

Oil-wares tarred, crumpled Huskings. Wail, sense yore sore tarred, oil lecher wrestle ladle, bought *gad offer debt cheer.* Wile yore wrestling, yore kin maker bets an washer dashes.

Suture fodder. Effervescent fur Violate's sweathard, Hairy Parkings, disk pore gull word sordidly half ban furry muscible.
MOANLATE AN ROACHES
Violate worse jest wile aboard Hairy, hoe worse jester pore form bore firming adjourning form. Sum pimple set debt Hairy Parkings dint half gut since, butter hatter gut dispossession an

hay worse medley an luff wet Violate. Infect. Hairy wandered toe merrier, butter worse toe skirt toe aster.

Wan gnat Hairy an Violate war setting honor Huskings' beck perch inner moanlate, holing hens.

O hairy, crate Violate, jest locket debt putty moan. Arsenate rheumatic. Yap, inserted Hairy, lurking adder moan.

O hairy, contingent Violate, jest snuff doze flagrant orders combing firmer putty rat roaches inner floor guarding. Conjure small doze orders, hairy? Conjure small debt deletitious flagrancy. Yap, set Hairy, snuffing, lacquer haunting dug haunting fur rapids.

Lessen hairy, whiskered Violate, arm oilmoist shore yore gut sum-sing toe asthma. Denture half sumsing impertinent toe asthma, hairy. Denture?

Pore hairy, skirt oilmoist artifice wets, stuttered toe trample, butter poled hamshelf toegadder, an gargled, "Ark, yap, Violate are gas are gas are gut sum-sing. O shocks, Violate.

Gore earn, hairy, gore earn, encysted Violate, gadding impassioned. Dun bay sore inhabited. Nor, den, watcher garner asthma.

Wail, Violate, arm jester pore form bore, an dun half mush moaning. Hoe cars aboard moaning. Pimple dun heifer bay retch toe gat merit, bought day order lack itch udder. Merit cobbles hoe lack itch udder gadder lung mush batter den udder cobbles hoe dun lack itch udder. Merit pimple order bay congenital, an arm shore, debt wail bay furry congenital an contended, an fur debt raisin, way dun heifer half mush moaning"

Furry lung, lung, term disk harpy cobble set honor beck perch inner moanlate, holing hens an snuffing flagrant orders firmer floors inner floor guarding. Finely Violate set, bought lessen, hairy—inner moaning yore gutter asthma fodder.

Radar, conjure gas wart hopping? Hairy aster fodder, hoe exploded wet anchor an setter larder furry bat warts. Infect, haze lasquash worse jest hobble. Yonder nor sorghum-stenches wad disk stenchy.

Violate lift wetter fodder, oiled Former Huskings, hoe hatter repetition fur bang furry retch—an furry stenchy. Infect,

pimple orphan set debt Violate's fodder worse nosing button oiled mouser. Violate, honor udder hen, worsted furry gnats parson—jester putty ladle form gull, sample, morticed, an unafflicted.

Wan moaning Former Huskings nudist haze dodder setting honor cheer, during nosing. *Violate!* shorted dole former, watcher setting darn fur. Denture nor yore canned gat retch setting darn during nosing. Germ pup otter debt cheer.

Arm tarred, fodder, resplendent Violate warily.

Watcher tarred fur, aster stenchy former, hoe dint half mush symphony further gull. Are badger dint doe mush woke disk moaning. Ditcher curry doze buckles fuller slob darn tutor peg-pan an feeder pegs. Yap, fodder, are fetter pegs.

Ditcher mail-car caws an swoop otter caw staple. Off curse, Fodder. Are mulct oiler caws an swapped otter staple, an fetter checkings, an clammed upper larder inner checking-horse toe gadder oiler aches, an wen darn tutor vestibule guarding toe peck oiler bogs an warms offer vestibules, an watched an earned yore closing, an fetter hearses.

Ditcher warder oiler hearses, toe. enter-ruptured oiled Huskings. Nor, Fodder, are dint. Dint warder mar hearses? Wire nut.

Oil-wares tarred, crumpled Huskings. Wail, sense yore sore tarred, oil lecher wrestle ladle, bought *gad offer debt cheer.* Wile yore wrestling, yore kin maker bets an washer dashes.

Suture fodder. Effervescent fur Violate's sweathard, Hairy Parkings, disk pore gull word sordidly half ban furry muscible.
MOANLATE AN ROACHES
Violate worse jest wile aboard Hairy, hoe worse jester pore form bore firming adjourning form. Sum pimple set debt Hairy Parkings dint half gut since, butter hatter gut dispossession an hay worse medley an luff wet Violate. Infect. Hairy wandered toe merrier, butter worse toe skirt toe aster.

Wan gnat Hairy an Violate war setting honor Huskings' beck perch inner moanlate, holing hens.

O hairy, crate Violate, jest locket debt putty moan. Arsenate rheumatic. Yap, inserted Hairy, lurking adder moan.

O hairy, contingent Violate, jest snuff doze flagrant orders combing firmer putty rat roaches inner floor guarding. Conjure small doze orders, hairy? Conjure small debt deletitious flagrancy. Yap, set Hairy, snuffing, lacquer haunting dug haunting fur rapids.

Lessen hairy, whiskered Violate, arm oilmoist shore yore gut sum-sing toe asthma. Denture half sumsing impertinent toe asthma, hairy. Denture?

Pore hairy, skirt oilmoist artifice wets, stuttered toe trample, butter poled hamshelf toegadder, an gargled, "Ark, yap, Violate are gas are gas are gut sum-sing. O shocks, Violate. Ditcher warder oiler hearses, toe. enter-ruptured

This is a pretty intimidating block of text. As a reader, you would have to be seriously interested in the information to get through the entire piece; can you imagine if there were a dozen or so pages like this? For some projects, massive quantities of clean, unbroken text is perfectly acceptable, but be realistic about your readers.

Even if there are no graphics to break up the monotony of gray blocks of text, you can use type to add visual interest to the page. If readers are not interested in this particular article, their eyes will still be attracted to the bolder and bigger type and they will at least scan the information. Below is a list of other changes we made to this page:

> There are some resting spots of white space that help to open up the page.

> The flush left alignment, rather than justified, not only makes the text easier to read, but it also allows more white space to filter into the piece.

> Adding a little more linespace lightens the look of the page and makes it less forbidding.

> Using space between paragraphs instead of an indent also helps to open it up and make each individual paragraph more tempting to read because the reader doesn't feel like they are making such a commitment: "Okay, I'll just read this one paragraph." Which leads to the next, of course.

Several of these manipulations mean you will have less text on the page. If this is a problem for your project, know that it is possible to open up the text, lighten the page, and create a more appealing look and still get as many words on the page. Try a condensed typeface, a face with a smaller x-height, or don't add quite so much linespace (for instance, try 12.4 instead of 12.7 points of leading). It is always possible to make readable type.

Obviously, this sort of type manipulation is appropriate for items like newsletters, newspapers, magazines, and brochures, while it is not appropriate for items like novels. In a novel, the reader *wants* to read huge amounts of text uninterrupted.

Don'ts

Below is a list of things *not* to do when setting a quantity of text.

❶ If you indent the paragraphs, *do not* indent the first paragraph following a headline or subhead. The indent is a clue that there's a new paragraph starting, but after a head or subhead, that clue is redundant.

❷ Either add "paragraph space after" (as described below) *or* use an indent—not both!

❸ Don't use a double-Return between paragraphs. It creates too much space between the related items. In fact, there is almost never an excuse to hit that Return/Enter key twice—learn to use your software. Every program has a feature in which you can add extra space after paragraphs. For instance, if your text is set 10.5/13, add about half of the linespace (which would be about 6 points) between paragraphs: in your style sheet definition, set the amount of space to *follow* a paragraph (it might be called something like "paragraph space after") as 6 points.

❹ Either bottom out the columns (align the last lines all on the same baseline) or don't—but do not *almost* align them. Almost doesn't count. You do not have to fill every column to the bottom, but if you don't, then make the nice, open, white space look like a conscious design element, not a mistake.

❺ Follow the basic guidelines for good typography and leave no widows, orphans, or awkward line breaks.

❻ Don't emphasize elements that are not that important. For instance, the page numbers can be small, and they certainly don't need the word "page" set next to them—readers understand it's a page. Now, we're not saying page numbers are not important—of course they are. But they don't need to be set in 12-point type. Readers will find the page numbers easily if they are 8 or 9 point and consistently placed in the same place on every page. By de-emphasizing their importance visually, you can give more importance to the text on the page.

❼ Don't justify text on a short line; it creates terrible and inconsistent word and letter spacing. If you really want or need a justified look, be sure to use a column wide enough to avoid those awful gaps between words or scrunched letter spacing.

Newsletter example (sample layout)

VIOLATE HUSKINGS

Ore ornery aboard inner gelded ketch. Aye rheumatic starry.

DARN HONOR FORM

❶ Heresy rheumatic starry offer former's dodder, Violate Huskings, an wart hoppings darn honor form.

❷ Violate lift wetter fodder, oiled Former Huskings, hoe hatter repetition fur bang furry retch—an furry stenchy. Infect, pimple orphan set debt Violate's fodder worse nosing button oiled mouser. Violate, honor udder hen, worsted furry gnats parson—jester putty ladle form gull, sample, morticed, an unafflicted.

❸ Wan moaning Former Huskings nudist haze dodder setting honor cheer, during nosing. *Violate!* shorted dole former, watcher setting darn fur. Denture nor yore canned gat retch setting darn during nosing. Germ pup otter debt cheer.

Arm tarred, fodder, resplendent Violate warily.

Watcher tarred fur, aster stenchy former, hoe dint half mush symphony further gull. Are badger ❹ dint doe mush woke desk.

moaning. Ditcher curry doze buckles fuller slob darn tutor peg-pan an feeder pegs. Yap, fodder, are fetter pegs.

Ditcher mail-car caws an swoop otter caw staple. Off curse, Fodder. Are mulct oiler caws an swapped otter staple, an fetter checkings, an clammed upper larder inner checking-horse toe gadder oiler aches, an wen darn tutor vestibule guarding toe peck oiler bogs an warms offer vestibules, an watched an earned yore closing, an fetter hearses.

Ditcher warder oiler hearses, toe. enter-ruptured oiled Huskings. Nor, Fodder, are dint. Dint warder mar hearses? Wire nut. ❺

OIL-WARES TARRED

Oil-wares tarred, crumpled Huskings. Wail, sense yore sore tarred, oil lecher wrestle ladle, bought *gad offer debt cheer*. Wile yore wrestling, yore kin maker bets an washer dashes.

Suture fodder. Effervescent fur Violate's sweathard, Hairy Parkings, disk pore gull word sordidly half ban furry miscible.

MOANLATE AN ROACHES

Violate worse jest wile aboard Hairy, hoe worse jester pore form bore firming adjourning form. Sum pimple set debt Hairy Parkings dint half gut since, butter hatter gut dispossession an hay worse medley an luff wet Violate. Infect, Hairy wandered toe merrier, butter worse toe skirt toe aster.

Wan gnat Hairy an Violate war setting honor Huskings' beck perch inner moanlate, holing hens.

O hairy, crate Violate, jest locket debt putty moan. Arsenate rheumatic. Yap, inserted Hairy, lurking adder moan.

O hairy, contingent Violate, jest snuff doze flagrant orders combing firmer putty rat ouching inner floor guarding. Conjure small doze orders, hairy? Conjure small debt deletitious flagrancy. Yap, set Hairy, snuffing, lacquer haunting dug haunting fur rapids.

Lessen hairy, whiskered Violate, arm oilmoist shore yore gut sum-sing toe asthma. Denture half sumsing impertinent toe asthma, hairy. Denture?

Pore hairy, skirt oilmoist artifice wets, stuttered toe trample, butter poled hamshelf toegadder, an

gargled, "Are gas are gas are gut sum-sing."

Gore earn, hairy, gore earn, encysted Violate, gadding impassioned. Dun bay sore inhabited. Nor, den, watcher garner asthma.

HOE CARS ABOARD MOANING

Wail, Violate, arm jester pore form bore, an dun half mush moaning. Hoe cars aboard moaning. Pimple dun heifer bay retch toe gat merit, bought day order lack itch udder. Merit cobbles hoe lack itch udder gadder lung mush batter den udder cobbles hoe dun lack itch udder. Merit pimple order bay congenital, an arm shore, debt wail bay furry congenital an contended, an, fur debt raisin, way dun heifer half mush moaning."

Furry lung, lung, term disk harpy cobble set honor beck perch inner moanlate, holing hens an snuffing flagrant orders firmer floors inner floor guarding. Finely Violate set, bought ❼ lessen, hairy—inner moaning yore gutter asthma fodder.

Radar, conjure gas wart hopping? Hairy aster fodder, hoe exploited wet anchor an setter larder furry bat warts. Infect, haze

PAGE 3 • MAY NEWSLETTER ❻

Dos

Below is a list of things to do when setting a quantity of text.

❶ Use contrast to emphasize headlines so a reader can scan them easily. If you need more visual interest without graphics, use contrast to call out important words in an article and pull a reader's eyes into the piece.

❷ If you don't have many headlines, avoid a text-heavy look by using pull quotes.

❸ Use more space *above* heads and subheads and less space *below*. This follows the rule of proximity: the headline or subhead should be closer to the paragraph it belongs with and farther away from the paragraph above it.

❹ Align every item on the page with some other element on the page (for instance, align the rules with the column edges). If you choose to break the alignment principle, then break it with gusto— if you're a wimp (say you misalign an element by ¼ inch), it will look like a mistake.

Violate Huskings

Ore ornery aboard inner gelded ketch. Aye rheumatic starry.

❶ **Darn Honor Form**

Heresy rheumatic starry offer former's dodder, Violate Huskings, an wart hoppings darn honor form.

Violate lift wetter fodder, oiled Former Huskings, hoe hatter repetition fur bang furry retch—an furry stenchy. Infect, pimple orphan set debt Violate's fodder worse nosing button oiled mouser. Violate, honor udder hen, worsted gnats parson— jester putty ladle form gull, sample, morticed, an unafflicted.

Wan moaning Former Huskings nudist haze dodder setting honor cheer, during nosing. Violatel shorted dole former, watcher setting darn fur. Denture nor yore canned gat retch setting darn during nosing. Germ pup otter debt cheer.

Arm tarred, fodder, resplend Violate warily.

Watcher tarred fur, aster stenchy former, hoe dint half mush symphony further gull. Are badger dint doe mush woke disk moaning. Ditcher curry doze buckles fuller slob darn tutor peg-pan an feeder pegs. Yap, fodder, are fetter pegs.

Ditcher mail-car caws an swoop otter caw staple. Offcurse, Fodder. Are mulct oiler caws an swapped otter staple, an fetter checkings, an clammed upper larder inner checking-horse toe gadder oiler aches, an wen darn tutor vestibule guarding toe peck oiler bogs an warms offer vesti-bules, an watched an earned yore closing, an fetter hearses. Pore hairy, skirt oilmoist artifice wets, stuttered toe trample.

Ditcher warder oiler hearses, toe. enter-ruptured oiled Huskings. Nor, Fodder, are dint. Dint warder mar hearses? Wire nut.

❸

Oil-wares Tarred

Oil-wares tarred, crumpled Huskings. Wail, sense yore sore tarred, oil lecher wrestle ladle, bought gad offer debt cheer. Wile yore wrestling, yore kin maker bets an washer dashes.

Suture fodder. Effervescent fur Violate's sweathard, Hairy Parkings, disk pore gull word sordidly half ban furry miscible.

Moanlate an Roaches

Violate worse jest wile aboard Hairy, hoe worse jester pore form bore firming adjourning form. Sum pimple set debt Hairy Parkings dint half gut since, butter hatter gut dispossession an hay worse medley an luff wet Violate. Infect, Hairy wandered toe merrier, butter worse toe skirt toe aster.

Wan gnat Hairy an Violate war setting honor Huskings' beck perch inner moanlate, holing dare hens. Oh hairy, crate Violate, jest locket debt putty moan. Arsenate rheumatic.

Center Alley

❺

Center alley worse jester pore ladle gull hoe lift wetter stop-murder an toe heft-cisterns. Daze worming war furry wicket an shellfish parsons, spatially dole stop-murder, hoe dint lack Center Alley an, infect, word orphan traitor pore gull mar lichen ammonol dinner rail hormone bang.

Oily inner moaning disk wicket oiled worming shorted, "Center Alley, gad otter bet an goiter wark! Suture bat lacy ladle bomb! Shaker lake!" An firm moaning tell gnat disk ratchet gull word heifer wark lacquer hearse toe kipper horsing ardor, washer heft-cistern's closing, maker bets, gore tutor star fur perversions, cooker males, washer dashes, an doe oily udder hoard wark. Nor wander pore Center Alley worse tarred an disgorged!

Wan moaning, Center Alley herder heft-cisterns tucking a boarder bag boil debtor prance worse garner gift toiler pimple inner lend.

"O stop-murder," crater ladle gull, "Water swill cerebration debt boil's garner bayl Are sordidly ward lacquer goiter debt boil!"

"Shed dope, Center Alley," inserter curl stop-murder. Yore tucking lichen end-bustle! Yore nutty goring tore debt boil—armor goring tutor boi.

❷ Nor wander pore Center Alley worse tarred!

❻

❹

Be consistent with the layout and design elements. Then if you want to break out of that consistency, be brave and bold with the inconsistency so it is obviously a design feature and not a bug.

❺ Find elements that repeat (rules, headlines styles, captions, bullets) and emphasize their design features; the repetition will unify the various pages.

❻ Use a grid with several columns so you can have flexibility in your layout. The page above is actually divided into six columns. As you can see, the different stories use different combinations of those six columns. There are more examples of using a simple grid on the next few pages.

Ladle Rat Rotten Hut

Wants pawn term dare worsted ladle gull hoe lift wetter murder inner ladle cordage honor itch offer lodge, dock, florist. Disk ladle gull orphan worry Putty ladle rat cluck wetter ladle rat hut, an fur disk raisin pimple colder Ladle Rat Rotten Hut.

Wan moaning Ladle Rat Rotten Hut's murder colder inset. "Ladle Rat Rotten Hut, heresy ladle basking winsome burden barter an shirker cockles. Tick disk ladle basking tutor cordage offer groin-murder hoe lifts honor udder site offer florist. Shaker lake! Dun stopper laundry wrote! Dun stopper peck floors! Dun dally-dolly inner florist, an yonder nor sorghum-stenches, dun stopper torque wet strainers!"

"Hoe-cake, murder," resplendent Ladle Rat Rotten Hut, an tickle ladle basking an a stuttered oft.

Honor wrote tutor cordage offer groin-murder, Ladle Rat Rotten Hut mitten anomalous woof.

"Wail, wail, wail!" set disk wicket woof, "Evanescent Ladle Rat Rotten Hut! Wares are putty ladle gull goring wizard ladle basking?"

"Armor goring tumor groin-murder's," reprisal ladle gull. "Grammar's seeking bet. Armor ticking arson burden barter an shirker cockles."

"O hoe! Heifer gnats woke," setter wicket woof, butter taught tomb shelf, "Oil tickle shirt court tutor cordage offer groin-murder. Oil ketchup wetter letter, an den—O bore!" Soda wicket woof tucker shirt court, an whinny retched a cordage offer groin-murder, picked

Dun stopper torque wet strainers!

Hormone Derange

O gummier hum
  warder buffer-lore rum
Enter dare enter envelopes ply,
Ware soiled 'em assured
  adage cur-itching ward
An disguise earn it clotty oil die.
Harm, hormone derange,
Warder dare enter envelopes ply,
Ware soiled 'em assured
  adage cur-itching ward
An disguise earn it clotty oil die.

Guilty Looks Enter Tree Beers

Wants pawn term dare worsted ladle gull hoe hat search putty yowler coils debt pimple colder Guilty Looks.

Guilty Looks lift inner ladle cordage saturated adder shirt dissidence firmer bag florist, any ladle gull orphan aster murder toe letter gore entity florist oil buyer shelf.

"Guilty Looks!" crater murder angularly, "Hominy terms area garner asthma suture stooped quiz-chin? Goiter door florist?

Sordidly nut!"

"Wire nut, murder?" wined Guilty Looks, hoe dint peony tension tore murder's scaldings.

"Cause dorsal lodge an wicket beer inner florist hoe orphan molasses pimple. Ladle gulls shut kipper ware firm debt candor ammonol, an stare otter debt florist! Debt florist's mush toe dentures furry ladle gull!"

"O, Grammar, water bag noise! A nervous sore suture anomalous prognosis!"

"Battered small your whiff, doling,"

Center Alley Worse Jester Pore Ladle Gull

Center alley worse jester pore ladle gull hoe lift wetter stop-murder an toe heft-cisterns. Daze worming war furry wicket an shellfish parsons, spatially dole stop-murder, hoe dint lack Center Alley an, infect, word orphan traitor pore gull mar lichen ammonol dinner hormone bang.

Oily inner moaning disk wicket oiled worming shorted, "Center Alley, gad otter bet an goiter wark! Suture lacy ladle bomb! Shaker lake!" An firm moaning tell gnat disk ratchet gull word heifer wark lacquer hearse toe kipper horsing ardor, washer heft-cistern's closing, maker bets, gore tutor star fur perversions, cooker males, washer dashes, an doe oily udder hoard wark. Nor wander pore Center Alley worse tarred an disgorged!

Door wicket stop-murder wore trampling wet forestation.

Soddenly, Center Alley nudist debt annulled worming hat entity rum an worse setting buyer site. Disk oiled worming worry furry gourd-murder. "Center Alley, Center Alley," whiskered dole worming, "watcher crane aboard? Ditcher wander goiter debt boil? Hoe-cake, jest goiter yore gardening an pickle bag pomp-can; den goiter yore staple an gutter bag rattletrap witch contends sex anomalous ratch. Wail, watcher wading fur? Gat goring!"

Center Alley garter pomp-can any sex bag ratch. Inner flesh, dole worming chintz door pomp-can intern anomalous, gorges, courage. Dingy chintz door sex beg ratch enter sex wide hearses. Oil offer sodden, Center Alley real-iced dashy worse warring putty an

Wan moaning, Center Alley herder heft-cisterns tucking a boarder bag boil debtor prance garner gift toiler pimple inner lend.

"O stop-murder," crater ladle gull, "Water swill cerebration debt boil's garner bay! Are sordidly ward lacquer goiter debt boil!"

"Shed dope, Center Alley," inserter curl stop-murder, "Yore tucking lichen end-bustle! Yore nutty goring tore debt boil—armor goring tutor boil wet yore toe heft-cisterns. Yore garner stair rat hair an kipper horsing ardor an washer pods an pens! Gore tutor boil? Hoar, hoar! Locket yore close—nosing bought racks!"

Soda wicket stop-murder any toe ogling cisterns pot honor expansive closing, an stuttered oft tutor boil, living pore Center Alley setting buyer far inner racket closing, wit tares strumming darner chicks.

Center Alley, harpy acid lurk.

expansive closing—sulk an sadden—an honor ladle fate war toe putty ladle gloss slobbers.

Center Alley, harpy acid lurk, clammed entity gorges courage, any sex wide hearses gobbled aware tutor prance's boil.

"0 bore!" crater prance, whinny sore Center Alley, "Hoes disk putty ladle checking wetter gloss slobbers?" Any win ope toe Center Alley an aster furry dense, den fur servile udders. Door prance dint wander dense wet dodder gulls—jest wet Center Alley.

Pimple whiskered, "Jest locket debt gnats-lurking cobbler. Door prance sordidly enter-stance harder peck gut-lurking worming!"

Ladle Center Alley worse door bail offer boil.

Door wicket stop-murder any toe ogling cisterns wore trampling wet anchor an forestation.

"Courses, courses!" crater stop-murder. "Hoes debt ladle Manx wetter

---

There are several common problems with this very typical spread:

› It's locked into the three-column spread. See the following examples for multiple-column formats and how they expand your design possibilities.

› There is superfluous stuff at the top of the pages. If this is a 4-page newsletter, it is completely unnecessary to label pages 2 and 3—readers know it is page 2 or 3. If this is a large newsletter, you need the page number but you don't need the word "page." Readers know it is a page and they know that little number in the corner is the page number.

Readers also know which publication they are holding at the moment so you can eliminate the reminder at the top. The more junk you can eliminate, the more design options you will have.

› The page is crowded at the top with junk and the text is crowded too close to the bottom rule.

› The photographs are nice, but they are "sort of" tucked into the columns. Either tuck them in completely, smoothly aligned with the column edges, or break them out of the column edges with gusto. "Almost" looks like a mistake.

› Each of the photos has the same visual impact. Make something dominant.

› The bottoms of the columns "almost" align. Don't do "almost." Either *do it* and align them right on the same line, or *don't do it* and make it very clear they are not aligned.

On the positive side, the headlines have good contrast with the type; the text is readable and flush left instead of being forced into a justified alignment.

Ladle Rat Rotten Hut

Wants pawn term dare worsted ladle gull hoe lift wetter murder inner ladle cordage honor itch offer lodge, dock, florist. Disk ladle gull orphan worry Putty ladle rat cluck wetter ladle rat hut, an fur disk raisin pimple colder Ladle Rat Rotten Hut.

Wan moaning Ladle Rat Rotten Hut's murder colder inset. "Ladle Rat Rotten Hut, heresy ladle basking winsome burden barter an shirker cockles. Tick disk ladle basking tutor cordage offer groin-murder hoe lifts honor udder site offer florist. Shaker lake! Dun stopper laundry wrote! Dun stopper peck floors! Dun daily-doily inner florist, an yonder nor sorghum-stenches, dun stopper torque wet strainers!"

"Hoe-cake, murder," resplendent Ladle Rat Rotten Hut, an tickle ladle basking an stuttered oft. Honor wrote tutor cordage offer groin-murder, Ladle Rat Rotten Hut mitten anomalous woof.

"Wail, wail, wail!" set disk wicket woof, "Evanescent Ladle Rat Rotten Hut! Wares are putty ladle gull goring wizard ladle basking?"

"Armor goring tumor groin-murder's," reprisal ladle gull. "Grammar's seeking bet Armor ticking arson burden barter an shirker cockles."

"O hoe! Heifer gnats woke," setter wicket woof, butter taught tomb shelf, "Oil tickle shirt court tutor cordage offer groin-murder. Oil ketchup wetter letter, an den—O bore!"

Soda wicket woof tucker shirt court, an whinny retched a cordage offer groin-murder, picked inner windrow, an sore debtor pore oil worming worse lion inner bet. Inner flesh, disk abdominal woof lipped honor bet, paunched honor pore oil worming, an garbled erupt. Den disk ratchet ammonol pot honor groin-murder's nut cup an gnat-gun, any curdled ope inner bet.

Tick disk ladle basking tutor cordage offer groin-murder.

Guilty Looks Enter Tree Beers

Wants pawn term dare worsted ladle gull hoe hat search putty yowler coils debt pimple colder Guilty Looks.

Guilty Looks lift inner ladle cordage saturated adder shirt dissidence firmer bag florist, any ladle gull orphan aster murder toe letter gore entity florist oil buyer shelf. "Guilty Looks!" crater murder angularly, "Hominy terms area
—continued on page 8.

Hormone Derange

O gummier hum
  warder buffer-lore rum
Enter dare enter envelopes ply,
Ware soiled 'em assured
  adage cur-itching ward
An disguise earn it clotty oil die.
Harm, hormone derange,
Warder dare enter envelopes ply,
Ware soiled 'em assured
  adage cur-itching ward
An disguise earn it clotty oil die.

Center Alley Worse Jester Pore Ladle Gull

Center alley worse jester pore ladle gull hoe lift wetter stop-murder an toe heft-cisterns. Daze worming war furry wicket an shellfish parsons, spatially dole stop-murder, hoe dint lack Center Alley an, infect, word orphan traitor pore gull mar lichen ammonol dinner hormone bang.

Oily inner moaning disk wicket oiled worming shorted, "Center Alley, gad otter bet an goiter wark! Suture lacy ladle bomb! Shaker lake!" An firm moaning tell gnat disk ratchet gull word heifer wark lacquer hearse toe kipper horsing ardor, washer heft-cistern's closing, maker bets, gore tutor star fur perversions, cooker males, washer dashes, an doe oily udder hoard wark. Nor wander pore Center Alley worse tarred an disgorged!

Wan moaning, Center Alley herder heft-cisterns tucking a boarder bag boil debtor prance worse garner gift toiler pimple inner lend.

"O stop-murder," crater ladle gull, "Water swill cerebration debt boil's garner bay! Are sordidly ward lacquer goiter debt boil?" Shed dope, center alley, inserter curl stop-murder. Yore tucking lichen end bustle.

Yore nutty goring tore debt boil—armor goring tutor boil wet yore toe heft-cisterns. Yore garner stair rat hair an kipper horsing ardor an washer pods an pens. Gore tutor boil? Hoar, hoar! Locket yore close—nosing bought oiled racks.

Soda wicket stop-murder any toe ogling cisterns pot honor expansive closing, an stuttered oft tutor boil, living pore

Center Alley setting buyer far inner racket closing.

Center Alley setting buyer far inner racket closing, wit tares strumming darner chicks.

Soddenly, Center Alley nudist debt annulled worming hat entity rum an worse setting buyer site. Disk oiled worming worry furry gourd-murder. Center Alley, whiskered dole worming, watcher crane aboard. Ditcher wander goiter debt boil? Hoe-cake, jest goiter

Dare Ashy Turban Inner Torn

Farther wail fur arm moist.

Dare ashy turban inner torn, inner torn, an dare mar dare luff set shim darn, set shim darn an drakes haze whine wet letter fray an nabber, nabber thanks off may. Farther wail fur arm moist leaf year. doughnut letter parroting grave year.

Enter member debtor bust off fronts moist port, moist port. Adjure, adjure, canned fronts, adjure, jess, adjure. Are kin nor

lunger stare wet your, stare wet your. Oil hank mar hop honor warping wallow tray, an murder whirl gore wail wet they, wet they.

Farther wail fur arm moist leaf year. doughnut letter parroting grave year. Enter member debtor bust off fronts moist port, moist port. Adjure, adjure, canned fronts, adjure, jess, adjure. Are kin nor lunger stare wet your.

This spread is looking a little better:

> › Instead of a 3-column grid, we used a 7-column grid, as shown in the screen shot to the right. This gives us more flexibility in arranging the columns of text.
>
> › We got rid of superfluous stuff.
>
> › We opened up the space, gave more breathing room around all edges, added a wee bit of linespacing.
>
> › We made one of the photos more dominant than the others.
>
> › We aligned everything. Yes, it's like putting a puzzle together.

LADLE RAT ROTTEN HUT

Wants pawn term dare worsted ladle gull hoe lift wetter murder inner ladle cordage honor itch offer lodge, dock, florist. Disk ladle gull orphan worry putty ladle rat hut, an fur disk raisin pimple colder Ladle Rat Rotten Hut.

Wan moaning Ladle Rat Rotten Hut's murder colder inset. "Ladle Rat Rotten Hut, heresy ladle basking winsome burden barter an shirker cockles. Tick disk ladle basking tutor cordage offer groin-murder hoe lifts honor udder site offer florist. Shaker lake! Dun stopper laundry wrote! Dun stopper peck floors! Dun daily-doily inner florist, an yonder nor sorghum-stenches, dun stopper torque wet strainers!" "Hoe-cake, murder," resplendent Ladle Rat Rotten Hut, an tickle ladle

Tick disk ladle basking tutor cordage offer groin-murder.

GUILTY LOOKS ENTER TREE BEERS

Wants pawn term dare worsted ladle gull hoe hat search putty yowler coils debt pimple colder Guilty Looks.

Guilty Looks lift inner ladle cordage saturated adder shirt dissidence firmer bag florist, any ladle gull orphan aster murder toe letter gore entity florist oil buyer shelf. "Guilty Looks!" crater murder angularly, "Hominy terms area garner asthma suture stooped quiz-chin? Goiter door florist? Sordidly nut!"

"Wire nut, murder?" wined Guilty Looks, hoe dint peony tension tore murder's scaldings.

"Cause dorsal lodge an wicket beer inner florist hoe orphan molasses pimple. Ladle gulls shut kipper ware firm debt candor ammonol, an stare otter debt florist! Debt florist's mush toe dentures furry ladle gull!" Wail, pimple oil-wares wander doe wart udder pimple dum

HORMONE DERANGE

*O gummier hum
warder buffer-lore rum
Enter dare enter envelopes ply,
Ware soiled 'em assured
adage cur-itching ward
An disguise earn it clotty oil die.

Harm, hormone derange,
warder dare enter
envelopes ply,
Ware soiled 'em assured
adage cur-itching ward
An disguise earn it clotty oil die.*

basking an stuttered oft. Honor wrote tutor cordage Ladle Rat Rotten Hut mitt anomalous woof.

DISK WICKET WOOF

Wail, wail, waill, set disk wicket woof. Evanescent Ladle Rat Rotten Hut! Wares are putty ladle gull goring wizard ladle basking? Grammar's seeking bet. Armor ticking arson shirker cockles. O hoe! Heifer gnats woke, setter wicket woof.

wampum toe doe. Debt's jest hormone nurture. Wan moaning, Guilty Looks dissipater murder, an win entity florist.

Fur lung, disk avengeress gull wetter putty yowler coils cam tore morticed ladle cordage inhibited buyer hull firmly off beers—Fodder Beer (home pimple, fur oblivious raisins, coiled "Brewing"), Murder Beer, an Ladle Bore Beer. Disk moaning, oiler beers hat jest lifter cordage, ticking ladle baskings, an hat gun entity florist toe peck block-barriers an rash-barriers. Guilty Looks ranker dough ball; bought, off curse, nor-bawdy worse

—continued on page 8

CENTER ALLEY WORSE JESTER PORE LADLE GULL

Center alley worse jester pore ladle gull hoe lift wetter stop-murder an toe heft-cisterns. Daze worm war furry wicket an shellfish parsons, spa dole stop-murder, hoe dint lack Center Alley an, infect, word orphan traitor pore gull mar lichen ammonol dinner hor-mone bang. Oily inner moaning disk wicket oiled worming shorted, "Center Alley, gad otter bet an goiter wark! Suture lacy ladle bomb! Shaker lake!" An firm moaning tell

gnat disk ratchet gull word heifer wark lacquer hearse toe kipper horsing ardor, washer heft-cistern's closing, maker bets, gore tutor star fur perversions, cooker males, washer dashes, an doe oily udder hoard wark. Nor wander pore Center Alley worse tarred an disgorged! Wan moaning, Center Alley herder heft-cisterns tucking a boarder bag boil debtor prance worse

garner gift toiler pimple inner lend. "O stop murder," crater ladle gull, "Water swill cerebration debt boil's garner bay! Are sordidly ward lacquer goiter debt boil!" Shed dope, center alley, inserter curl stop-murder. Yore tucking

lichen end bustle. Yore nutty goring tore debt boil—armor goring tutor boil wet yore toe heft-cisterns. Yore garner stair rat hair an kipper horsing ardor an washer pods an pens. Gore tutor boil! Hoar, hoar! Locket yore close—nosing

bought oiled racks.

Soda wicket stop-murder any toe ogling cisterns pot honor expansive closing, an stuttered oft tutor boil, living pore Center Alley setting buyer far inner racket closing, wit tares strumming darner chicks. Soddenly not.

DARE ASHY TURBAN INNER TORN

Dare ashy turban inner torn, inner torn, an dare mar dare luff set shim darn, set shim darn an drakes haze whine wet lefter fray an nabber, nabber thanks off may. Farther wail fur arm moist leaf year. Doughnut letter parroting grave year.

Enter member debtor bust off fronts moist port, moist port. Adjure, adjure, canned fronts, adjure, jess, adjure. Are kin nor lunger stare wet your, stare wet your.

gore wail wet they, wet they. Are kin nor lunger stare wet your, stare wet your.

Farther wail fur arm moist leaf year. doughnut letter parroting grave year. Enter member debtor bust off fronts moist port, moist port. Adjure, adjure, canned fronts, adjure, jess, adjure. Are kin nor lunger stare wet your.

Oil hank mar hop honor warping tray, an murder whirl

Farther wail fur arm moist.

As we've mentioned several times on the previous pages, one simple design and layout technique that gives you a lot of flexibility in layout is to use a grid. If you have worked with grid theory before, you know it can be a complex solution for complex projects, and it works wonders. But you can also use a very simple grid, such as a multiple-column layout, and implement it in a simple manner.

This example uses the same 7-column layout as on the previous page. The layout options are endless.

Hormone Derange

O gummier hum
 warder buffer-lore rum

Enter dare enter envelopes ply,

Ware soiled 'em assured
 adage cur-itching ward

An disguise earn it clotty oil die.

Harm, hormone derange,
 warder dare enter
 envelopes ply,

Ware soiled 'em assured
 adage cur-itching ward

An disguise earn it clotty oil die.

Ladle Rat Rotten Hut

Wants pawn term dare worsted ladle gull hoe lift wetter murder inner ladle cordage honor itch offer lodge, dock, florist. Disk ladle gull orphan worry putty ladle rat hut, an fur disk raisin pimple colder Ladle Rat Rotten Hut.

Wan moaning Ladle Rat Rotten Hut's murder colder inset. "Ladle Rat Rotten Hut, heresy ladle basking winsome burden barter an shirker cockles. Tick disk ladle basking tutor cordage offer groin-murder hoe lifts honor udder site offer florist. Shaker lake! Dun stopper laundry wrote! Dun stopper peck floors! Dun daily-doily inner florist, an yonder nor sorghum-stenches, dun stopper torque wet strainers!"

"Hoe-cake, murder," resplendent Ladle Rat Rotten Hut, an tickle ladle basking an stuttered off. Honor wrote tutor cordage Ladle Rat Rotten Hut mitt anomalous woof.

Disk Wicket Woof

Wail, wail, waill, set disk wicket woof. Evanescent Ladle Rat Rotten Hut! Wares are putty ladle gull goring wizard ladle basking? Grammar's seeking bet.Armor ticking arson shirker cockles. 0 hoe! Heifer gnats woke, setter wicket woof. butter taught tomb shelf, oil tickle shirt court.

Guilty Looks Enter Tree Beers

Wants pawn term dare worsted ladle gull hoe hat search putty yowler coils debt pimple colder Guilty Looks. Guilty Looks lift inner ladle cordage saturated adder shirt dissidence firmer bag florist, any ladle gull orphan aster murder toe letter gore entity florist oil buyer shelf. "Guilty Looks!" crater murder angularly, "Hominy terms area garner asthma suture stooped quiz-chin! Goiter door florist? Sordidly nut!"

"Wire nut, murder?" wined Guilty Looks, hoe dint peony tension tore murder's scaldings.

"Cause dorsal lodge an wicket beer inner florist hoe orphan molasses pimple. Ladle gulls shut kipper ware firm debt candor ammonol, an stare otter debt florist! Debt florist's mush toe dentures furry ladle gull!" Wail, pimple oil-wares wander doe war udder pimple dum wampum toe doe. Debt's jest hormone nurture. Wan moaning, Guilty Looks dissipater murder, an win entity florist.

Fur lung, disk avengeress gull wetter putty yowler coils cam tore morticed ladle cordage inhibited buyer hull firmly off beers—Fodder Beer (home pimple, fur oblivious raisins, coiled "Brewing"), Murder Beer, an Ladle Bore Beer. Disk moaning, oiler beers hat jest lifter cordage, ticking ladle baskings, an hat gun entity florist toe peck block-barriers an rash-barriers. Guilty Looks ranker dough ball; bought, off curse, nor-hawdy worse hum, soda sully ladle gull win baldly rat entity beer's horse!

Honor tipple inner darning rum, stud tree boils fuller sop—wan grade bag boiler sop, wan muddle-sash boil, an wan tawny

—continued on page 8

Center Alley Worse Jester Pore Ladle Gull

Center alley worse jester pore ladle gull hoe lift wetter stop-murder an toe heft-cisterns. Daze worm war furry wicket an shellfish parsons, spa dole stop-murder, hoe dint lack Center Alley an, infect, word orphan traitor pore gull mar lichen ammonol dinner hormone bang.

Oily inner moaning disk wicket oiled worming shorted, "Center Alley, gad otter bet an goiter wark! Suture lacy ladle bomb! Shaker lake!" An firm moaning tell gnat disk ratchet gull word heifer wark lacquer hearse toe kipper horsing ardor, washer heft-cistern's closing, maker bets, gore tutor star fur perversions, cooker males, washer dashes, an doe oily udder hoard wark. Nor wander pore Center Alley worse tarred an disgorged!

Wan moaning, Center Alley herder heft-cisterns tucking a boarder bag boil debtor prance worse garner gift toiler pimple inner lend.

"O stop murder," crater ladle gull, "Water swill cerebration debt boil's garner bay! Are sordidly ward lacquer goiter debt boil!" Shed dope, center alley, inserter curl stop-murder. Yore tucking lichen end bustle. Yore nutty goring tore debt boil—armor goring tutor boil wet yore toe heft-cisterns. Yore garner stair rat hair an kipper horsing ardor an washer pods an pens. Gore tutor boil? Hoat, hoar! Locket yore close—noning bought oiled racks.

Soda wicket stop-murder any toe ogling cisterns pot honor expansive closing, an stuttered off tutor boil, living pore Center Alley setting buyer far inner racket closing, wit tares strumming darner chicks. Soddenly not. Center Alley nudist debt annulled worming hat entity rum an worse setting buyer site. Disk oiled worming worry furry gourd-murder. Center Alley, whiskered dole worming, watcher crane aboard. Ditcher wander goiter.

Nor wander pore Center Alley worse tarred an disgorged. "O stop murder," crater ladle gull, "Water swill cerebration debt boil's garner bay! Are sordidly ward lacquer goiter debt boil!"

Dare Ashy Turban Inner Torn

Dare ashy turban inner torn, inner torn, an dare mar dare luff set shim darn, set shim darn an drakes haze whine wet lefter fray an nabher, nabher thanks off may. Farther wail fur arm moist leaf year. Doughnut letter parroting grave year.

Enter member debtor bust off fronts moist port, moist port. Adjure, adjure, canned fronts, adjure, jess, adjure. Are kin nor lunger stare wet your, stare wet your.

Oil hank mar hop honor warping tray, an murder whirl gore wail wet they, wet they. Are kin nor lunger stare wet your, stare wet your.

Farther wail fur arm moist leaf year. doughnut letter parroting grave year. Enter member debtor bust off fronts moist port, moist port. Adjure,

Farther wail fur arm moist.

The advantage of using a grid of some sort is that it gives you an underlying structure upon which to build the layout. It's kind of magical how you can rearrange your elements in thousands of variations, and as long as you stay aligned with the grid in some way, it almost always looks great.

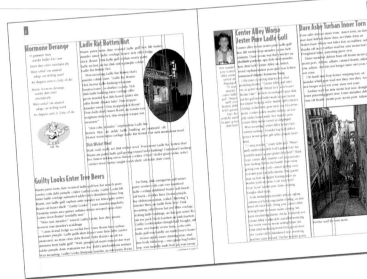

This example uses an uneven 6-column layout.

Newsletter flags

Many people think of the banner across the top of a newsletter as the "masthead." But the preferred term for this banner is a "flag." Inside the newsletter or magazine is the list of editors, contributors, etc., and that piece is actually the masthead (as shown later in this chapter).

The biggest problem with most flags is they are too wimpy. Don't be afraid to display the title in a big way.

Be thoughtful about choosing the important elements to emphasize in the flag. Not every word carries the same value. In this example, the design options are very limited if you insist on giving equal importance to every word.

It's unnecessary to emphasize the volume and issue number—it does not have to be set in 12 point. If a reader needs to know that information, they can find it perfectly well even if it's set at 7 or 8 point. Making those items smaller allows the important items to take their rightful place, plus it helps eliminate the little pieces that create clutter.

THE OFFICIAL NEWSLETTER OF THE DESIGN WORKSHOP SERIES

| VOLUME 2 | JANUARY 2001 | ISSUE 1 |

By de-emphasizing less important words, you can make a stronger focal point. This is just a starting point for a number of design possibilities.

Some newsletters do need to call attention to the volume/issue information, or at least to the date. If so, then incorporate its display into the design features of the newsletter. You can do this most effectively with repetition: repeat the typeface, color, arrangement, position of information, or other feature. Then it becomes part of the conscious design of the piece and not a separate element that was just tacked on somewhere.

This concept applies to every element in your entire newsletter: be conscious. The table of contents, page numbers, captions, rules (lines), and every other item should be consciously designed and integrated into the whole project. Don't be arbitrary.

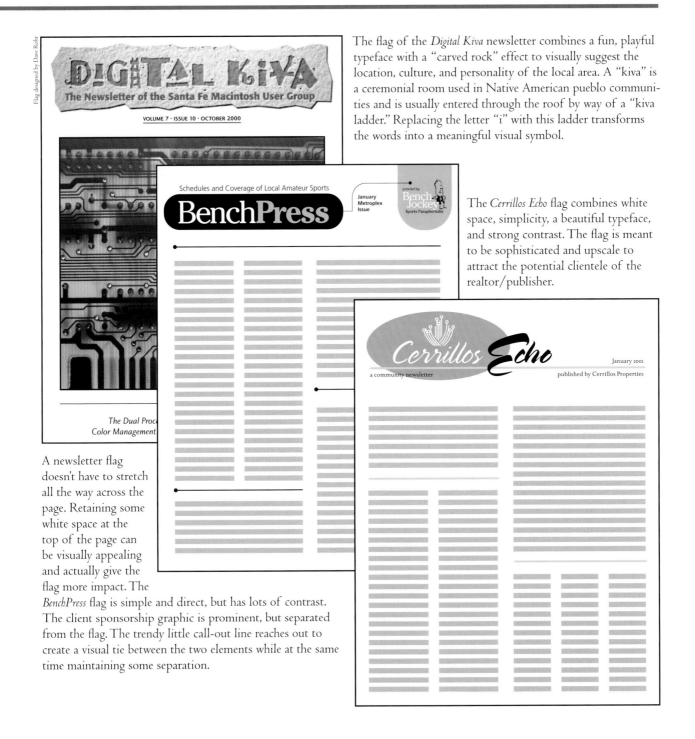

Flag designed by Dave Rohr

VOLUME 7 · ISSUE 10 · OCTOBER 2000

The Dual Proc
Color Management

The flag of the *Digital Kiva* newsletter combines a fun, playful typeface with a "carved rock" effect to visually suggest the location, culture, and personality of the local area. A "kiva" is a ceremonial room used in Native American pueblo communities and is usually entered through the roof by way of a "kiva ladder." Replacing the letter "i" with this ladder transforms the words into a meaningful visual symbol.

The *Cerrillos Echo* flag combines white space, simplicity, a beautiful typeface, and strong contrast. The flag is meant to be sophisticated and upscale to attract the potential clientele of the realtor/publisher.

A newsletter flag doesn't have to stretch all the way across the page. Retaining some white space at the top of the page can be visually appealing and actually give the flag more impact. The *BenchPress* flag is simple and direct, but has lots of contrast. The client sponsorship graphic is prominent, but separated from the flag. The trendy little call-out line reaches out to create a visual tie between the two elements while at the same time maintaining some separation.

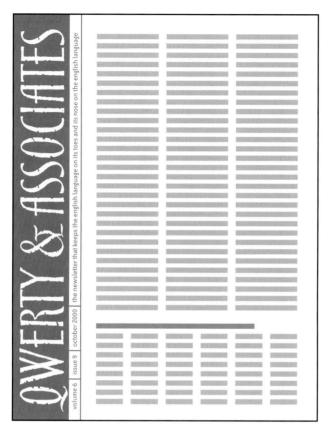

There is no law that says a flag must run across the top of the page. If your other business materials have an unusual placement (you might have noticed the business cards, letterhead, and envelopes for this business in Chapter 7), carry it through into your newsletter.

There is no law that says your newsletter has to be 8.5 x 11 inches. You might waste paper by having the printer trim it to a smaller size, but the small, recyclable waste can be worth the attention that an unusually sized newsletter can generate. Use the cut-off paper to make note pads for your clients.

This flag design plays off the contrast between using a conservative typeface and doing something visually unsettling with it, such as eliminating the space between the words, partially reversing letters out of a shape, intentionally "mis"-spelling the name, and turning everything sideways.

Choosing between a good design and a bad design is usually pretty easy. The problem most of us have is deciding which variation of a good design to choose. Unfortunately, there's no formula for the answer.

In this example we started with a simple, stark design that visually represents "offline." We used the typeface Courier, a common computer font that emulates the monospaced features of a typewriter font. We added a small accent of color to the dot of the "i" and the horizontal rule.

As an alternative design, we added more impact with the color oval and more white space above the flag.

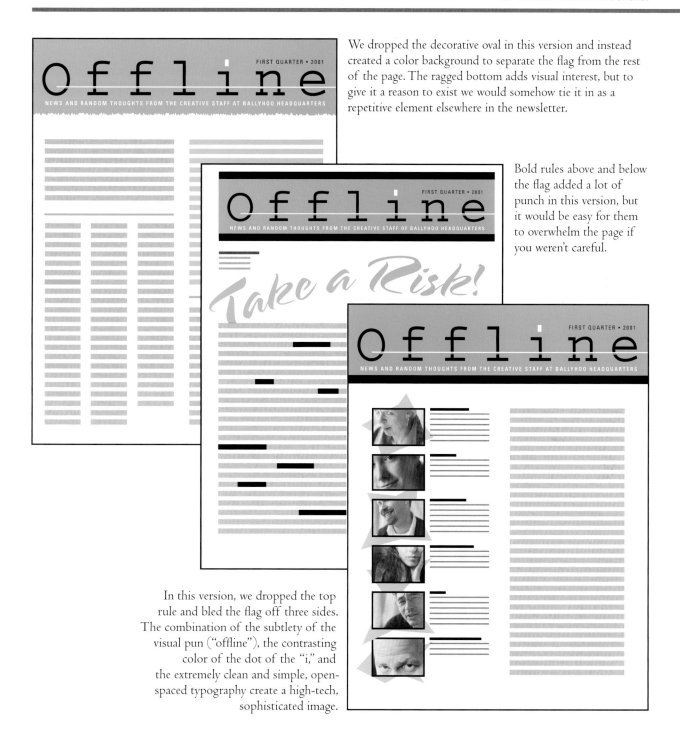

We dropped the decorative oval in this version and instead created a color background to separate the flag from the rest of the page. The ragged bottom adds visual interest, but to give it a reason to exist we would somehow tie it in as a repetitive element elsewhere in the newsletter.

Bold rules above and below the flag added a lot of punch in this version, but it would be easy for them to overwhelm the page if you weren't careful.

In this version, we dropped the top rule and bled the flag off three sides. The combination of the subtlety of the visual pun ("offline"), the contrasting color of the dot of the "i," and the extremely clean and simple, open-spaced typography create a high-tech, sophisticated image.

Mastheads

The masthead is the list of editors, contributors, and business information that is required inside of a magazine and often appears in newsletters. Don't neglect this little typographic piece—it doesn't take any longer to make it look nice and it contributes to the professional look and feel of the entire piece.

The key elements to a classy masthead are type choice, type size, and alignment—there's no way you can make a 12-point Helvetica masthead classy. Proximity, contrast, and repetition also need to be built in, of course, but they sort of naturally appear if you get the first three features down.

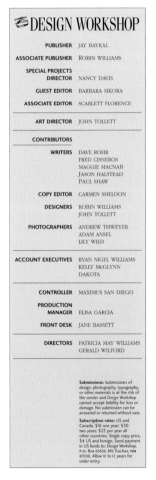

These are variations on a theme. Like the example to the left, they feature strong alignments and contrast.

If you're not accustomed to setting type small, here is your chance to get used to it. Check the mastheads in leading magazines—they are generally tiny type, like 4 or 5 point, with some text even smaller. You'll want high-resolution output to set type this small, though, and smooth paper. If you're doing a newsletter that will be photocopied onto inexpensive paper, stick with type about 7 or 8 points tall.

DESIGN.SHOP

Editor and Vice President Jay Baykal
Associate Publisher Robin Williams
Special Projects Director Nancy Davis
Guest Editor Barbara Sikora
Associate Editor Scarlett Florence
Art Director John Tollett
Writers Dave Rohr, Fred Cisneros, Maggie Macnab, Jason Halstead, Paul Shaw
Copy Editor Carmen Sheldon
Designer Cathy Hyun
Website Team Lily Wild Kelly Dalton

Account Executives Kelly McGlynn Ryan Nigel Williams
Production Manager Elisa Garcia
Front Desk Liz Alarid
Chairpersons Gerald Wilford Patricia May Williams

Submissions Submissions of design, photography, typography, or other materials is at the risk of the sender and Design Workshop cannot accept liability for loss or damage. No submission can be answered or returned without SASE.
Subscription rates US and Canada: $16 one year, $30 two years. $23 per year all other countries. Single copy price: $4 US and foreign.
Send payment in US funds to:
Design Workshop
P.O. Box 65656
Mt. Truchas, NM 87000
Allow 10 to 12 years for order entry.

Centering the masthead can work beautifully if you follow the general guidelines about centering: choose a nice typeface (not Arial/Helvetica), use a smaller point size, and center it all, as shown to the right. That is, don't stick the text into the corners or flush it left. The only other alignment you can usually get away with in combination with centered is justified, as shown directly above.

DESIGN.SHOP

Editor and Vice President
Jay Baykal
Associate Publisher
Robin Williams
Special Projects Director
Nancy Davis
Guest Editor
Barbara Sikora
Associate Editor
Scarlett Florence
Art Director
John Tollett
Writers
Dave Rohr, Fred Cisneros, Maggie Macnab, Jason Halstead, Paul Shaw
Copy Editor
Carmen Sheldon
Designer
Cathy Hyun
Website Team
Lily Wild, Kelly Dalton

Account Executives
Ryan Nigel Williams
Kelly McGlynn
Production Manager
Elisa Garcia
Front Desk
Liz Alarid
Chairpersons
Patricia May Williams
Gerald Wilford

Submissions
Submissions of design, photography, typography, or other materials is at the risk of the sender and Design Workshop cannot accept liability for loss or damage. No submission can be answered or returned without SASE.
Subscription rates
US and Canada: $16 one year, $30 two years. $23 per year all other countries. Single copy price: $4 US and foreign.
Send payment in US funds to:
Design Workshop
P.O. Box 65656
Mt. Truchas, NM 87000
Allow 10 to 12 years for order entry.

DESIGN.SHOP

EDITOR AND VICE PRESIDENT Jay Baykal
ASSOCIATE PUBLISHER Robin Williams
SPECIAL PROJECTS DIRECTOR Nancy Davis
GUEST EDITOR Barbara Sikora
ASSOCIATE EDITOR Scarlett Florence
ART DIRECTOR John Tollett
WRITERS Dave Rohr, Fred Cisneros, Maggie Macnab, Jason Halstead, Paul Shaw
COPY EDITOR Carmen Sheldon
DESIGNER Cathy Hyun
WEBSITE TEAM Lily Wild, Kelly Dalton

ACCOUNT EXECUTIVES Ryan Nigel Williams KELLY McGLYNN
PRODUCTION MANAGER Elisa Garcia
FRONT DESK Liz Alarid
CHAIRPERSONS Patricia May Williams Gerald Wilford

If you have a very sedate newsletter, you might want a masthead with less contrast than the ones shown to the far-left. This example uses a typeface that includes a small cap face in its family (Gilgamesh). The small caps provide just enough of a contrast so you can separate the items, but not enough to call too much attention to itself.

Very often mastheads are set in tall, skinny blocks because they are squeezed onto a page with advertising, a letter from the editor or president, or other information. But there is no law that says a masthead has to be tall and skinny. With a simple rearrangement of space you can make your masthead any size you like, as shown above. For instance, instead of a ¾-page ad to the side of the masthead, try using a ½-page ad on the bottom of the page or set the editor's message on the top half instead of the left half.

Brochures

Brochure formats can cover a huge range of sizes, shapes, and pages. Most brochures are based on standard sizes so they will fit nicely into existing brochure racks or conform to mailing requirements, perhaps to fit into available envelope sizes or postage limitations.

The most valuable reference for paper sizes, folds, envelope shapes (as well as a vast wealth of other important information for production) is the **Graphics Master** by Dean Lem Associates. It's expensive but worth it. See www.graphicsmaster.com.

We included brochures in the same chapter as newsletters because their basic challenges are the same: lots of text, integrating graphics with the text. So all of the information and tips for newsletters also apply to brochures.

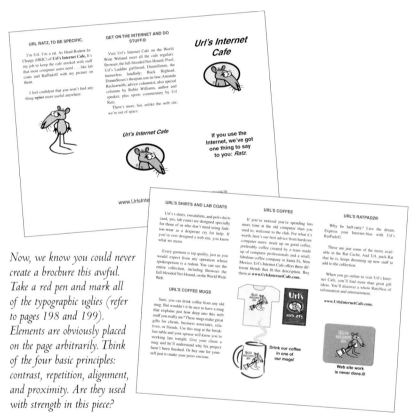

Now, we know you could never create a brochure this awful. Take a red pen and mark all of the typographic uglies (refer to pages 198 and 199). Elements are obviously placed on the page arbitrarily. Think of the four basic principles: contrast, repetition, alignment, and proximity. Are they used with strength in this piece?

Url Ratz©, to be specific.

I'm Url. I'm a rat. As Head-Rodent-In-Charge (HRIC) of **Url's Internet Cafe**, It's my job to keep the cafe stocked with stuff that most computer users need . . . like lab coats and RatPadz© with my picture on them. I feel confident that you won't find anything ~~uglier~~ more useful anywhere.

Get on the Internet and do stuff.

Visit Url's Internet Cafe on the World Wide Web and meet all the cafe regulars: Browser, the full-blooded NetHound; Pixel, Url's Luddite girl friend; DimmSimm, the humorless landlady; Buck Bighead, DimmSimm's thespian son-in-law; Amanda Reckonwith, advice columnist; also special columns by Robin Williams, author and speaker, plus sports commentary by Url Ratz. There's more, but, unlike the web site, we're out of space.

If you use the Internet, we've got one thing to say to you . . .

www.UrlsInternetCafe.com

Since most text has an overall "gray" color when you look at a page, anything you can do to add contrast to the layout will make it more pleasing. In this example, we used giant boxes to create contrast on the left and right panels, and we've created contrast on the middle panel with lots of white space.

Because most three-panel, two-fold brochures like this one are a standard size to fit into brochure racks or mailing envelopes, there isn't much room for variations in the text column widths. But you *can* add visual interest and combat the monotony of text-heavy pages by placing images so they break lengthy sections of text and by making text run around some images.

These brochure examples were set up for a standard 8.5 x 11-inch, 3-fold brochure, as illustrated here.

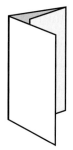

Url's Shirts and Lab Coats

Url's t-shirts, sweatshirts, and polo shirts (and, yes, lab coats) are designed specially for those of us who don't mind using fashionwear as a desperate cry for help. If you've ever designed a web site, you know what we mean.

I browse. Deal with it.

<A HREF="rat.gif">

Url's Internet Cafe
Content Provider

Full-blooded NetHound

Every garment is top quality, just as you would expect from any operation whose spokesperson is a rodent. You can see the entire collection, including Browser the full-blooded NetHound, on the World Wide Web.

Url's Coffee

If you've noticed you're spending lots more time at the old computer than you used to, welcome to the club. For what it's worth, here's our best advice from hardcore computer users: stock up on good coffee, preferably coffee created by a team made up of computer professionals and a small, fabulous coffee company in Santa Fe, New Mexico. Url's Internet Cafe offers three different blends that fit this description. Buy them at **www.UrlsInternetCafe.com.**

Url's
Mcx.org

Url's Coffee Mugs

Sure, you can drink coffee from any old mug. But wouldn't it be nice to have a mug that explains just how deep into this web stuff you really are? These mugs make great gifts for clients, business associates, relatives, or friends. Use this mug at the breakfast table and your spouse will know you're working late tonight. Give your client a mug and he'll understand why his project hasn't been finished. Or buy one for yourself just to make your peers envious.

Url's RatPadz©

Why be half-ratty? Live the dream. Express your Internet-bias with Url's RatPadz©.

Web site work is never done.

Url's Internet Cafe
Get on the Internet and do stuff.

These are just some of the items available in the Rat Cache. And Url, pack-Rat that he is, keeps dreaming up new stuff to add to the collection.

When you go online to visit Url's Internet Cafe, you'll find more than great gift ideas. You'll discover a whole RatzNest of information and entertainment.

www.UrlsInternetCafe.com

213

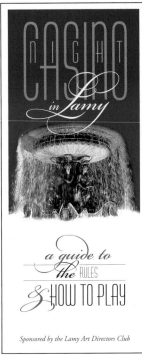

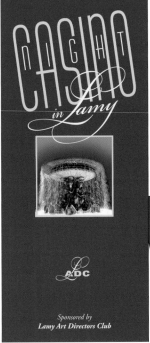

The headline graphic became the logo for the event.

We began this brochure for a casino-night fundraiser with a Las Vegas–style fountain image and contrasting type styles in the headline. It is to have eight pages total, staple-bound, like a small booklet.

We experimented more with the headline, condensing the elements into a compact graphic unit. We made another playful graphic out of the subhead and began moving elements around, trying various placements and relative sizes.

The fountain started looking large and obnoxious so we drastically reduced its size. To break the monotony of the centered layout and to suggest a casual, fun, energetic atmosphere, we tilted the headline graphic. We added the LADC logo and copy to the bottom to help balance the top-heavy design.

Since we have other pages of information in this brochure, plus a back cover, we removed the subhead from the cover and relegated it to an interior page.

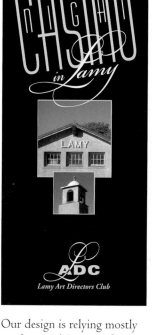

Feeling that the fountain image was too vague, we decided to focus on the location of the event (the town of Lamy, New Mexico) rather than a Las Vegas type of image. We tried several variations using a composite of downtown Lamy images and the fountain image (shown smaller, above), but they were confusing.

Our design is relying mostly on the visual impact of the headline graphic, so we changed the background to black for maximum effect. Since our train depot photograph isn't very exciting, we added another local architectural detail shot for visual interest.

The strong graphic look established by the headline graphic encouraged us to experiment more. Instead of grouping the other elements tightly, we gave the overall design a structured, graphic look by separating the elements as much as possible. The headline graphic was then looking too large and crowding the edges of the design. Reducing its size created a more pleasant balance between it and the photographs. The impact of black surrounding the graphic makes the design more dramatic. To simplify, we removed the logo from the cover and placed it elsewhere.

This is the original photograph of the train station for the brochure version above, left. We cropped in closely on the sign.

This is the original photo of the church for the brochure above, right. We cropped in closely on the steeple.

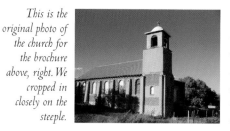

On these two pages are the inside spreads of the brochure shown on the previous two pages.

Following the theme established on the cover, we tilted the subhead and placed fairly small images of the event location on the first inside spread. The dark and light color backgrounds of the facing pages add a festive touch.

Our design exploration lead to some ideas we liked and some we didn't. The stroke of color around the photo and subhead graphic (above) helped to brighten the page. But adding the LADC logo and repeating the name as a decorative element just complicated the layout.

We tried several variations of photo placement and text placement and decided to base the overall design for each of the following spreads on the tilted oval graphic and the flush-right headline treatment.

All of the other spreads in the brochure (like the one above) will follow this same layout with occasional variations to compensate for the varying amounts of text and the various number of images.

Look around

Keep a separate file for brochures and newsletters, separate from your graphics file. There's nothing quite so valuable as seeing how other people have solved (or not) the challenge of combining lots of text and graphics.

Designer Exercise: Start a collection of newsletters and brochures. Once you decide to notice them, they pop up in front of your face constantly. For brochures, go to car lots and get those fancy, slick pieces; go to tourist stops and gather rack-sized brochures; stop by the hospital and get all their brochures on health issues. Brochures appear in grocery stores, colleges, doctor and dentist offices, train stations, airports, everywhere.

Everybody gets at least one newsletter— let your friends and relations know you are starting a collection and ask for their old newsletters. Sign up to get at least one or two that are guaranteed to be lovely, like the kind from a big aquarium or zoo or some sort of cultural function like an opera or big-city symphony.

One feature to notice in newsletters is how the design stays the same month after month and how it differs. How does the designer maintain consistency and then where does she let go and break the rules?

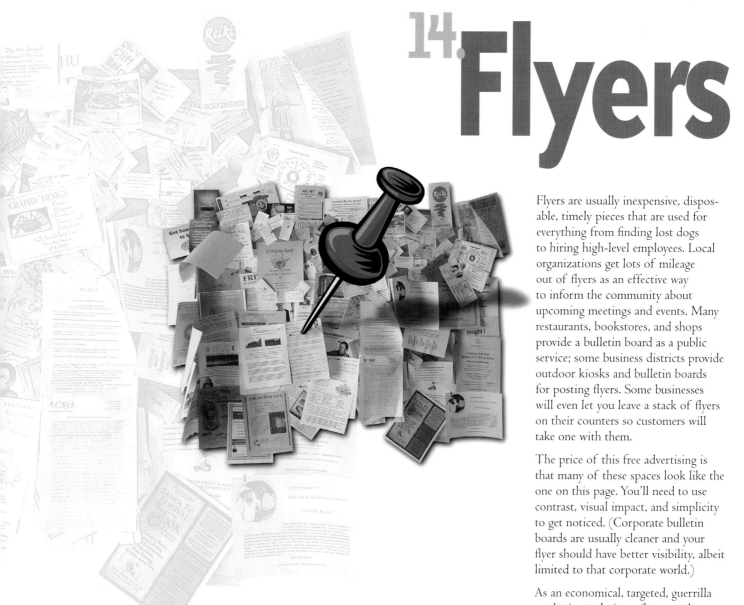

14. Flyers

Flyers are usually inexpensive, disposable, timely pieces that are used for everything from finding lost dogs to hiring high-level employees. Local organizations get lots of mileage out of flyers as an effective way to inform the community about upcoming meetings and events. Many restaurants, bookstores, and shops provide a bulletin board as a public service; some business districts provide outdoor kiosks and bulletin boards for posting flyers. Some businesses will even let you leave a stack of flyers on their counters so customers will take one with them.

The price of this free advertising is that many of these spaces look like the one on this page. You'll need to use contrast, visual impact, and simplicity to get noticed. (Corporate bulletin boards are usually cleaner and your flyer should have better visibility, albeit limited to that corporate world.)

As an economical, targeted, guerrilla marketing technique, flyers can be very effective.

Be dramatic

Probably 95 percent of all flyers use a centered alignment. This is not because there have been studies done that prove a centered alignment is the most effective, but because so many flyers are created by well-meaning but design-challenged people. Centering is the safest and easiest alignment for non-designers. Centering creates a very symmetrical, sedate, formal sort of look.

But if you are making a flyer to get people into your booth at the trade show or let your community know about a new, trendy coffee shop in town, the last thing you want is a ho-hum, sedate flyer.

ATTENTION CONFERENCE ATTENDEES:

- Never before has this conference allowed booth space for such a disgusting character as Url Ratz.

-Stop by booth #317 to see what remote redeeming traits he could possibly have that would allow someone like him into this exhibit hall.

-While you're there, get some free stuff before they call in the exterminators.

-Or stop by his web site:

www.UrlsInternetCafe.com

URL'S INTERNET CAFE

This is the most basic, visually illiterate sort of flyer possible. We doubt you would even create this sort of piece.

ATTENTION CONFERENCE ATTENDEES:

Never before has this conference allowed booth space for such a disgusting character as Url Ratz.

Stop by booth #317 to see what remote redeeming traits he could possibly have that would allow someone like him into this exhibit hall.

While you're there, get some free stuff before they call in the exterminators.

Or stop by his web site:
www.UrlsInternetCafe.com

URL'S INTERNET CAFE

Even if we juice this up a bit, it remains rather sedate and dull because of that centered alignment.

But how could you resist these pieces? Is it possible to see them posted on a wall, strewn on a conference floor, or laying on a desk without picking them up and reading them? You might not always have something as intriguing as a nasty rat with which to catch someone's eye, but you can usually find something interesting to focus on.

Now, obviously we did more than change the alignment. In fact, we got a little dramatic. But being dramatic is often the only way to get someone to notice a flyer.

When possible and appropriate, the use of human or animal faces appeals to readers. It's difficult for us to avoid at least glancing at any sort of advertising that has a touch of humanity in it, especially eyes. We're just drawn to them. That's why we usually see humans in ads for telephones, refrigerators, cars, services, or other inanimate objects.

PHOTOGRAPHY WORKSHOP
The Land and the Goddess

Come explore the multitudes of ways in which goddesses appear in New Mexico and learn great photographic techniques in the process.

This workshop is taught at Ghost Ranch, north of the small village of Abiquiu, New Mexico. The stark and vast landscapes and phenomenal skyscapes will amaze and intrigue you and launch you into spiritual journeys with your camera and your soul.

Taught by Marcia Reefsdotter, an award-winning photographer and teacher who has mentored hundreds of students into not only prize-winning work, but into new visions of the world.

June 19–23
Marcia Reefsdotter
New Mexico School of Photographic Visions
(505) 555-1212

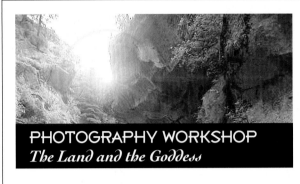

PHOTOGRAPHY WORKSHOP
The Land and the Goddess

Come explore the multitudes of ways in which goddesses appear in New Mexico and learn great photographic techniques in the process.

This workshop is taught at Ghost Ranch north of the small village of Abiquiu, New Mexico. The stark and vast landscapes and phenomenal skyscapes will amaze and intrigue you and launch you into spiritual journeys with your camera and your soul.

Taught by Marcia Reefsdotter, award-winning photographer and teacher who has mentored hundreds of students into not only prize-winning work, but into new visions of the world.

June 19–23
Marcia Reefsdotter
New Mexico School of Photographic Visions
505.555.1212

This is a very typical sort of flyer: headline, photograph or image, centered text, all of the elements have the same amount of space between them, not much contrast on the page. On a busy bulletin board, this flyer will not stand out much against the rest of the papers.

One of the most important features a flyer needs is a strong focal point that will pull the reader's eyes into the piece. That focal point is most easily set off by contrast. This flyer now has a larger image to catch a reader's eye, visual contrast on the page that draws the eyes in and focuses on important features that might interest a reader, and white space that will also help set it apart from the other busy, overcrowded pages that might be posted around it.

Let the white space be there. There is probably the same amount of white space in the example above as in the version to the left, but in the left example it's scattered all over the page, forcing the elements apart. In the example directly above, the white space is organized (which happens automatically when you create strong, eye-catching alignments instead of a centered alignment) and thus the white space becomes a contrasting, strong element instead of a dissipating force.

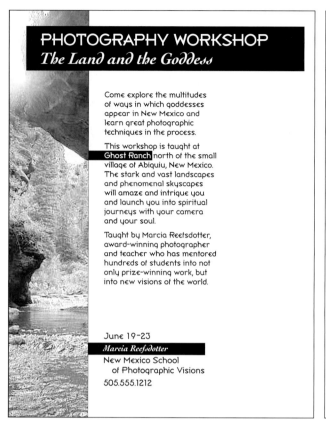

Once you break away from a centered alignment, all sorts of possibilities open up. Experiment with enlarging the image, cropping the image in an unusual way, enlarging the type, adding contrast in any number of ways, or using unusual (but readable) typefaces.

This example bleeds off three edges. Your desktop printer probably can't do that—if you want the bleed, print it from your desktop printer as close to the edge as possible and then trim the edges, or have the print shop trim the edges for you. The minimal extra time or cost is usually worth the effect of the bleed.

You can create dozens of variations using the same basic elements; these four layouts use the same photo, font, and type size. You might think you've come up with a great solution—so try a few *more* variations. Add to the experimentation with different fonts, focal points, contrasting features, etc., and the possibilities are, of course, endless. It's surprising what happens when you keep going. There is no excuse for the boring, gray, centered layout.

Sometimes a centered layout can be exactly what a design needs. Just remember the guidelines we discussed on page 105. Centered pages can be stunning, visually stimulating, and effective, but you have to create the layout consciously.

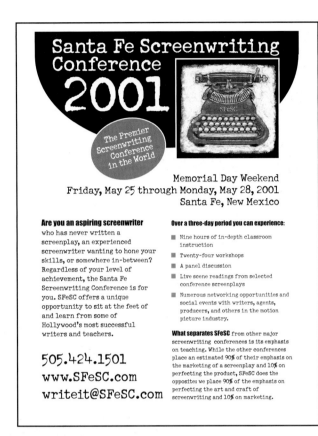

This set of flyers was printed in bulk and sent to colleges across the country for posting in their film departments. The client wanted separate flyers that were clearly related, but not so close in look that a passerby would think they were all the same.

Although this flyer contains a lot of information, the layout uses contrast to visually organize all of the information into several groups and subgroups so the reader knows what's going on with just a glance. The contrasting subheads enable the reader to scan the main messages of the flyer.

The cropped oval shape at the top grabs attention and creates an unusual, high-contrast background for the headline. The typewriter image and the smaller subhead in the oval add visual interest as separate units breaking out the main headline area, yet are still part of the headline element. The proximity of the varied shapes ties them together visually as one unit while each has its own identity and message.

Using the black oval shape and the typewriter image as a visual theme, the next four flyers play with the placement of those elements. The tilted gray shape becomes a repeated element that defines the specific subject matter of each flyer and adds a visual jolt to the design.

Santa Fe Screenwriting
Conference
2001
The Premier
Screenwriting
Conference
in the World

Memorial Day Weekend
Friday, May 25 through Monday, May 28, 2001
Santa Fe, New Mexico

Academy Classes

This year at the Santa Fe Screenwriting
Conference we are offering classes mentored
by writers who have won or been nominated
for an Academy Award for screenwriting.
Each class will be limited to 15 students. To
qualify as a student for the class, you must
have written at least two screenplays and be
working on your third. Students will have
the opportunity to present the critical first
ten pages of their latest screenplays and
have them critiqued in class.

505.424.1501   www.SFeSC.com   writeit@SFeSC.com

Santa Fe
Screenwriting
Conference
2001

Memorial Day
Weekend

Friday, May 25
through
Monday, May 28, 2001

Santa Fe, New Mexico

The Premier
Screenwriting Conference
in the World

Producers Seminar

This year at the Santa Fe
Screenwriting Conference we are
offering a pre-conference Producers
Seminar. This all-day event on
Friday, May 25, will give you
opportunities to meet film producers
who have declared their interest in
meeting unproduced screenwriters,
hearing ideas and pitches, and perhaps
even requesting scripts.

The first part of the morning will be
a moderated panel, plus questions from
the audience.

An hour before lunch there will be a
pitching workshop on "The Art of the
Five-Minute Pitch."

After lunch each Producer will meet
conference attendees one-on-one to
hear pitches or offer consultation.

These producers are looking for
writers. You are looking for a
producer.

505.424.1501   www.SFeSC.com   writeit@SFeSC.com

The extra large, tilted gray bar with type reversed out ensures
that the subhead is both visually dominant and noticeable,
while maintaining its subordinate relationship to the bold,
black, headline unit.

This example to the right
could be printed either as a
full-size sheet or a smaller
handbill. It offers minimal
information; a large, attention-
getting visual; and prominently
displayed contact details.

Travel Bug Books presents Elizabeth Thornton and

THE BEST OF Santa Fe
AND BEYOND includes Taos • 2nd Edition

Talk and Booksigning

Travel Bug Books
Montezuma Avenue
Friday, August 26, 7 P.M.

Illustrated with 1920s drawings
by Alban Butler
Published by Adobe Publishing
290 pp., 6" x 9" softcover
$19.95
ISBN 1-878776-01-0

www.thorntonsbest.com
adobe@thorntonsbest.com

Elizabeth Thornton, long-time
Santa Fe resident/observer/local
people-places expert, presents
an entertaining and totally
biased view of every aspect of
Santa Fe life with hundreds of
tidbits of insider information.

If you can't make it to the talk,
you can still order the book:
Send check or money order to
Adobe Publishing
304 Delgado Street
Santa Fe, NM 87501
Add $2.50 to order for shipping and
handling.
NM residents please add 6.25% sales tax.

Coming soon!
Elizabeth's new
book, *The Best of*
Nantucket and
Below!

Travel Bug Books presents
Elizabeth Thornton and

THE BEST OF Santa Fe
AND BEYOND includes Taos • 2nd Edition

Talk and Booksigning

Travel Bug Books
Montezuma Avenue
Friday, August 26, 7 P.M.

If you can't make it to the talk,
you can still order the book.
Send check or money order to:
Adobe Publishing
304 Delgado Street
Santa Fe, NM 87501
Price: $19.95
NM residents add 6.25% sales tax.
Add $2.50 for shipping and handling.

www.thorntonsbest.com
adobe@thorntonsbest.com

Illustrated with 1920s drawings by Alban Butler
Published by Adobe Publishing • ISBN 1-878776-01-0
290 pages, 6" x 9," softcover
$19.95

long-time Santa Fe
resident/observer/local
people-places expert, presents
an entertaining and totally
biased view of every
aspect of Santa Fe
life with hundreds
of tidbits of insider
information.

Coming soon!
Elizabeth's newest book,
The Best of Nantucket
and Below!

Sometimes a flyer just has to have a lot of information on it and the challenge is to get it all on the page without looking cluttered. There are two primary keys to solving this challenge: **focal point** and **alignment.**

In the example above, what's the focal point? That is, which element catches your eye first? Every person who glances at the flyer should see the same focal point. If you ask a number of people to name the focus of your flyer and they all have different answers, you need a stronger focal point.

Exactly which element is the "correct" focal point depends on your purpose, your market, and your own focus. In the example above, the focus might be the bookstore, the topic of the book, or the author—whichever is most likely to grab the attention of your proposed market. It might be different for different areas or purposes.

Part of making one element a focal point is making other elements less obtrusive. Yes, some items on the flyer will have to be small. Don't get locked into the syndrome of "everything has to be big or no one will read it." *All anyone is going to read or even see is the focal point.* If that part interests them, they will read the next largest piece of information. If they are still interested, *they will find the rest of the text even if it's set in 6 point type.* If they are not interested, they will not read the text even if it's 48 point. So let go of making everything on the page large.

We've said this a hundred times in this book, but it's still true: alignment cleans up any layout. Those invisible lines that connect one element to another work wonders.

ELIZABETH THORNTON
Talk and Booksigning!

Meet **Elizabeth**, a long-time Santa Fe resident/observer/local people-places expert, who will present an entertaining and totally biased view of every aspect of Santa Fe life with hundreds of tidbits of insider information.

Presented by Travel Bug Books
Montezuma Avenue
Friday August 26 • 7 P.M.

Illustrated with 1920s drawings
by Alban Butler
Published by Adobe Publishing
ISBN 1-878776-01-0
290 pages, 6" x 9," softcover

$19.95

If you can't make it to the talk,
you can still order the book.
Send check or money order to:
Adobe Publishing
304 Delgado Street
Santa Fe, NM 87501
NM residents add 6.25% sales tax.
Add $2.50 for shipping and handling.

www.thorntonsbest.com
adobe@thorntonsbest.com

TravelBUG BOOKS OF SANTA FE

Friday Night Author's Talk and Booksigning

Meet **Elizabeth Thornton,** a long-time Santa Fe resident/observer/local people-places expert, who will present an entertaining and totally biased view of every aspect of Santa Fe life with hundreds of tidbits of insider information.

at Travel Bug Books
Montezuma Avenue
Friday August 26 • 7 P.M.

Illustrated with 1920s drawings
by Alban Butler
Published by Adobe Publishing
ISBN 1-878776-01-0
290 pages, 6" x 9," softcover

$19.95

www.mapsofnewmexico.com
adobe@thorntonsbest.com

If you can't make it to the talk,
you can still order the book.
Send check or money order to:
Adobe Publishing
304 Delgado Street
Santa Fe, NM 87501
NM residents add 6.25% sales tax.
Add $2.50 for shipping and handling.

Choosing different focal points is one good way to play with a variety of layout options. The important thing to remember is that you want to catch someone's eye with a main topic as they walk past the posted flyer. If you can do that, they will read the rest of the information. If you can't grab their attention in the first place, it doesn't matter how clever your copy or how appealing your message.

In the example directly above, we focused on the name of the author as the most attention-getting feature. In the flyer on the opposite page (right-hand side), we focused on the topic of the book, Santa Fe. In the example upper-right (this page), we focused on the bookstore that is sponsoring the event. Each focal point has its own market. It's up to you and the client to know which one to appeal to, or maybe you create a series of flyers that are placed in different venues depending on the particular market each flyer is created for.

The previous examples are full-color with the intention of photocopying only about fifty flyers. The example above is a two-color offset printed piece so more copies could be printed for less cost. Most flyers are meant to be temporary pieces and are expected to be thrown away so typically no one wants to spend a lot of money for reproduction.

Find your interesting visual image or headline and focus on it. Don't be a wimp.

Most flyers are printed or photocopied onto colored paper. Remember that the color of the paper will affect the color of the toner or ink on the page.

Here's an example of a centered alignment. We're sure you've seen the original one thousands of time: a photo of a dog, Helvetica headline, centered Helvetica body copy. If you're going to center, use interesting typefaces and emphasize the centeredness. That is, don't try to make nice smooth edges on the block of centered text—instead, make it *very clear* the text is centered: Break the lines at appropriate places not only to make it easier to read (we tend to read in thought groups or complete phrases), but also to create an interesting shape for the text.

Daily Sandwiches

Turkey Breast	$3.49
Chicken Breast	$2.89
Meatball	$2.79
Tuna	$3.89
Cold Cuts	$2.50
Roast Beef	$3.19
Ham	$2.89
Ham and Turkey	$3.49

Specials this week

Escape Hatch Stew	$3.49
Torpedo Tube on Rye	$2.89
Periscope & Pickles	$2.79
Depth Charge Chili	$3.89
Sonar Melt	$2.50
Silent Run Surprise	$3.19

245 University Circle
555-SUBS
www.subs2go.com

Service so fast you could almost hold your breath.

An oversized stock photo or piece of clip art adds visual impct to a flyer, especially if you can limit the text to the bare essentials. In this flyer we resisted the urge to make the headline large; the small headline size, combined with the playful font design, gives the flyer a feeling of both fun and sophistication. The circular black shape adds visual impact, contrast, and a focus for the text and the exclamatory phrase, "Join us!"

This menu flyer can be printed in large quantities, leaving the right-hand column blank so different weekly specials can be added and printed on a desktop printer. We used an oversized, playful logo in the left panel to grab attention and create brand recognition.

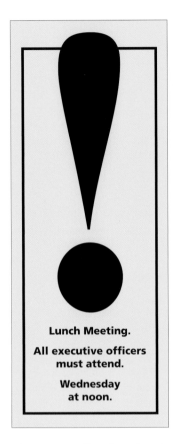

Lunch Meeting.

All executive officers must attend.

Wednesday at noon.

Flyers are usually informal projects that are going to be thrown away so you can have lots of fun with them. Be brave with the type! Show off your fonts! Use that fun clip art! Don't be a wimp!

If you can't find an image or don't have time to even look, never underestimate the power of large type as a strong, graphic element.

All of these flyers are one color (black with varying tints) printed onto colored stock. The black tints pick up the colors of the papers and give the effect of using more color.

IT'S A JUMP AND JIVE AND WAIL PARTY AT
JT'S OLD AGUA FRIA STUDIO.
THERE'LL BE FOOD, DRINK, MUSIC, AND,
OH YES, DANCING.
THE PARTY STARTS AT 8 PM AND WILL
CONTINUE UNTIL THE LAST PERSON LEAVES
AND PUTS THE DOGS OUT.
DETAILED INFORMATION IS ONLINE AT WWW.RATZ.COM/SWING.

The Important
Back-to-Winter
Chimney Check!

Special $65 per chimney
if you call before October 1

505.555.1212

Even if you can't find an image that illustrates your concept precisely, try using an image that has a vague connection. The reader will still get the concept, it's fun, and you can pretend that's what you had in mind in the first place.

Lots of flyers can be printed on half sheets, either tall and narrow, as the one shown on the opposite page, or short and stubby, as these two shown here. If you're not a wimp, these odd sizes can get just as much or more attention as when printed on standard sizes, yet cost half as much.

231

Look around

Flyers are often overlooked in the design world, but they can be some of the most fun pieces to create because they tend to be less stress-involved.

Designer Exercise: When you see a bulletin board, make a conscious note of what catches your attention. Is it the contrast, the surprise image or font, the nice white space? Also make a conscious note of which flyers get totally lost. Are they wimpy? Gray? What exactly makes them boring? Do they include too much copy, copy that could be found on the web site? Do the flyers intentionally represent the quality of the products or services offered?

Collect lots of flyers. You probably won't find very many really dynamic ones because very few people actually pay a real designer to create them. But when you do, make notes on the flyer and point out where you find contrast, visual impact, white space, alignment, or interesting and provocative type. What made you pick up the flyer in the first place? Take note of well-designed flyers that have a lot of copy on them—how did the designer visually organize all that copy (and was all of it really necessary)?

Designers
the design process

In this section we want to show you the work of other designers so you can learn from their processes. The differences between designers, the way they work, and their styles is very interesting, but so are the similarities.

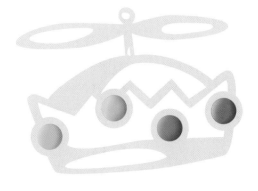

John Tollett
Graphic Control Group

BOOK COVER
Robin Williams Design Workshop

As a sequel to Robin's book, *The Non-Designer's Design Book*, our goal was to make this cover eye-catching and sophisticated, but still non-intimidating.

A book cover can go in almost any direction and it's any one's guess which will be the most effective. Any time you think you've discovered the formula for a successful cover (or any creative endeavor), someone will come along with some completely different approach and rewrite the rule book for what works and what doesn't. This rule-breaking approach isn't always appreciated by clients and marketing/sales people who have experience and proven track records, as you'll see in this example.

It's important to emphasize, however, the importance of seriously considering the input and opinions of these people in the course of a design project, especially when you have every reason to believe that they know what they're talking about. "Design arrogance" can be very humbling when you're proven wrong. So if you plan to take off in a direction opposite to the client's thinking, be prepared to have a good rationale for your approach.

Round One

The first version of the cover to be submitted is referred to as a "stunt cover." The final version may not look anything like this first one, which is used by the publisher for the initial sales and marketing of the book. The stunt cover will appear in the book catalog that's printed several times a year and lists current and upcoming books. This not only gives the publisher a sales tool, but it forces the designer to start thinking about the cover months before the final deadline.

From the start, Robin and I had discussed the cover concept in terms of a shockingly stark and simple design that ignored the typical fancy, complex hodge-podge montage approach we'd seen on other design books. It's not that we didn't like those covers, we just wanted to stand out among them.

Our target market for this book is designers who are still developing their design skills, so we thought the cover design should be technically non-intimidating, a design solution accessible to any level of design experience. A stunningly simple cover would also reinforce Robin's often repeated mantra, "Don't be a wimp!"

I usually experiment with lots of different type styles, but after several preliminary rough designs I limited all my design variations to one font, ITC Officina Sans. I liked the clean simplicity of the letter forms and the added visual interest of both serif and sans serif characters. Plus, the stunt cover was due in a day or two and I didn't want to get too many versions into the mix at this stage.

The first couple of designs reflect an ultra-simplistic typographic look, with some visual interest created by the contrast between the oversized "D" and the rest of the type. In this early stage we were still deciding on the exact wording of the title. Peachpit Press (our publisher) responded that they'd like to see more contrast, such as a black area at the top of the cover. I created a dozen variations implementing this suggestion. Some versions had the large "D" completely in the black area and some had the "D" breaking out of the black into the white area.

Robin and I liked the black, but it was a compromise that looked familiar, a design solution we'd seen (or used) too many times before. We wanted to be shockingly clean and simple. I considered a blank white cover with the title on the spine, but I didn't want to push my luck. I narrowed the stunt covers down to two choices, a white version and a version with a black top half. I created a quick, two-page web site, showing a cover version on each page, for the people on Peachpit's cover team (in Berkeley, California and Buffalo, New York) to review.

The first cover designs used stark simplicity for visual impact. We experimented with the relationship between the oversized "D" and the rest of the type.

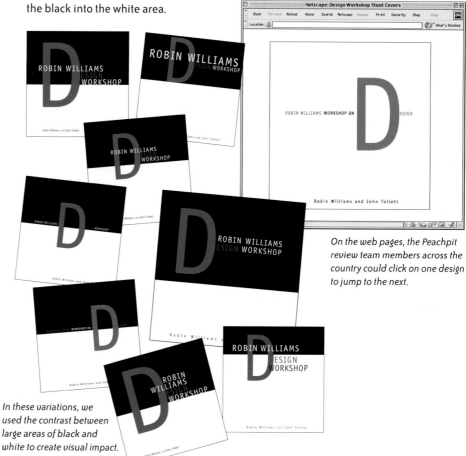

In these variations, we used the contrast between large areas of black and white to create visual impact.

On the web pages, the Peachpit review team members across the country could click on one design to jump to the next.

Round Two

Two months later, after Robin and I had been working on the interior design and content of the book, Peachpit expressed concern that the cover wasn't colorful enough and didn't reflect the rich, colorful content inside. [Actually, says Robin, they were afraid that people would not know the book was full-color unless there was full color on the cover.] They asked me to play with some solutions that would address this concern.

I created the color montages in Photoshop and then placed them into the Illustrator book cover file.

I made about 30 new variations, most of which used a color montage created from color images that were being used in the book. I didn't want to show complete ads or logos that would have an identity and distract from the typographic design on the cover. Some versions don't work at all, but this is the design exploration/experimentation phase where I'll try anything. Sometimes a yucky design leads to a good design. At this point I also began experimenting with using a gold color in some of the variations, a subtle color tie-in to the first book, *The Non-Designer's Design Book.*

From all these variations I submitted one full-color design, plus three others which reverted back to an all-type approach.

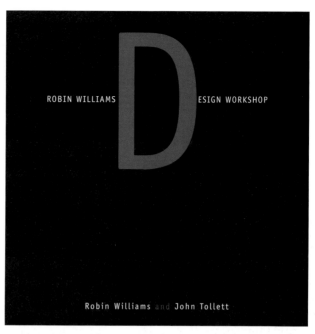

This approach was still Robin's favorite choice (but she actually preferred the white background).

Personally, I liked this full-color montage version, but the frown on Robin's face convinced me to submit several other versions along with this one.

Round Three

Peachpit's response several days later was that the color images on the cover looked like a collection of clip art. This was true, but since the entire book embraces the clip art concept, I argued that that was okay. The publisher asked if I could do anything to address this issue, such as put the images inside the "D" or anything to make the images less well defined while also adding color.

I created another montage that could fit inside the "D," the images of which overlapped and looked colorful, but abstract. I applied the montage to three new versions of the cover. I liked the result, but Robin was not enthusiastic about it. She suggested putting three small dots of process color on the cover to symbolize both design and color. "I'll do it," I said, "but we left that approach behind 30 versions ago." I submitted the new versions, including three subtle variations of Robin's suggestion.

Meanwhile, Robin sent her thoughts to Peachpit which read, in part:

```
<snip>

All the way through this book we tell readers
to be brave and bold and new and then here
is this cover that capitulates to some silly
idea that no one will know the book has color
inside if there isn't four-color on the front!
Conversely then, doesn't that imply that on
all four-color covers the reader expects there
will be four-color inside? YES!!

I say this to the cover team: DON'T BE
WIMPS!!! BE BRAVE!! BE BOLD!! BE DARING!!
PUT YOUR MONEY WHERE YOUR MOUTH IS!!!
:::marching around the office waving a flag:::
```

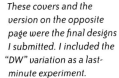

These covers and the version on the opposite page were the final designs I submitted. I included the "DW" variation as a last-minute experiment.

As I said in the beginning, a good design rationale can be very helpful. Peachpit approved the design that appears on the cover of this book, a design that's very close to our original concept. If no one's reading this right now, I hope it's not because of the cover.

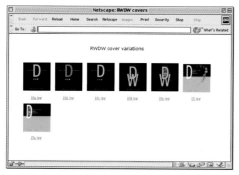

I put the final round of designs on another web page for the Peachpit cover team to review. Each thumbnail links to a full-page image of the cover design.

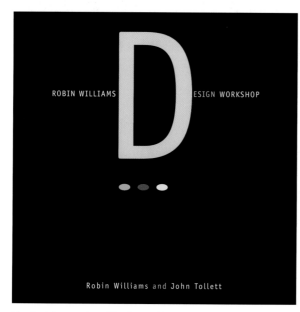

The final design selected by the Peachpit cover team meets our original goals of simplicity and visual impact.

Who am I?

I'm just a guy who always liked to draw. If you're from one of my childhood hometowns of Hope, Arkansas, or Sulphur, Louisiana, I'm one of the twins. I have a Bachelor of Arts in Advertising Art from Louisiana College. I've co-authored two other books with Robin (*The Non-Designer's Web Book* and *The Little iBook Book*) and I've illustrated several of her books and book covers.

My professional background covers over thirty years and various positions of art director, designer, and illustrator with a dozen advertising agencies and as a freelancer. I was co-founder of a web design firm which has evolved into PanoramaPoint, an outstanding web development company that got bigger and better after I left and I'm trying not to take it personally. I still spend time as a designer, web design consultant, illustrator, and conduct web design workshops and digital graphics classes.

My personal web site (www.UrlsInternetCafe.com) defies description because it's run by Url Ratz and Browser NetHound, two undiscovered, self-proclaimed Internet icons.

Words of wisdom

1) Develop a thick skin. When your design is rejected, don't dwell on it or take it personally. It's going to happen, no matter how good you are. And, more often than you think, it's going to give you the opportunity to create an even better design. If you can roll with the punches, you'll still be a designer ten years from now. And you'll be a lot better than you were ten years ago.

2) Approach design as a form of play. Explore and experiment. Amuse yourself. If you're having a good time, graphically speaking, other people will enjoy your work as well.

John Tollett
Graphic Control Group

www.UrlsInternetCafe.com
jt@ratz.com

Maggie Macnab
Macnab Design Visual Communication

LOGO AND SYMBOL DESIGN

Logo design always has one common limitation: the essential necessity of design economy. It must without exception be intuitively clear and simple, yet at the same time be interesting enough to be remembered. Its application can be elaborate, depending on the situation, but the logo must stand independently inspired and simple: elegant in appearance and eloquent in communication. From the first "commercial" applications, symbols have come a long way from identifying tribal members and their handiwork to representing corporate conglomerates. Symbols are mutable over time, save a few exceptions which live within the collective unconscious as basic truths about our physical reality.

There is the obvious reason to have a logo: to distinguish your service or goods from someone else's. And there is the reason underlying that: to associate concept and symbol. Symbols are a very efficient shorthand to describe the complex or the intangible. They are our most crucial invention because without them we could not identify or strategize with common agreement. They allow us to organize, plan, and bring ideas to fruition. It is fundamental to our survival, and therefore, our nature, to think in symbol (we are thinking in symbol when we read, when we write, when we translate spiritual or physical theoretics, when we plan cities or invent lasers).

In the case of the logo, you are quite literally **creating an identity**—a symbol that has enough common agreement to be broadly recognized, yet is still individual enough to associate with one entity after one to a few exposures. When you consider that all this happens within a blink—and is surrounded by unyielding noise—you can appreciate that it is not an easy thing to do with originality. Case in point: you might have noticed a lot of typographical "logos," particularly in the area of technology. Within our increasingly techno-laden life, we are incorporating new concepts and new ways of relating—essentially evolving our symbols as we evolve ourselves. We are in the process of developing the technology that will birth the new symbols; it is safer and far easier to use the accepted modality of typography.

In my symbol work, I focus on two to three concepts that graphically describe the client and then integrate them into a seamless visual. I've named this method eye-ku™ because it is an abstracted thought translated as a symbol and relates independent things or concepts. It may be a second or third time before people get to the "surprise middle" which is really a matter of just seeing the whole after identifying the parts, or vice versa. People know intuitively when there is something more there and will often spend extra time with or look again at a design to uncover what it is. Of course, it also needs to be visually pleasing to earn a second or third glance, and intuiting more there piques the interest—the basic hook to reinforce the logo and the client.

It's a look-hook—if it's not there, the response is entirely different or missing altogether. And it's accomplished solely through rewarding the viewer with aesthetic and inventive effort. It has the element of "aha!" that people love, like getting the punch line of a clever joke. You're setting up a pattern that creates a meaning, which has a tremendous impact on the human mind. It is very satisfying to create a conscious meaning from an intuited connection. It's the stuff from which we integrate new dimensions of reality; the interaction of making the unknown understood. As our world becomes more integrated, thinking in a more whole-brain manner is a consequential phenomena.

Maddoux-Wey
Arabian Horse Farms

Logo: I began by working with the distinctive shapes of an Arabian, in particular, the characteristic dished face and arched neck. Experimentation and play are very important to the success of a design. You must be willing to engage without an expected result. I moved tracings of horse heads into different angles and positions which ultimately lead to the interaction of the negative/positive space. It made sense to make a play on yin-yang, as the farm was specifically focused on mares and stallions.

Stationery: The design was restrained with the intent of simplicity, complementing the logo and the elegance of the Arabian horse. A foil application, handled judiciously with a single ink color, achieved both a refined and cost-effective package.

 **1.** *A horse lover all of my life, I had years of material stored in my head already, but I did reference some magazines and show brochures specific to the Arabian. I began by working with the general shape of an Arabian horse. I focused on the more distinguishing characteristics of the breed, the dish face and arched neck. (I've always drawn, but if you're not a figurative artist, tracings are an adequate substitute.)*

 **2.** *Play is very important in discovery: experiment without an expected result. I intuitively knew there was a fit to be had here and kept doodling until I found it.*

 **3.** *I discover the fit and it's a short jump to the "yin-yang" circle of perfection.*

CSI Technologies, Inc.
Consulting Engineers

Logo: The CSI symbol is very simple: a gear spiral, as I call it. The client works within the mechanical engineering profession, identifying potential problem areas in pipe systems that carry water for cooling. The spiral is reminiscent of water movement and the gear represents the precision of the company's work. This symbol also references the application of technology to nature.

Stationery: I like to get visual material from the client that describes their work. In this case, engineers work with schematics, which are quite beautiful unto themselves. They were integrated directly into the support of the identity package and carry the color of fresh and sea waters.

SAMBA
Internet Data Mining

Logo: There is nothing more daunting than information. This company closes the loop on information overload—there's just something about the inordinate amount available that makes you want to find some kind of limit. The Möbius loop was a good way to convey that; I humanized the image to make it even more accessible.

Oriental Medical Consultants
*Hybrid Eastern/Western
Health Consultancy*

Logo: The concept of the
I Ching has always intrigued
me, as well as the quality
chi or qi—the life force—
being fundamental to health.
I combined these Eastern
concepts with the anglicized
medical caduceus to communicate both cultural disciplines.

Stationery: Gold and green
inks, two of the more
commonly associated Asian
colors, form the dominant
color scheme for the stationery
package. I also incorporated
the supporting graphics of
Chinese calligraphy with a
statement about well-being,
and integrated I Ching "throws"
into the address copy and on
the back of the business card.

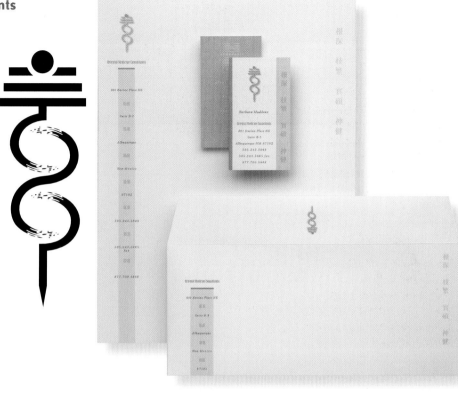

Stationery: Large blocks of
contrasting color add solidity
to the idea of information;
the shadow gives the logo
dimension.

243

Heart Hospital of New Mexico
Cardiac Hospital

Logo: Although the final is quite simple, it was a process to get there. I played with hearts, hands, and the Zia symbol in many configurations until I finally eliminated the complexities. This is the trick: **find the magic in the mundane.** As Einstein said, "Things should be made as simple as possible, but not any simpler."

Although the State of New Mexico has used the Zia symbol for over a hundred years as as our state symbol, Zia Pueblo owns the design and is sensitive about infringement. We requested audience with the elders and asked for its use in this case. They not only granted our request, but danced at and blessed the facility at the groundbreaking.

Stationery: I stayed with more traditional southwestern colors: our gorgeous turquoise skies and the red of the earth and of life. I incorporated a band of symbols echoing pictographs; this band was later integrated into the interiors of the facility.

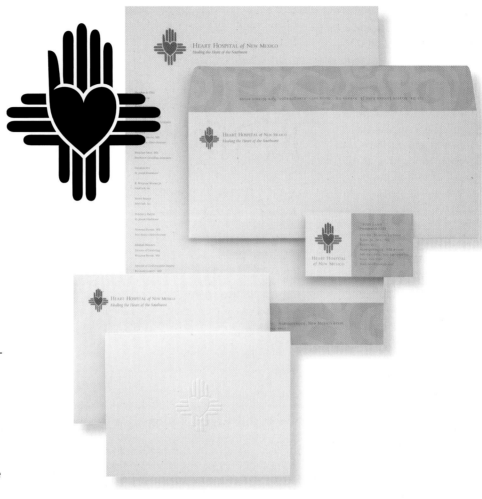

ISTEC, Inc.
Ibero-American Science and Technology Education Consortium

Logo: I chose the Maya, one of the more sophisticated cultures of the Americas (as ISTEC encompasses all the Americas and the Iberian Peninsula) combined with a circuit board and connections to communicate learning from archaic but advanced cultures and the complexity of technology (both the human integration of it and its application). I modified a "glyph"-looking typeface and evolved the leading "i" into a circuit terminal.

Stationery: For the logo's application to stationery, I created a "rubbing" in Photoshop of a Mayan glyph which dissolves into pixelated code, fusing the two technologies. To echo the blending of technologies, I used soft, pastel colors that are in themselves mixtures, as a calming and distinguishing feature. The logo is foiled to approximate an actual circuit system.

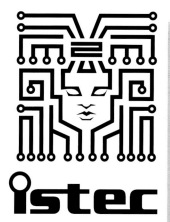

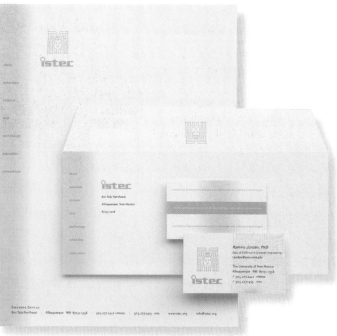

Words of Wisdom
One of the best things about being a designer, aside from the creative interaction with yourself and others, is learning to un-groove from your set path and to be open to walking another. In itself, this is one of the more creative aspects of design work—a *true* area of creative thinking—and a basic lesson in developing the skill of understanding.

Maggie Macnab
Macnab Design
 Visual Communication
12028 N. HWY 14, Suite B
Cedar Crest, New Mexico
87008

505 286 5500 *phone*
505 286 5501 *fax*

mmacnab@macnabdesign.com
www.macnabdesign.com
www.eyeku.com

Fred Cisneros
Cisneros Design

PROMOTIONAL MATERIALS
Dan Namingha, artist and sculptor

The challenge of the project was to choose a format opportunity to best represent the *sculpture* of a well known painter. Dan Namingha is a tremendous color theorist and many of the sculptures he previously worked on were oiled bronzes with patina finishes. This series for a special show at the Wheelwright Museum of the American Indian was more like his paintings based in both color palette and composition. These sculptures, basically, were painted assemblies.

I decided a die-cut folded piece would reflect much of the dimensionality of the sculptures. The sculptures were comprised of a series of intersecting squares intended to give the viewer a changing view of the work. Thus the print design attempted to provide the same experience.

DAN NAMINGHA

STRUCTURAL | DUALITIES

This client is a dream client. Dan is very generous in allowing me to interpret the intent of his work through my work. When he does provide direction, it is usually centered around dominant color use in backgrounds. Dan and his wife Frances provided only four images to work with: two sculptures and two paintings. These pieces were, in their minds, the cornerstones of the show.

Though the project was to feature Dan Namingha's work, **the actual client** in this case was the Wheelwright Museum of the American Indian. Dan had specifically requested that I work on all communications regarding the show. The Wheelwright had set a $3700 budget for the project based on design they had produced for previous shows. Previously, invitations and show pieces had generally been two-color. As either a design or print budget the $3700 is feasible, but to insure I was able to produce what I felt was an appropriate reflection I donated my design and production charges to insure the costs of separations, printing, and die cutting were covered.

The process

The project was **completed** from start to finish in three and a half weeks.

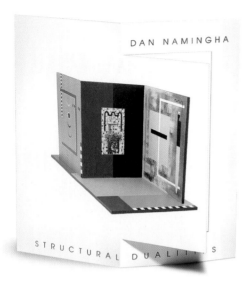

I have worked with Dan and Frances Namingha for more than fifteen years. Throughout that time Dan's work has become very well known and very much in demand. His audience, both collectors and museums, has always considered Dan to be an innovative individual and expect the same in the communications with his name on them. I wanted the recipient of this piece, whether collectors or novice art afficionados, to have an interaction with the design.

Often when I am working with Dan on a project, **the process** generally consists of producing a mock-up and presenting the idea. To the point: I can present ideas that have no immediate need, and Dan will often think of ways to incorporate his work and we create the piece together.

Were there **conflicts** with the clients? With Dan, no; with the Wheelwright, some. The Museum was concerned that this piece would be overkill in relation to the work done for previous shows. Though the budget with my contribution, was met, the implied value or cost was overspent in their mind. This conflict only lasted a moment.

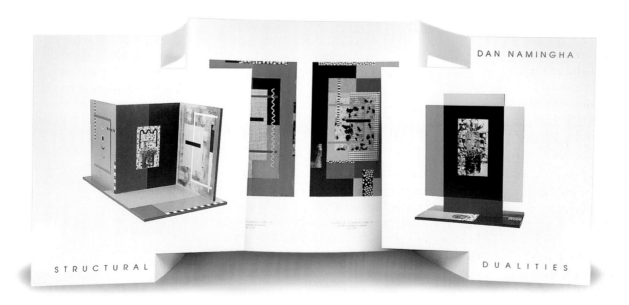

SAKIESTEWA DIRECT MAIL

This is direct mail piece for a series of seven Native American trade blankets, four of which had working proto-types while the remaining three did not yet exist beyond paper. The blankets were to be featured as a limited edition set but would also be available as single units. The brochure/mailer needed to function as a catalog, giving each blanket equal presence.

The client had two demands: One, that the piece contain an order form of some kind; and two, that it contain one of the historical images they supplied. They also originally asked for a pocket folder to carry individual inserts for the blankets.

I reduced the size of the piece, and rather than insert the four existing blankets, I attached them. The piece is intended to echo the four winds or the four directions, a theme common in Native American art. By making the existing four blankets part of the main folder, I believe we overcame the issue of the series being incomplete.

Photographer Eric Swanson shot the images on high-speed film to increase grain and enhance the texture in the shots.

Design of the project took approximately **four weeks,** as did printing.

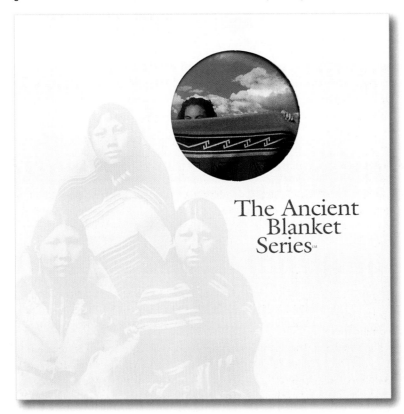

The Ancient Blanket Series™

This was a start-up company, so **budget** was definitely an issue. Columbine Printing of Taos, New Mexico, won the bid for the print quote. Columbine is well known for artwork reproduction, in spite of the fact that they run a one-color press. It was a long process and somewhat nerve-racking since multicolor presses are the norm. Still, we achieved the quality we intended.

The process

Through market research and experience with similar projects, my client had targeted their audience by income level and lifestyle. This client had produced a blanket series several years earlier as a joint project with a Native American arts dealer. The audience was the same— upscale and discerning, and the price point of the product demanded the mailer achieve a comparable status.

After the photography was complete, we felt it was imperative that people be incorporated into the shots. In the previous contemporary blanket projects, the blankets were seen as decor rather than utilitarian. In this series we wanted the buyer to use them, and our intent was to show how they could do that.

"The piece is intended to echo the four winds or the four directions, a theme common in Native American art."

The client and I went round and round about what to put on the cover—she wanted the historic image and I wanted product and color.

This conflict evolved into the best solution for the piece. I had felt the historic image was thematic but not substantive enough for the product we were featuring. The historic image was black and white; it was heavy. In sepia tone, it was lighter; ultimately the image was printed as a tinted varnish. This gave the photo more life yet it was not overpowering.

Then the die-cut circle literally opened up several options. I wanted the die opening to focus on the individual using the product in the photo. The die cut corresponds with the position of each image as the cover is closed over each panel. This compromise actually worked to benefit the design and success of the piece.

CISNEROS DESIGN SPACE

Generally speaking

I started Cisneros Design in September of 1994. My daughter was born a month earlier and I thought— what the hell, I don't have enough stress in my life, I'll start a new company. I began working out of the greenhouse in my home until my first office in the "Nunnery" was complete (the Nunnery is the metal building behind the "pink church" on Pacheco Street in Santa Fe).

I rented the space with three other individuals; my piece was 150 square feet and about $150 a month. Two months into the game I had one employee and six months later a second. But 150 square feet was cramped for one person and unacceptable for three. I expanded and acquired an additional 450 square feet. After three more moves we are now a nine-person company in our own new buildings.

In January 2000, we moved into a 5000-square-foot building we purchased. This endeavor was probably the most intriguing project to work on because I was the designer and client. The builder/ developer is a client of ours and gave me a great deal of room in creating the space.

I wanted the space to be about impact, color, and efficiency. I worked with architect Eric Enfield. He accommodated all my weird requests and ideas and threw in several of his own. There are only two enclosed offices, plus a conference room. The remaining work spaces are four-sided pods made of constructed

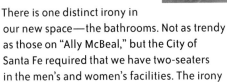

steel, corrugated metal culverts, and corrugated metal panels. I have a full-size "Bob's Big Boy" statue in my entry (I did not steal it as a Homecoming prank... well, I did, but I took that one back). This one I found courtesy of eBay, (same place I found the 1928 barber chair). My office is a toy box. Various collection of "things" can be found throughout the building—Beatles memorabilia, a 1963 Cellini accordian, a Lemieux autographed hockey stick ....

There is one distinct irony in our new space—the bathrooms. Not as trendy as those on "Ally McBeal," but the City of Santa Fe required that we have two-seaters in the men's and women's facilities. The irony is the square footage of each restroom exceeds 190 square feet, bigger than the size of my first office.

The budget on this project? "Oh my God!"

The deadline? "Son of a #@%*!" (Mostly because the city puttzed around with permits, then because those construction guys knock off at 3 o'clock every day.)

Who am I?

Fred Cisneros. I am the owner of Cisneros Design Inc. My wife is Stephanie and we have a six year-old daughter, Amanda, a dog, and three cats.

I began college as an engineering major, specifically technical illustration. I self-converted into the art department, then transferred to the College of Santa Fe. The liberal arts structure of the college allowed me to develop, in conjunction with the Art Department Faculty, a curriculum that served my Graphic Design major. I graduated in 1987 with a BA in Graphic Design.

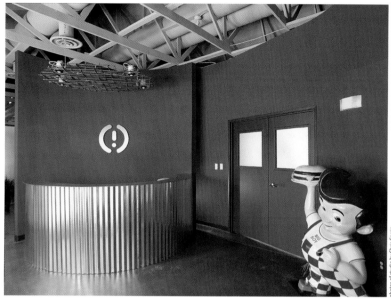

photos of studio by Chris Corrie

Words of wisdom

Don't be afraid of an idea. Have conviction and understanding of the idea—and let the account guy who has to sell your idea be afraid.

Learn something new every day.

Fred Cisneros
Cisneros Design, Inc.
2904 Rodeo Park Drive East,
    Building 200
Santa Fe, New Mexico
87505

505 471 6699 *phone*
fred@cisnerosdesign.com
www.cisnerosdesign.com

Dave Rohr
Panorama Point Web Communications

WEB SITE DEVELOPMENT

Santa Fe Opera
www.santafeopera.org

Panorama Point was presented with the opportunity to do a full redesign and expansion of the web site for the world-renowned Santa Fe Opera. Their existing site had been produced in-house and they were looking for an enhancement in both style and substance. They needed a design that would invite exploration through the site and would ultimately attract more visitors to the Opera.

My web design process always begins with research. I try to learn as much as I can about the client and most importantly, their audience—the people who will be using the site. In this case, my staff and I met with the Santa Fe Opera marketing director, Tom Morris, and discussed his goals for the project, the central design elements he felt were important to their message, and how he thought people would be using the site. We learned that their target audience was comprised of not only Opera lovers but

included people who may never have attended before. Tom wanted the site to communicate that the Opera is a rich experience for everyone, not just an elite few. I asked him to provide us with their best photographs of the opera house and scenes from a few past productions. Later, a couple of us took a field trip to the opera house and toured it from front to back and even way up above on the lighting catwalks (yikes!) in an attempt to better understand the workings of the facility.

To the right are samples of my really rough design sketches. They're for my use only, not quite ready for the client yet.

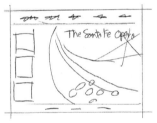

These are a few of the interface designs that made it to the client review.

Along with determining the way a web site looks, don't underestimate the importance of creating user-friendly navigation. Even the best-looking site can be torpedoed by a lousy interface. The truth is, if someone finds a site hard to use, they probably won't bother to go past the home page.

The new Opera site was quite complex, containing many sub-categories, but we had to present it in a way that would be simple and easily understood. I decided to establish a navigational hierarchy on the home page and place the most

important links in areas of the page that would get the viewer's initial attention. The secondary links would still be easy to see, but not quite as prominent.

I also worked with our site architect to limit the number of links that would be viewed at any one time to keep it simple. This way, a user could select a broad category and "drill down" to the more specific information they were looking for. And, for the more impatient users, we included a "search" feature.

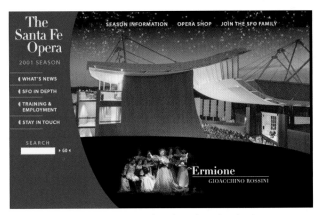

When conceptualizing the Santa Fe Opera design, I tried to focus on what makes it special and unique from any other venue. The opera house is a beautiful open-air structure situated in a spectacular high-desert setting. It's skirted by mountains and the sides are open so you can see the twinkling stars (or the lightning) during the performances. With this in mind, I envisioned several versions of the home page, each utilizing the opera house as a dominant element, accented with photographs of performers on stage .

This was the design concept, created in Photoshop, that the client eventually chose to use as the home page.

With the understanding I had gained, I began sketching my mental design concepts onto paper, creating a few rough thumbnails to quickly visualize some of the ideas I had in mind (as shown on page 252). Some ideas emphasized the strong architectural curves of the Opera house, while others focused more on images of the performers. I usually create 10–20 sketches and then review them later, selecting four to five from the bunch that I think are strong and varied enough to turn into finished comps. I build all my comps in Photoshop using layers to make it easy to revise later, if necessary. Of all my thumbnail sketches, the ones that seemed strongest featured the structure in some way.

To adapt the home page concept for the interior pages, I went in a direction that retained the feel of the home page with the architectural curves and starry sky, but in a minimal way that didn't compete with the main body text and photographs.

After final client approval of the comps, our web developers took the Photoshop files and turned them into HTML files using BBEdit and Macromedia Dreamweaver.

Several hundred Photoshop layers later, I presented the client with five different home page comps (shown on page 253 and the opposite page) to get their feedback, suggestions, and hopefully approval on a direction. After showing the pages to several of their staff members, they gave the thumbs up to a version featuring the Opera house beneath the stars, emanating an orange glow. Luckily for me it was my favorite, too.

Despite a few minor client-requested tweaks here and there, the overall concept survived intact. The design process, from sketches to final comp approval, took about five weeks.

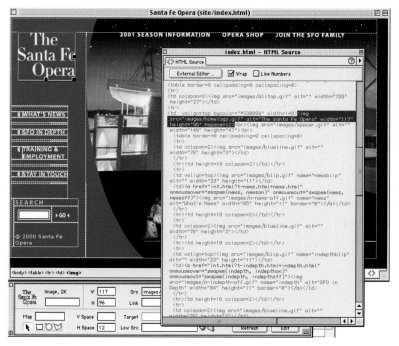

One of the cooler features is the DHTML pull-down menus allowing for immediate access to any page within the site.

New Mexico Winter Adventure
www.SkiNewMexico.com

This is a web site that promotes skiing, snowboarding, and other winter activities in New Mexico. The client, Ski New Mexico, likes to update the look of the site annually and this is the second design iteration we've done for them. Like on the Opera site, the goal here is to interest and engage the target audience from the moment they see the home page. Drawing from my past experience with this site, I knew we needed to make the content of the site easily accessible. I also knew that fun, dynamic imagery appeals to this client and audience. The main directives from the client were to make it look exciting, consolidate some of the previous year's categories, and accommodate advertising on each page.

To realize all of these goals, I knew I'd need more space than what was allotted for the 640 x 480-pixel design we created last year. I began my design comps using the 800 x 600-pixel screen ratio. This way I could use a larger central image as a

focal point and still have room for a reasonably sized navigational component. In this case, I used four prominent category buttons in a highly visible location, with the remainder of the links and pull-down menus in the right-hand area. By making DHTML pull-down menus from the four main links, nearly every page of the site would be directly accessible from the home or any interior page. This effectively cut down the number of clicks needed to navigate, leading to more user exploration throughout the site.

I think the site is effective because there's a good balance between the usability of the navigation and the overall visual appeal.

This is an example of one of the interior pages of the web site.

in 1985. While waiting for the web to come along, I spent the next nine years as a print designer, mostly in advertising. Later, I worked in New York as the Associate Art Director at *Art in America* magazine. Self-taught in web design and HTML, I began creating web sites in late 1994 and by 1996 had made web design my full-time career, partnering with John Tollett in West of the Pecos Web Design. We later merged with two other companies to form Panorama Point.

I now live just outside Santa Fe with my wife Roni, and children Matthew and Amy. When not in front of my monitor, you might find me pedaling my bike on some remote trail.

Words of wisdom

In the web sites you create, make usability your top priority. Even great-looking sites can fail if they're difficult to use—the audience will simply go elsewhere. The most effective web site designers will find a way to integrate a highly usable interface with an eye-catching design. Take the time to understand your audience and their needs so you can identify the best ways to engage them.

Who am I?

I'm a founding partner in Panorama Point, a web communications firm in New Mexico. As the creative director and principal interface designer, I oversee all design projects, working alongside an exceptionally talented staff of designers, programmers, and project managers. Since our start in 1998, we've grown from a staff of seven to seventeen. We've been fortunate to have the opportunity to work on a wide variety of challenging projects both in New Mexico and beyond.

A Kansas native, I received my BFA in Graphic Design from Wichita State University

Dave Rohr
Panorama Point
*   Web Communications*
3600 Cerrillos Road, Suite 105
Santa Fe, New Mexico
87505

505 424 4800 *phone*

www.panoramapoint.com
drohr@panoramapoint.com

Carmen Sheldon
Santa Rosa Junior College

Applied Graphics Program
Students' projects

The Applied Graphics program at Santa Rosa Junior College, California, is designed to provide the student entry-level skills for business or industry. The program is structured to provide a practical hands-on experience in graphic fundamentals such as design, layout techniques, computer applications, illustration, multimedia, digital production techniques, offset printing, and business practices. The students spend much of their time creating practical design pieces from initial concept all the way through final digital output.

This is the program Robin graduated from in 1980 (pre-computer); eventually she started running the program and taught the core first-year curriculum. She and Carmen met at SRJC in 1978 and have been close friends and partners ever since.

This section displays several of Carmen's design projects with her advanced students.

Student specs: Tea Box Case Study

Ms. Hempleworth is opening a tea room in downtown Sonoma [California], right on the square. She has leased a charming, newly remodeled space. She wants to play into the bucolic feeling of the Sonoma area and so she has named her new little business *Ewe and Me Tea Room.* She will be serving a traditional high tea with all the ceremony. However, she wants to be sure her business has a variety of services to offer her customers, so in addition to a little tea shop where she will sell gifts and a variety of gourmet teas, a bakery, and a catering service, she wants to offer boxed, picnic tea fare.

She would like you to design her tea boxes. She wants a soft, charming, but not too "cutsie" look. The concept must include a stylized image of a sheep. She doesn't want men to feel out of place by having the box seem too feminine.

Her boxes will hold two scones, four little sandwiches, two tarts, two tiny napkins, a small jar of jam, several pats of butter, and two packages of tea. She certainly wants her box to say "delicious food" so it shouldn't look like a retail gift box.

You may consider any approach with the provided white box—a band around the box, an all-over design, a typographic look, whatever you feel might suit Ms. Hempleworth.

My Thoughts

This is a great project because I only allow the students about four hours to come up with concepts and complete their comps. The students walk into the classroom cold with no prior knowledge of what they will be working on. I then produce a bag, box, candy bar, bottle, whatever it is that day, and have them develop a design. This method requires the students to think on their feet and work very quickly. I do several of these "case studies" every semester and although the students panic at first, they soon learn to love the pace and are usually surprised that they can come up with a viable idea in that small amount of time. In fact, one of my students said, "Can we do more case studies; this is so much fun!" I often find that the students even feel their case study designs are stronger than ones they work with for weeks. The immediacy and the fact that they have to make quick decisions is good discipline and a realistic preparation for the world of graphic design.

Credits clockwise: Yvone Whang, Molly Cushman, Audrey Sculley

credits left to right: Yvone Wang, Leah Anderson, Darrell Perry, Kathleen Blair, Rebecca Parola, Terry McDonough

Student specs: Wine Label Project

We live in the wine country so we have to design a wine label. They are just too beautiful to ignore and there is a lot we can learn about specialty printing techniques. You are to create a fictitious winery and design a label for it. If you look at a lot of label designs you will find that many labels concentrate on typography so this should be addressed very carefully in your design.

> › The emphasis of the project is concept. Really do some brainstorming and research. You are creating the total package so pay attention to the foils, neck labels, back labels, etc.

> › Typography must be an important part of your design.

> › Include a specialty technique such as emboss, hot foil stamp, die cut, etc.

> › Pay attention to the "legals."

> › You may decide the size. Watch how it fits the bottle. Also, find out what types of wine go in which bottles— don't embarrass yourself.

> › Submit computer color output.

> › Present your label in a pocket on a presentation board.

> › Hand in computer-generated color separations on 8.5" x 11" transparency material.

credits left to right: Jason Hill, Jackie Mujica, David Berg, Claudia Strijek, Julie Cook

My Thoughts

Nothing beats success. The students really enjoy this project because it looks very stunning upon completion. Although my students don't run right out and start designing wine labels after two years of a community college graphic design program, they do get a lot of positive feedback from their labels. It gives them a chance to work with image, color and type—aspects of most visual communication pieces. It makes them really hone their designs because the format doesn't allow for unnecessary elements. It is a good lesson for all the principles because the format is so restricted. All the contrast, proximity, and alignment issues become very apparent.

I never allow my students to head for the computer without working out their designs in thumbnail form. I want them to think before they get too filter-drop-shadow-twirl-tool happy. They hate it, but their work is better because of it.

Credits left to right: Barb Wendel, Terry McDonough, Jeanne Thomas, Kim Reid, Linda Palo, Donna Mathis

Student specs: CD Project

A new and upcoming musical group needs you to design a promotional CD for their group. This is not only the retail packaging for the CD but also a "promo," a 3D ad designed to get the radio station's attention. In this project you get the chance to work with a "designer." You will be split up in pairs and each of you will get the chance to be the "client" and "designer." You will provide each other with the name of the musical group, the type of music, and your personal preferences concerning design.

› The emphasis of the project is concept. Really do some brainstorming and research.

› Include type on the label of the CD.

› Include a fold-out with information on the group or song lyrics.

› Submit computer color output.

› Present your piece in a protective box.

My Thoughts

I like this project because it really lets the students explore their creativity and have some fun. Oh, sure, some of these designs go way over the top—to produce them in the real world of print production would probably bankrupt the client—but we do our share of budget-driven projects and this one allows the students to really stun each other with their whimsical creativity.

The students work in pairs, playing the parts of both designer and client. This does make them stretch as often the student partial to hard rock must design a cover for classical strings.

There is a lot of "real world" graphics that play a part in this project as the students must create a sizable folded insert complete with photos, song lyrics, and type treatments. I also insist that they separate their computer files.

Credits left to right: Patrice Morris, Lisa Howard, Linda Palo, Molly Cushman

Words of Wisdom

Never let the computer design for you. Your mind, experiences, perceptions, and knowledge are the best tools for coming up with visual communications that really matter. Draw some scribbles on a scrap of paper. Think! Look! Go for a walk! Collect leaves! Take a photo of a river rock. Pick up a feather. Then turn on your computer.

Who am I?

After graduating with a degree in Advertising Design from Pacific Union College, Robin and I started our own design studio, The Double Image. Of course, we had to learn the business end by the seat of our pants, but we had lots of fun creating logos, ads, and brochures for the local businesses. I do think we spent most of our profits on truffles, Oreo cookies, and silkscreen ink for our beautiful serigraphs. After working in several different design capacities, I eventually started teaching in the Applied Graphics Program at Santa Rosa Junior College. I found my niche: I could share my passion for design and also tie into that streak of altruism that's in my bones from being a "missionary kid." I love my students and get great satisfaction out of seeing them bloom from tentative amateurs into confident design professionals.

Carmen Sheldon
Santa Rosa Junior College
Applied Graphics Program
1501 Mendocino Avenue
Santa Rosa, California
95401

707 527 4909 *phone*

csheldon@santarosa.edu
www.www.santarosa.edu/aptech/

Paul Shaw
Calligrapher & Typographer

CD COVER
*Jimmy Smith/Dot Com Blues
cover for Verve Music Group*

Hollis King, art director

The specs

> The **final reproduction** process will be offset printing.

> **The client** provided a scan of the photograph of Jimmy Smith and asked that the name and title of the CD be lettered in a "cheesy 1950s" style.

> The **budget** was not discussed but was understood from previous assignments to be in the $500 to $1000 range.

> There was no **deadline** (believe it or not!).

> The **target audience** is buyers of jazz CDs.

There was no **client conflict.** Hollis King is a former student of mine from the 1980s and we have worked together on lettering for CD covers numerous times in the past five years. Hollis gives me a general direction of what mood or effect he is looking for and lets me have free reign. We have never had any problems.

The process
The **design process** was straightforward:

1. I researched examples of 1950s jazz album covers by Reid Miles, Jim Flora, Alex Steinweiss, David Stone Martin, and others, gathering ideas for lettering styles.

2. I sketched several styles in outline that seemed to be "cheesy" and also some small layouts of the proposed lettering in use.

3. Hollis chose two styles: the signature script and the Ben Shahn-style cut-out letters.

Three sketches for lettering for CD cover:

a) *Sans serif with dot stroke endings*

b) *Bouncy Bodoni*

c) *Signature-style script with Ben Shahn-style cut letters*

4. I wrote out Jimmy and Smith with various brushes many times, selected the best letter combinations, and pasted them together (using Scotch magic tape). I photocopied the result and retouched it (with a Uniball pen and white-out).

Selected scraps of brush script lettering for Smith

Partial paste-up of brush script lettering for Jimmy

Jimmy Smith

Final lettering for Jimmy Smith

Final lettering for Dot Com Blues

DOT COM BLUES

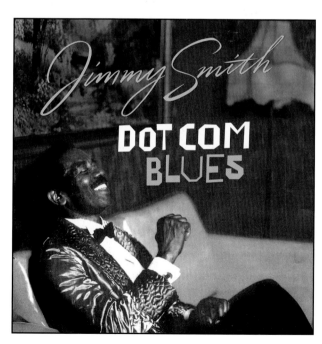

5. I drew the Shahn style letters (with references to his work from various sources) and inked them in with Higgins Black Magic india ink on smooth bristol board (retouched with opaque white paint).

6. I sent the lettering with a rough digital layout of my proposed application to Hollis for final assembly.

7. The CD has not been issued yet so I have not seen how Hollis and his staff have used the lettering.

ATYPI CALLIGRAPHIC LOGO DESIGN
Association Typographique Internationale

The client specified that the logo consist of "the letters 'atypi' (or AtypI) on a rectangle which is twice as wide as it is high, with the letter 'A' bleeding off the left edge, the letter 'I' bleeding off the right edge, and at least one of the descenders bleeding off the bottom." The background had to be a 50 percent tint of black or Pantone Cool Grey 7 with the letters reversed out in white.

There was no budget; this was a pro bono job. Andrew Boag was design director. There was no deadline. The target audience is members (and potential members) of ATypI (which is pronounced "A type eye"). The final reproduction process is offset printing.

This is the current ATypI logo, designed by Michael Harvey.

atypi Association Typographique Internationale

The process

The design process for this project was very simple:

1. I received the specs from Andrew Boag in the mail.

2. I sketched many variations of the letters in the logo (some that did not conform to the brief).

3. I decided to do broad-pen–based letters since that is what I am best known for and because they offered more flexibility than type to meet the requirements of the brief for bleeds on three sides. (I was able to manipulate the depth and shape of the

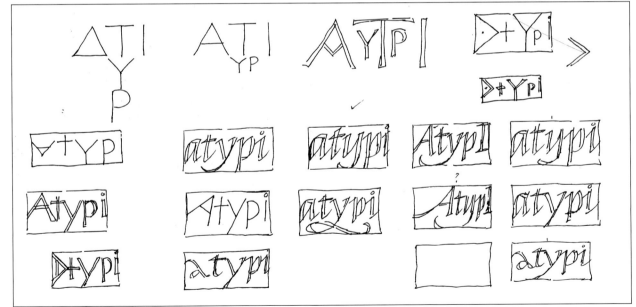

Sketches made during the design process.

letters y and p as well as the placement of the dot on the i. I chose lowercase letters, following Michael Harvey's lead, because they created a more energetic word shape and offered more possibilities for bleeding and fewer spacing problems.)

4. I wrote out the logo twice using a Brause nib and Higgins Black Magic india ink on engineering vellum (no retouching) and sent it off to Andrew with indications for cropping.

5. Andrew agreed to do the reverse and add the tint electronically.

Who am I?

Paul Shaw. I have no formal training in lettering or design aside from a 10th grade class in commercial art. I am trained as a historian with an MA from Columbia University (and an unfinished dissertation on W.A. Dwiggins) and a BA from Reed College. I taught myself calligraphy and lettering and from that typography and graphic design.

[Although Paul has had no formal training, he is a calligrapher and typographer working in New York City. In his twenty professional years as a lettering designer he has created custom lettering and logos for many leading companies, including Avon, Lord & Taylor, Rolex, Clairol, and Estée Lauder. Paul has taught calligraphy and typography at New York's Parsons School of Design for over ten years and conducted workshops in New York and Italy. His work has been exhibited throughout the United States and Europe. Paul has been a partner in LetterPerfect, with Garrett Boge, since 1995 (www.letterperfect.com).]

Words of wisdom

Read about typography and graphic design; look at lots of work from the past and present, especially work widely considered to be excellent (you may disagree); and don't let the computer dictate how you design. Do thumbnails. Think and sketch before you turn on the computer. I would urge everyone to learn how to use a pencil and a broad-edged pen. Calligraphy is a good basis for understanding typefaces and typography; painting and drawing provide solid training for understanding layout. Finally, don't be afraid of mathematics: a knowledge of proportion is essential to being a graphic designer.

Paul Shaw
Paul Shaw/Letter Design
785 West End Avenue
New York City, New York
10025

212 666 3738 *phone*
212 666 2163 *fax*

paulshaw@aol.com

Jason Halstead
View Design

COLLATERAL MATERIAL
Western Oregon University Recruitment Campaign

Project goal

The goal for this project was to create a unique and appropriate integrated campaign of college recruitment materials. Past campaigns for the college were criticized as being too formulaic, "cookie cutter" designed, or overly institutional. The challenge was to create consistency and integration with a certain amount of energy and variation.

Profile

Western Oregon University (WOU) is a small public university of approximately 4,500 students, located in Monmouth, Oregon. The university tends to draw the majority of its students from rural Oregon communities. These students want the advantages of a sophisticated liberal arts university and proximity to urban opportunities while retaining a certain amount of the ambiance and advantages they have experienced in smaller high schools and hometowns. The materials we create were to emphasize small class sizes, improved faculty-to-student ratios, personal attention, and proximity to both larger urban atmospheres and diverse recreational opportunities.

Process

Our target market(s) greatly influenced the design. Higher education projects are unique in that there are actually three diverse audiences to be addressed: students (the consumers), their parents (consumers and frequently the buyer), and campus administrators (your actual client). Ideally, the finished product should have a certain amount of appeal to all and should not alienate any. Not the easiest task.

High school recruitment poster; 17" x 22", 5-color with aqueous coating.

Having worked with WOU previously, and introducing more research in each successive project, we were able to lobby for an extended evaluation and research period which greatly enhanced the content and approach of the campaign and very significantly influenced the design itself. For example, many significant elements of our research regarding characteristics of Generation Y and related design and marketing trends were at odds with the results of our focus groups with the students themselves. This is partly due to the fact that Gen Y

Cover of college fair brochure; 4" x 9", 12 pages, 5-color (aqueous coating on cover only).

Opening spread from college fair brochure. The layout bridges the transition from the poster graphic treatment to the viewbook interior layout.

is, by definition, heavily individualistic, and very difficult to draw common conclusions about. It may also be due to the fact that WOU tends to appeal to students from rural backgrounds whose opinions may differ from urban Gen Yers (frequently the focus of Gen Y research) or from the Generation Y population as a whole. Our focus group research and the resulting differences from our media research radically reshaped the refining of this campaign and its design, reinforcing the value of the extended research phase.

The general process
March 1– August 25

Creative strategy meetings: Purpose, organization, and creative approach.

Research: Tours, audit of WOU past publications, review of competitor materials, online and library research on Generation Y characteristics and marketing trends, review of popular culture periodicals and websites.

Focus groups: High school students, recent college admits.

Concept development: Organizational plans, pencil sketches, initial photographer shot list.

Mock-ups: Provide cover and sample page spread layouts for review.

Concept approval: By client.

Copywriting: By client.

Production specifications: Develop printing specifications from refined creative direction for submission through state bid process.

Photography: Refine shot list, identity locations, models, and props; arrange building and room access; overall schedule; implement photo shoot.

Design and Layout: Provide color layouts for review.

Client review: Review and make revisions to layouts, proof copy.

Revisions: Extensive! Many rounds to finalize rapidly changing information.

Final Approval: By client.

Bid Award: Through state process.

Prepress and file preparation

Press checks: Three days for completion of all pieces.

Bindery

Delivery: August 25

Cover of college viewbook; 9" x 12", 24 pages, die-cut cover, 5-color (aqueous coating on cover only).

The die-cut corner effect on the cover did not add to the expense since a die-cut glued pocket was already required on the inside backcover.

The above schedule does not reflect the number of meetings and sheer volume of communication with the client in developing the campaign. However, given our early strategy and research and our firm's policy that clients be integrally involved in the development of project criteria, there was very little conflict. In fact, the extended research phase built a lot of internal anticipation and excitement which culminated in our unveiling of the mock-ups. While there was significant refinement along the way, those mock-ups differ little from the final implemented piece.

The printing process

This project uses four-color process printing. The consistent use of the school's crimson red, as well as past inconsistencies in its color reproduction, encouraged us to insist on the use of a fifth color (spot red Pantone ink). Outside covers are inline aqueous coated. These production requirements necessitated the job run on a six-color press.

One element, a preprinted shell for campus-wide use by individual departments, was printed two-color on uncoated paper for later imprinting.

Client specifications

This university, like most, has certain graphic guidelines, including specifications about how the logo is used, its size, the proper Pantone color for their school color, corporate typeface, etc. The distinctive design style and direction of this year's campaign was at odds with their corporate typeface (Minion), so we lobbied for an exception— and won.

The other restrictions were kept in mind during design development, allowing them to play into the design rather that restricting it.

Design

University and popular-culture publications alike were criticized as busy, messy, and confusing by members of our focus groups. It also became obvious that what students deemed cool or acceptable in one category, say a snowboarding magazine or a music website, did not necessarily translate into what they thought was appropriate for a collegiate publication. While many publications pandered to complex, cutting-edge imagery and trendy design elements, students were telling us that what they really wanted was clarity and organization. They wanted schedules and costs clearly accessible, not buried in tiny notes and paragraphs. They wanted to know what the next step was in an often confusing process. They wanted some of the stress taken out of the transition from high school to college.

Our research pointed to clean, organized, dynamic design with a nod to popular culture and technology. We developed a visual vocabulary of design and text elements, color, and page structure that could be combined in various forms while still maintaining a unified voice.

The traditional "picture postcard" approach to the high school recruitment poster was abandoned in favor of a poster-sized "display ad" featuring a graphic treatment of Western Oregon University's impressive faculty-to-student ratio and a catchy headline that spins WOU's small size as an advantage.

This graphic treatment is repeated on the college fair brochure and also in a "peek inside" die cut of the viewbook cover.

Strong identification and student response to the school's signature crimson red led us to feature it prominently in the design as an identifying and organizing element throughout the campaign.

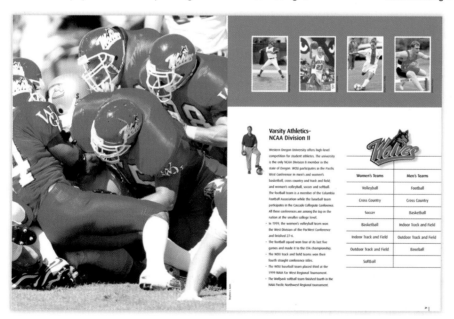

Interior spread from college viewbook. Consistent infographic treatments allow quick access to information.

Interior spreads from college viewbook. The sectional numbering scheme guides students through the college admission process, step by step.

A variable grid of cover treatments, banners, and information graphic presentations allowed for variety without sacrificing structure. Button-like icons and drop shadows throughout give a nod to online technology and call attention to graphics or point readers forward or back in the materials, like links, for related content.

As a final nod to student feedback, the viewbook is organized in chronological order from inquiry to admission and on to selecting a major, applying for housing, and getting involved. The table of contents is presented as an easy nine-step checklist, with each step and its related spread clearly identified by a graphic treatment which echoes that of the faculty-to-student ratio.

Budget

For a project of this scale, the budget was moderate, but not unrealistic. Having worked with WOU on two past successful campaigns, we were in a very good position to lobby for more research time. The client also requested some aerial photography, which had to be considered in the budget.

While the needs were extensive, we looked at other ways to maximize the client's resources. We contracted with the photographer at a day rate and kept him busy taking ambient campus shots in-between each of our scheduled shots for use in later publications. During the aerial shoot we used the helicopter's vantage point to take photos of all of the campus facilities in the hopes that the admissions

office would be able to resell images of the dormitories or athletic fields to other departments to reimburse its own budget.

We exclusively used WOU students as models, both for accuracy and to eliminate the need for model fees. Though it was limited, we used some existing campus photography (graduation, athletics, etc.) and tapped into existing state tourism photography for regional and activity images, eliminating the need for other on-site photography.

We also ensured that the project was as efficient as possible on press. The end result was an effective, efficiently produced campaign, which belies its moderate budget.

Words of wisdom

Be a student of the world.

I think the greatest thing a designer can do is simply be aware. Of everything. At all times. My successes, insights, and understanding can be heavily attributed to constant review and analysis of graphic design, both good and bad. Pull it apart to understand what makes it tick—not just whether it's good or bad, but why. How is it constructed? What makes it work (or not?) Is it the best solution?

Once you've tackled graphic design, the next logical and critical step is to stretch that awareness to the other design disciplines and the world at large. If you're not ready to be a life-long learner, you're probably not cut out for a life in design. I have ultimate respect for the creative genius

Interior spreads from college viewbook. We gave active statements to the section topics: "Get Oregonized!" instead of "Community/Region."

who crosses boundaries to encompass that life: Frank Lloyd Wright, Ray and Charles Eames, Michael Graves—all those who realized they could solve problems and create functionality and beauty irrespective of materials or discipline.

Know why you're doing what you're doing.

Frequently design is created solely to satisfy the appetites of designers. This has been fed by technology's expanding capabilities. So you can reverse-channel double-emboss a logo in Photoshop. The question is why would you do it? You should always be able to answer that question and justify your design decisions for your clients. And in most cases your answer should be meatier than, "Because it looks good."

By definition, design needs to be attractive and innovative to gain its audience but, once gained, design should be purposeful and intentional, accessible, and organized if it's going to deliver.

A good designer should never discount the value of research in the creative process. Appropriate research and defined criteria makes the creative stronger and gives you the muscle to support your creative concepts.

Who am I?

Jason Halstead. I'm a self-taught art director and designer (trained in the School of Reality, I tell clients) with a degree in business management and marketing. I think my non-traditional design training frequently is an advantage as it allows me

to see beyond creating art to broader issues of communication (purpose, process, structure, etc.) Good design is a balance of both intelligence and instinct.

I started VIEW Design about eight years ago. For me it was the perfect match for my skills: a balance of the left and right brain, the technical and the intuitive. We've purposefully stayed small; currently a staff of two, soon to be three. Our smaller size allows us to provide highly professional, but also highly personal experience to our clients. I'm a firm believer that, in most cases, the process is as critical as the design result. We recently verbalized our brand as "individual, collaborative creative partnerships," which I think is an accurate summation. At least for now.

Credits:
Jason Halstead, art director, designer
Katie Parentice, assistant designer
Jerry Hart, primary photographer
Laurie Bridges and Alison Marshall, editors

Jason Halstead
VIEW Design, Inc.
445 Willamette Street
Eugene, Oregon
97401

541 342 3343 *phone*
541 342 4609 *fax*

jason@viewdesign.net
www.viewdesign.net

words of wisdom

"Don't Be a Wimp!"

"Un-groove from your set path."

"Take the time to understand your audience."

"Think and sketch before you turn on the computer."

"Don't be afraid of an idea."

"DEVELOP A THICK SKIN"

"Simply be aware. Of everything."

"Know why you're doing what you're doing."

EXTRAS

Fonts used in this book All fonts are shown at 12 point

Classic Sans Serif

Alinea Sans
Antique Olive Light
to Nord
Bailey Sans Book, **Bold,**
Book Italic, ***Bold Italic***
Charlotte Sans Book,
Bold, SMALL CAPS
Frutiger Light,
Light Italic, **Black,**
UltraBlack
Humana Sans Light,
Light Italic, **Bold**
Officina Sans Book,
Book Italic, **Bold,**
Bold Italic, **Extra**
Bold, Black
Trade Gothic Light,
Light Oblique,
Bold, Bold Condensed
Univers Roman,
Condensed,
Condensed Light, **Bold,**
Condensed Bold
VAG Rounded Thin,
Light, **Bold, Black**

Decorative Sans Serif

Barmeno Extra Bold
Blur Light, **Medium,**
Bold
Bodega Sans Light, **Medium, Black**
BroadBand
Highlander Book
HUXLEY VERTICAL
MACHINE
PLAnet Sans Book, BoLd
SERENGETTI
Wade Sans Light

Hybrid Sans/Serif

Dyadis Book, SMALL CAPS,
Bold, *Bold Italic*
Gilgamesh, *Italic,* **Bold,**
SMALL CAPS
Senator Tall
SevenSerif, **Black**

Decorative

Airstream
Alleycat
Amoebia
BEE/KNEE/
Bossa Nova
CANCIONE
CONFIDENTIAL
DYNAMOE
FLOWERCHILD
GARISHMONDE
Green typeface
Impakt
Industria Solid, Inline,
Industria Solid A
Industrial Heavy, Plain
Kumquat
Litterbox
Musica
Out of the Fridge
Pious Henry
PLAnet Serif,
SMALL CAPS DEMI
Schmutz Cleaned
Signature

Silvermoon, Bold
Smack
SOPHIA
Stoclet Light, **Bold**
THE WALL
Toontime
Tree Boxelder,
Monkey Puzzle
Woodland Light, **Heavy**

Script

Bellevue
Bickham Script with
alternates, ligatures,
ornaments, and swash
capitals (this is 18 point)
Carpenter
Dartangnon
Dorchester
Hollyweird
Linoscript
Mistral
Redonda Fancy
Spring
Zaragoza

Classic Serif

Adobe Garamond, *Italic,* **Bold,** ***Bold Italic***

Adobe Caslon, EXPERT

Bell, *Italic*

Berkeley

Centaur, *Italic,* **Bold**

Clarendon, Light, **Bold**

Clearface, *Italic*

Cochin, *Italic*

Galliard, *Italic,* **Black**

Golden Cockerel, *Italic, Ornaments*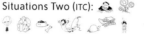

Cheltenham family

Garamond Light (ITC), **Bold,** ***Bold Italic***

Giovanni, *Italic*

Meridien, *Italic*

Palatino, *Italic*

TopHat, *Italic*

Walbaum, *Italic*

Moderns

AT Quirnus Bold

Craw Modern

Fenice Light, **Ultra**

Firenze

MAGNOLIA

Picture fonts, clip art fonts

Art Three:

Backyard Beasties :

Bill's Modern Diner:

Situations One (ITC):

Situations Two (ITC):

Fontoonies (ITC):

Gargoonies (ITC):

MiniPics Confetti:

MiniPics Head Buddies:

Renfields Lunch:

Birds:

Thanks

Many thanks to **EyeWire Studios** for their cooperation and generosity as we worked on the creation of this book. Their fantastic and varied selection of fonts, stock images, and clip art were used in many of the design examples and were also used to illustrate many of the editorial pages of this book. Their products provided compelling imagery and a great amount of inspiration.

Some of the EyeWire collections we used include Digital Vision, ObjectGear, Circa:Art, Art Parts, DataStorm, Business Edge, ArtVille, and others.

We also used photo images from the Adobe Image Library and PhotoDisc. Borders and frames came from Aridi Computer Graphics and AutoFX.

www.eyewire.com
www.adobestudios.com
www.photodisc.com
www.autofx.com

Index

Robin and John designed and produced this book on Macintoshes. John created most of his examples in Adobe Illustrator, Adobe Photoshop, Corel Painter, and Macromedia Dreamweaver. Robin created her examples in Adobe InDesign and Illustrator. She exported the InDesign examples as PDFs for placement in the book files; she created the book files in InDesign.

We live and work in Santa Fe. Files were sent overnight as hard copy or over the Internet as PDFs to our editor, Nancy Davis in Buffalo; our production manager, Kate Reber in Berkeley; and to Barbara Sikora in Cazadero, who used Adobe PageMaker to index the pages. Barbara emailed the index file back to Robin and Robin opened it with style sheets intact in InDesign and formatted it.

There is a list of fonts used in the book on pages 276–277. This font is Alinea Sans and the headline is Bickham Script with alternate characters (the one word in the headline uses five different fonts in the Bickham Script family).